Corporate
Strategy

Also by W. Stewart Howe

Competition in British Industry (with D. Swann *et al.*)
Case Studies in Competition Policy (with K. Blois)
Industrial Economics
Competition Policy, Profitability and Growth
(with D. P. O'Brien *et al.*)
The Dundee Textiles Industry 1960–1977

CORPORATE STRATEGY

W. Stewart Howe

MACMILLAN

First published 1986

Published by
MACMILLAN EDUCATION LTD
Houndmills, Basingstoke,
Hampshire RG21 2XS
and London
Companies and representatives
throughout the world

Printed in Hong Kong

British Library Cataloguing in Publication Data
Howe, W. Stewart
Corporate strategy.
1. Corporate planning
I. Title
658.4′012   HD30.28
ISBN 0–333–36900–9
ISBN 0–333–36901–7 Pbk

*To the memory of
my Father and Mother*

Contents

Acknowledgements

Although writing this book has been very largely a solo effort, I am nonetheless grateful for this conventional opportunity to acknowledge various debts of gratitude to those who through their writings or otherwise have influenced or assisted me in writing this book.

There are many intellectual debts. I have drawn heavily upon the existing textbook, monograph and journal literature in the field of corporate strategy. Where I have taken a point from that literature into this text directly I have made the usual acknowledgement through appropriate reference. I am also grateful at a more general level to these writers for the stimulus with which their work has provided me. On occasion I have reproduced diagrams or tables from journals and books, and I am grateful to the editors of the *Journal of Marketing, Long Range Planning* and *Management Today* and to the publishers Harper & Row, McGraw-Hill and John Martin for their permission to reproduce these. I am also particularly grateful to the editor of the *Financial Times* for permission to reproduce the article from that newspaper which appears in Chapter 6. Although time has prevented me from benefiting from the views of others on draft chapters of this text I am indebted to a number of colleagues for their advice and help in directing me to references in the literature and discussing these with me. I am particularly grateful in this context to my Management Faculty colleagues Kishen Srinivasan, Robert Pemble, Tina Walley, Ian Glover and Roy Hutchison. I am also indebted to the library staff at Dundee College of Technology for their assistance in obtaining access to a wide range of literature in the corporate strategy field which I have used in my teaching and which has been incorporated into this text.

My wife and family have again borne with me in the writing of this book, which was largely carried out during what some other professions would regard as unsocial hours. This domestic support and assistance is much appreciated.

June 1985   W. Stewart Howe

The author and publishers wish to thank the following who have kindly given permission for the use of copyright material:

Philip Allan Publishers Ltd for tabulated points from *Business Policy*, by R. E. Thomas, 2nd edn 1983, p. 114.

American Marketing Association for a table from an article by G. S. Day in the *Journal of Marketing*, April 1977, p. 32.

Financial Times Business Information Limited for 'The Long Search that Led to Howard Johnson's Door'.

Harvard Business Review for a exhibit from 'The Industrial State: Old Myths and New Realities' by Bruce R. Scott, March – April 1973.

B. Hedley for 'Strategy and the "Business Portfolio"' in *Long Range Planning*, February 1977, p. 10; B. W. Denning for 'Strategic Environmental Appraisal' in *Long Range Planning*, March 1973, p. 26; and D. E. Hussey for 'Portfolio Analysis: Practical Experience with the Directional Policy Matrix', *Long Range Planning*, August 1978, pp. 3–4.

Managing Today for the article 'The Strategy of Merging' by John Kitching, *Management Today*, October 1969.

Every effort has been made to trace all the copyright holders, but if any have been inadvertently overlooked the publishers will be pleased to make the necessary arrangement at the first opportunity.

Introduction

This text is concerned with the topic of corporate strategy, which is about the decisions which senior management make regarding how a business organisation should relate to its product market environment. The book is designed to be of use to business or management students following a one-year course in the subject area who have previously studied economics, accounting and behavioural sciences, and who also have some knowledge of functional areas of business such as marketing. The author has used the material in the text with final-year business studies students and also those studying for the part-time Diploma in Management Studies.

Practitioners of corporate strategy need to have an understanding of the variables which they should take into account in arriving at strategic decisions, of the strategies open to businesses, and of how possible strategies should be evaluated. They also require to know something of how particular business strategies such as vertical integration or divestment work, and the problems surrounding the appraisal and undertaking of these strategies. For these reasons the text is divided into two parts. Part I, Chapters 1–6, is concerned with the strategic decision-making process: a sequence of analysis, choice and implementation through which senior management should go in determining corporate strategy. Part II of the book offers an analysis of a range of individual business strategies, applying the understanding of the strategy-making process covered in Part I. Part II concludes with a general

appraisal of the role and significance of corporate strategic decision-making. The advantage claimed for this two-part analysis is
that it enables the student to grasp within a relatively short space
of time – in the author's experience about ten weeks – the role of
the strategic decision-making process. Thereafter in Part II individual business strategies are considered, and readers may choose
to study all or part of this section according to their interests and
the time available. As a result of this structure a slight degree of
repetition is involved in reading the text as a whole. Strategic
possibilities outlined in Part I are considered in detail in Part II,
and, for example, some common reference to diversification by
acquisition appears both in the analysis of the strategy of diversification and in the consideration of acquisition strategies. It is
believed that this small degree of repetition will be of value in
consolidating an understanding of the strategic management process.

Two further characteristics of the text deserve mention. First,
except in one particular case, appropriate examples of the
strategies considered have been built into the text rather than
isolated or provided by means of separate case histories. It is
intended in this way not only to illustrate the use of strategies
discussed by means of practical examples, but also to integrate
these fully into the text without disturbing the flow of the analysis.
Second, a fairly generous list of references is included at the end of
each chapter. These are provided not to indicate how widely the
author has read, but to allow the interested reader to follow up in
detail the individual studies and illustrations relating to any
particular strategy. Only in a very few instances is the argument in
the body of the text amplified in the references, and the reader
whose time is limited may disregard these references without
significant loss.

The Strategic Management Process

I

1

The Strategic
Management
Process

Strategic Management 1

The story of any great industrial enterprise is full of interest. All the elements of high adventure are contained in it – the vision of some distant goal to be won, the planning of the expedition, the struggle against human inertia and material difficulties, the freaks of luck, the triumphs and the reverses, and in the end the glory of achievement, greater perhaps than the vision of the pioneer. — A. G. Whyte, Introduction to *Forty Years of Electrical Progress* (London: Ernest Benn, 1930).

1.1 Definitions

This book is concerned with strategic management and the strategic management process. Determining the strategy of an organisaton is only one of the functions of management. It is, however, arguably the most significant area of management decision-making, and the most important one in which to make the right decisions. Management is defined in one text as 'the process of planning, organizing, leading and controlling the efforts of organization members and of using all other organizational resources to achieve stated organizational goals'.[1] Strategic management decisions in fact precede all of the management functions above. Indeed, in the absence of strategic management decisions none of the above management functions can be carried out.

3

Strategic management and the strategic management process is concerned with arriving at decisions on what the organisation ought to be doing and where it should be going. Ansoff, one of the most influential writers in the field, defines strategic decisions as those pertaining to the relationship between the firm and its environment, and involving 'decisions on what kind of business the firm should seek to be in'.[2] Chandler, the business historian, refers to strategy as involving 'the determination of the basic long-term goals and objectives of an enterprise, and the adoption of courses of action and the allocation of resources necessary for carrying out these goals'.[3] In the context of the modern business organisation the editor of the *Harvard Business Review* described strategic decision-making as follows:

> **agreements reached by top management about how the company should position itself to take advantage of future market opportunity and to outdo its competitors ... [as a result of having] investigated market opportunity, appraised and invested in the distinctive competence and total resources of the company, and combined opportunity and resources, consistent with the economic goals, personal values, and ethical aspirations that define the character of the company.[4]**

These definitions of strategy and strategic management emphasise both the prime nature of the strategic decision within the total management process, and also that there is a logical process to be gone through before arriving at the strategic decision itself.

1.2   Comparisons

One way in which to gain further insight into the strategic decision is to contrast such decisions with other management decision areas. Ansoff distinguishes three such areas: strategic, administrative and operating.[5] Operating decisions in any organisation are concerned with the resource conversion process itself, and involve, for example, allocating operating resources, setting price and output levels, and making decisions about necessary marketing and research and development expenditures. Decisions at this level are being made all the time in an organisation, and a stream

of such decisions constantly presents itself to be made by managers. Actual decision-making in this area thus tends to be decen-
tralised within the organisation. Many of such decisions are
repetitive, and while they involve risk and uncertainty they are
also characterised by a relatively short time period between
recognising the need to make such decisions and the completion of
all of the effects following from them. Administrative decisions
within an organisation are essentially facilitative. They establish
procedures for acquiring resources, for ensuring an appropriate
internal structure of authority and responsibility among those
working within the organisation, and for managing the flow of
information within the business.

Strategic decisions, in contrast to the first two areas above,
relate to the interface between the business and its external
environment. Such decision-making is inevitably centralised at the
top of the organisation as the decisions are concerned with the
general disposition of the total resources of the business. Strategic
decisions, in contrast to operating ones, are made relatively
infrequently, and their effects will normally be felt by the business
over a considerable period of time. Perhaps the most challenging
of all of the characteristics of strategic decisions is that top
management does not receive any forewarning that such decisions
require to be made. Ansoff refers to them as 'non self-generative'.
This means that although strategic decisions are relatively few in
number, the organisation must be constantly aware of the need to
make such decisions, and must ensure that a mechanism exists for
drawing the need for making these decisions to the attention of
senior management. This is particularly true in an environment
where lead times relating to such decisions – involving, for
example, capital building programmes – are increasingly long.

Although there may be occasions when a firm's short-term
survival is more immediately determined by its operating or
administrative efficiency, in the longer term business success or
failure is much more dependent upon making the right strategic
decisions – upon doing the right things rather than upon doing
things right. Indeed, one of the problems faced by senior management, arising from the non self-generative nature of the strategic
decision, is that of tending to concentrate upon day-to-day operating and administrative issues and neglecting strategic decision-
making. Two American authors contrast the relative importance

and outcome of efficiency in the areas of operations and strategy in the form of the matrix shown in Table 1.1. The goal of senior management is of course to be both strategically and operationally efficient; but while efficient operations without a correct strategy may ensure short-term survival for the business, in the longer term no organisation can survive without a clear and appropriate strategy.

Tregoe and Zimmerman also stress the need in arriving at strategic decisions to make a distinction between strategy and

Table 1.1
Comparison of Operations and Strategy

What How		Strategy *Clear*	*Unclear*
OPERATIONS	**Effective**	I Clear strategy and effective operations have equaled success in the past and will in the future	II Unclear strategy but effective operations have equaled success in the past, but success is doubtful in the future
	Ineffective	III Clear strategy but ineffective operations have sometimes worked in the past in the short run, but increasing competition makes success doubtful in the future	IV Unclear strategy and ineffective operations have equaled failure in the past and will in the future

Source: B. Tregoe and J. Zimmerman, *Top Management Strategy* (London: John Martin, 1980) p. 20.

long-range planning – one which is at first glance less obvious.[6] Planning in business, these authors point out, is in most cases carried out on the assumption that current environmental factors relating to the firm will continue to affect it in the same way as in the past, and is often simply a forward projection of existing operations. Business plans are normally set down in purely financial terms, and by their nature are built up from the lower levels of the organisation. By contrast strategy begins by asking what activities the business *should* be in and what its goals should be on the basis of the present and likely *future* resources and opportunities available to the organisation. Such strategy-making must be carried out on the basis of a very wide range of data, and is inevitably concentrated at the top of the organisation. Thus the annual business planning cycle is not an appropriate context in which to develop corporate strategy. Strategic decision-making cannot normally be fitted into the inevitable timetable constraints of the annual business planning cycle. Strategic decision-making is probably better carried out in a much less structured framework than that appropriate to corporate planning, and may also require different skills on the part of the management concerned.[7]

1.3   The Strategic Management Process

It was emphasised at the beginning of this chapter that this book was to be concerned not simply with strategic decisions but with the process by which such decisions are arrived at. Indeed the first part of the book beyond this chapter is structured around this strategic decision-making process.

The strategic decision-making process in our view comprises six distinct but interrelated steps, as shown in Table 1.2[8]. A strategic decision should only be made and implemented after the senior management of the organisation has gone through the strategic decision-making process outlined in the table.

At *Stage 1*, mission and objective identification, the management must answer for itself questions about the nature of the business in terms of its basic mission or purpose. It must also decide in broad terms its corporate financial objectives over the next five or ten years. The basic mission or purpose of the organisation should be expressed in terms of the market in which

Table 1.2
The Strategic Decision-Making Process

Stage	Steps	Process
1	Mission and objective identification	Establishment of basic mission or purpose of the organisation, and determination of broad goals.
2	Analysis of the business environment	Appraisal of the opportunities and threats relating to the business arising from its external environment.
3	The internal business audit	Review and assessment of strengths and weaknesses of the organisation.
4	Review of strategic opportunities	Identification of all possible strategies open to the business.
5	Comparison of strategic options	Evaluation of all possible options and final making of the strategic decision.
6	Implementation, evaluation and control of strategy	The translation of strategic into administrative and operating decisions, and ongoing monitoring of strategy.

the business sees itself operating – industrial textiles, banking services, information processing, travel/tourism, etc. – while the business goals should at this stage be thought of in broad terms along dimensions of profitability, growth, stability of earnings, etc.

Stage 2 of the strategic decision-making process, analysis of the environment – involves the business in an appraisal of its current and likely future external environment: its market opportunities and threats. Opportunities for the business may include new market areas into which to sell existing products, or the appearance of new market demands which match the company's unique strengths. Threats might be posed by the decline of markets upon which the business has been dependent in the past, upward movements in raw material costs, or demographic changes likely to have an adverse impact upon the organisation.

By contrast *Stage 3* of the strategic decision-making process involves the organisation's analysing its own internal capabilities – its unique strengths and weaknesses. Such an analysis will enable the business to identify the key factors upon which its success in exploiting markets and surviving against its competitors depends, and also the weaknesses that should be remedied if the business is to continue to operate in such markets and survive against competitors. For example, a firm may have particular strengths arising from possession of a nationally recognised name, or considerable financial resources accumulated as a result of past profitability. Such a business may correspondingly have recognised weaknesses in the areas of production efficiency or its physical distribution network. In choosing its strategy any organisation will wish to capitalise upon the former strengths while at the same time remedying, or in the short term minimising the exposure of, its competitive weaknesses.

At *Stage 4* of the strategic planning sequence the business should identify and consider as wide a range of strategic options open to it as possible. These may be thought of in very broad terms such as expansion or consolidation of existing activities, innovation, diversification, or divestment and restructuring. This range of options will need to be narrowed down at a later stage to more specific strategies. Indeed, *Stage 5* of the strategic decision-making process is the point at which the business evolves a particular strategy. At this stage the business seeks to match the goals which it has set for itself at Stage 1 with the results of the external and internal audit (Stages 2 and 3), and chooses which of the avenues identified at Stage 4 should actually be followed in the light of all of the circumstances. This is arguably the most difficult part of the whole strategic decision-making process, and although in Chapter 5 of this book we shall discuss techniques which may improve business decision-making in this area, there is undoubtedly a great deal about such decisions which must be left to the judgement of the business strategist. At the end of this stage the business will have decided upon one particular strategy.

Stage 6 of the sequence set out in Table 1.2 involves a process of putting the chosen strategy into effect and of monitoring its implementation in order to ensure the achievement of the business goals identified at Stage 1. This stage involves continuous monitoring of the strategy and its implementation in order, if necessary, to adjust the strategy to the changing circumstances of the business. We hope to show in the first part of this book that by following the sequence of steps in the strategic decision-making process senior managers can improve the quality of the difficult decisions which they have to make.

1.4   The Importance of Strategy

Making correct strategic decisions matters for the business; and it was emphasised above that it is probably more important for the long-term survival of the organisation for management to be efficient in terms of its strategy than in respect of its operating activities. The formal literature in this area has identified two approaches to examining the internal determinants of the performance of organisations. The former of these, the universalistic theory, holds that certain characteristics of an organisation are conducive to superior performance under all circumstances. The latter approach, contingency theory, suggests that the internal conditions most conducive to business success will vary from one firm to another depending upon the specific environmental characteristics of the organisation.[9] The contingency approach, which is of particular relevance to strategic decision making, suggests that given certain environmental conditions for the business an optimal strategy exists for the achievement of business goals. It is thus the job of senior management, in the light of these environmental conditions, to discern and implement the optimal strategy. At the universalist level there appears to be some evidence that certain management characteristics such as youth, type of strategic objectives set, the directions in which manpower resources are employed, and containment of bureaucracy are associated with superior profit and/or growth performance by businesses. Indeed, interestingly, such management characteristics would appear to be more useful in explaining economic performance than some more familiar economic or organisational variables such as company size

or the nature of the control group in the firm.[10] The evidence
supporting the contingency theory relationships suggests that
management can influence the economic performance of their
organisation by reacting to specific features of its environment;
and that a recognition of the need to take account of the variability
or turbulence of the environment, of the size of the organisation,
and of the type of technology employed and structuring the
organisation accordingly can enhance economic performance.

With specific regard to strategy, although the evidence is far
from robust, there are grounds for suggesting on the basis of
American and British research that there is a link between
strategic planning and profit performance in business.[11] In the case
of the British evidence the study by Grinyer and Norburn,
although it was not able to establish a relationship between
financial performance and the formality of business planning, nor
between financial performance and agreement upon objectives
within the organisation, did find a positive statistical relationship
between company financial performance and the detail of objective setting and the fixing of responsibility for long-term decisions.

While one would accept that in the short term there is nothing
which any business can do to mitigate the adverse effects of a
sudden and unpredicted change in its circumstances, such as the
dramatic quadrupling of crude oil prices in 1974, in the longer term
there can be significant differences between the performance of
businesses in similar environments arising from differences between managements in the quality of their strategic decisions. That
is to say, some organisations are better than others at interacting
with their environment – at making strategic decisions. A business
is not a prisoner of its past history or present environment; and to
emphasise the role of successful businessmen in building up their
organisations is not simply to glamourise the task of the chief
executive but to recognise the scope on the part of an individual or
group of individuals for choosing between possible strategies for
their organisations. The roles of Sir Robert Barlow at Metal Box
or Sir John Cohen of Tesco Stores in building up in competitive
conditions organisations which were later to play a dominant role
in their markets, the work of Lord Weinstock at GEC or Sir
Halford Reddish at Rugby Portland Cement in successfully creating and sustaining large organisations in mature and competitive
markets, or of Sir Alan Smith at Dawson International operating

successfully in a declining sector are merely a few illustrations of
the choice and implementation of successful business strategies in
the face of severe domestic or international competition, or in
industries facing rapid technological change or a general decline in
their fortunes.[12]

Leontiades, in his study of diversification, provides through
three short case studies very telling evidence from the American
business scene of the importance of making correct strategic
decisions.[13] Taking examples from the areas of computers and two
retailing sectors, Leontiades shows how in each case over a ten or
twenty-year period one of two organisations which were equally
placed in the market at the beginning of the period had succeeded
while the other had failed as a result of superior strategic decision-
making on the part of the former businesses. The successful
organisations are those which, as events have turned out, had the
correct vision of how things were to be in the future and deployed
their resources accordingly. The businesses which by comparison
failed did so not because of any obvious inherent disadvantage in
terms of size or financial resources, but because of poor strategic
decision-making. Numerous case studies of businesses operating
successfully in declining markets, of corporate acquisitions, and of
'turnaround' situations where businesses have been moved quite
rapidly from loss-making to profitability provide further examples
of the way in which companies can be made to succeed despite
adverse environments, of the important role in such situations of a
single chief executive officer, and thus of superior business
strategy-making.[14] That small firm size in a declining market
dominated by a single large producer is no barrier to a new
business succeeding through adopting the right strategy can be
seen by the case of Coloroll, operating in the UK wallcoverings
market still dominated by the Reed–International subsidiary,
Wallpaper Manufacturers. In this instance, commenting on the
results of successful strategy, *Management Today* wrote:

> **One remarkable example is provided by Coloroll, a small
> Lancashire firm, which has nearly trebled turnover and multi-
> plied profits six times over the last three years by abandoning its
> traditional product line and invading a market which was (and
> is) both ageing and declining: wall-coverings.**
>
> **While established manufacturers in this industry are closing
> factories, laying off workers and battling a profits squeeze,**

> Coloroll, led by a flamboyant and innovative entrepreneur
> named John Bray, is expanding production, increasing its sales
> force, investing in new machinery and confidently predicting a
> 60% boost to both turnover and profits this year . . . This success
> has not been built on the back of some brilliant technical
> breakthrough or the dynamism of a growing market . . . Most of
> the success undoubtedly stems directly from the personality of
> Bray himself.[15]

The author of this text has himself carried out a study of strategic
decision-making on the part of firms in one particular market
which has been subject to rapid decline in demand.[16] In this case
the very rapid contraction of the Dundee jute industry over the
period 1967–1974 in the face of competition from polypropylene
was met by a wide variety of reactions on the part of the thirty
firms which comprised the industry at the beginning of that period.
The variety of strategic reactions by these firms, the fact that
different strategies were adopted by similarly placed businesses,
and the varying degrees of success achieved by these businesses all
highlight again the way in which arriving at and implementing
correct strategies can have a significant impact upon the destiny of
business organisations.

1.5 Conclusions

The study of business strategy has come a long way over the past
thirty years. At the beginning of this period those wishing to learn
about business policy had to depend upon reading biographies or
autobiographies of successful businessmen in order to learn, after
the events, about how strategic decisions were arrived at.[17]
Valuable though such accounts of business still are for the insight
which they offer into top management decision-making, they
suffer from a lack of objectivity in their writing or an inability to
generalise from the experience. It would be unnatural, too, if
some of their conclusions were not clouded by an occasional
element of serendipity! By the late 1950s and the 1960s studies
were beginning to appear which, in addition to being based in part
upon the experiences of businessmen, offered a more systematic
analysis of business policy-making. The business history writings

of Chandler, the case histories and analyses assembled by Edwards and Townsend, and the economic studies by Penrose and by Carter and Williams are examples of the more systematic and objective work in this area appearing at this time but which was yet closely related to the business world.[18] Today business policy or strategy has become a field of study and writing in its own right; and although it would be rash to suggest that a 'theory' of any kind has emerged, during the 1970s a number of texts appeared on business strategy which offered an analysis of the topic within a rigorous framework which could be of help to students approaching the subject for the first time and also to practising business people. The text by Harvey to which reference has already been made is an excellent example of such studies emanating from America. The purpose of this present text is to continue the development of the subject of business strategy is this new direction by offering an analysis of strategic decision-making which is rigorous and at the same time capable of being put into practice. The study aims to be systematic, but at the same time draws upon current UK examples. The first part of the text, Chapters 2–6 takes the reader through the sequential steps of strategic decision-making. Part II, Chapters 7–12, considers individual areas of strategic decision-making. It is hoped that by this means readers will come to understand both the process of arriving at strategic decisions and also the major areas of business policy in which such decisions have to be made, and that both students and practitioners will benefit from this approach to the subject.

References

1. J. A. F. Stoner, *Management* (Englewood Cliffs, N.J.: Prentice-Hall, 2nd ed., 1982) p.8.
2. H. I. Ansoff, *Corporate Strategy* (Harmondsworth: Penguin, 1968) p. 9.
3. A. Chandler, *Strategy and Structure: Chapters in the History of the Industrial Enterprise* (Cambridge, Mass.: MIT Press, 1962) p.13.
4. K. R. Andrews, 'Corporate Strategy as a Vital Function of the Board', *Harvard Business Review*, November–December 1981, p. 180.
5. Ansoff, *Corporate Strategy*, pp. 17–22.
6. B. Tregoe and J. Zimmerman, *Top Management Strategy* (London: John Martin, 1980) pp. 23–7.

7. M. Leontiades, *Strategies for Diversification and Change* (Boston: Little, Brown & Co., 1980) pp. 105–7.
8. This sequence is based upon a more extended one in D. F. Harvey, *Business Policy and Strategic Management* (Columbus, Ohio: Charles E. Merrill Publishing, 1982).
9. See J. Child, 'Managerial and Organizational Factors Associated with Company Performance, Parts I and II', *Journal of Management Studies*, 1974, Vol. XI, pp. 173–89, and 1975, Vol. XII, pp. 12–27.
10. See W. S. Howe, *Industrial Economics* (London: Macmillan, 1978) pp. 86–8.
11. See S. Schoeffler *et al.*, 'Impact of Strategic Management on Profit Performance', *Harvard Business Review*, March–April 1974, pp. 137–45; and P. H. Grinyer and D. Norburn, 'Strategic Planning in 21 U.K. Companies', *Long Range Planning*, August 1974, pp. 80–8.
12. See W. J. Reader, *Metal Box: A History* (London: Heinemann, 1976); M. Corina, *Pile It High, Sell It Cheap* (London: Weidenfeld & Nicolson, 1971); G. Turner, *Business in Britain* (London: Eyre & Spottiswoode, 1969) pp. 308–25; G. Foster, 'Rugby after Reddish', *Management Today*, February 1981, pp. 42–9 and 124–5; and N. Newman, 'Dawson's Well-knit Whoosh', *Management Today*, March 1981, pp. 74–81, 162–3 and 168.
13. Leontiades, *Strategies for Diversification and Change*, pp. 63–4.
14. W. K. Hall, 'Survival Strategies in a Hostile Environment', *Harvard Business Review*, September–October 1980, pp. 75–85; M. L. Mace and G. G. Montgomery, 'The Chief Executive's Role in Acquisition Planning', in J. L. Harvey and A. Newgarden (eds), *Management Guides to Mergers and Acqusitions* (London: Wiley-Interscience, 1969) p.6; and D. Schendel *et al.*, 'Corporate Turnaround Strategies', *Journal of General Management*, Spring 1976, Vol. III, pp. 3–11.
15. D. Manasian, 'The Unwrapping of Coloroll', *Management Today*, March 1980, pp. 59–60 and 150.
16. See W. S. Howe, *The Dundee Textiles Industry 1960–1977: Decline and Diversification* (Aberdeen: Aberdeen University Press, 1982) Ch. 3.
17. A. G. Whyte, *Forty Years of Electrical Progress* (London: Ernest Benn, 1930); A. P. Sloan, *My Years with General Motors* (London: Sidgwick & Jackson, 1965).
18. See A. Chandler, *Strategy and Structure*; R. S. Edwards and H. Townsend, *Business Enterprise* (London: Macmillan, 1958); E. T. Penrose, *The Theory of the Growth of the Firm* (Oxford: Blackwell, 1959); and C. F. Carter and B. R. Williams, *Industry and Technical Progress* (Oxford: Oxford University Press, 1957).

Business Objectives 2

Probably the skill most nearly unique to general management
... is the intellectual capacity to conceptualize corporate purpose ... The installation of purpose in place of improvisation
and the substitution of planned progress in place of drifting are
probably the most demanding functions of the [company] president. — K. R. Andrews, *The Concept of Corporate Strategy*
(Homewood, Illinois: Irwin, revised edn, 1980) pp. 12–13.

2.1 Introduction

There is an old Greek saying that if the master of the ship doesn't
know which port he is making for then no wind is the right one for
him. Objectives, goals, purposes or missions give the business
organisation its major *raison d'être*. Indeed one author has defined
organisations as 'collectivities ... that have been established for
the pursuit of relatively specific objectives on a more or less
continuous basis'.[1] Although the definition of objectives is a
relevant starting point for a range of organisations, from amateur
charities through hospitals and local authorities to nationalised
industries, we shall be concerned in this text with the objectives of
manufacturing or service businesses in the private sector of the
economy, and with the role that objectives play in corporate
strategy.

Along with strategic decision-making, objective-setting is only one of the functions of senior management in an organisation. But equally, without objective-setting and strategic decision-making many of the other activities of senior management become pointless. None of the remaining traditional roles of top management – organising, staffing, directing and controlling – can be carried out unless organisation objectives have been set and a plan for their achievement drawn up.[2] Without a considered, communicated and verifiable set of objectives, positive management of the organisation – including management by objectives – becomes impossible. Thus every organisation should commence its strategic planning process with a set of objectives incorporating financial or accounting targets which it wants to achieve and also a broad and long-term view of the product-market area(s) in which the firm is to operate.

At the strategic level of the organisation goals or objectives perform four important functions. First, the statement of financial objectives in comparison with the existing performance of the organisation indicates the extent of strategic decision-making necessary. The comparison between these objectives and the current performance of the business reveals the gap, if any, to be filled in the future performance of the business; and the purpose of gap analysis is to lead to an understanding of why the shortfall in performance has occurred, to reveal the extent of strategic decision-making that is necessary, and to indicate what broad strategies might be adopted. Businesses with a minimal gap need to undertake less strategic analysis, whereas the existence of a significant gap indicates the need for a fundamental reappraisal of the firm's strategy.

Second, by providing, as they should, a statement of the broad mission of the organisation, objectives create a product-market focus for strategy. On this basis strategy-makers can analyse the relevant product-market environment and assess the appropriateness of the business resources (Stages 2 and 3 of the strategic decision-making process set out in Table 1.2 above). Product-market areas which are unlikely to satisfy the goals of the organisation need not be considered; and management's attention is drawn to the requirement to strengthen certain of the firm's resource areas if the corporate goals are to be achieved.

Third, a set of corporate goals established at the top of the organisation provides objectives for individual functions or areas of responsibility within the remainder of the firm. Such a set of corporate objectives or goals also facilitates, and is in turn dependent for its achievement upon, co-ordination and integration between these other business functions. By establishing a priority of objectives for the firm as a whole a rank order is created for the achievement of sub-objectives within the organisation. For example, if a priority in the firm over a stated time period is increased penetration of existing markets subject to some profit criterion, then not only should this become a priority for individual product divisions within the organisation, but activities in functional areas such as marketing or research and development should be directed to this end, and financial resources developed to ensure its achievement.

Finally, the objectives set for an organisation over a specified time period must be the means used to appraise the organisation and its managers: hence the requirement for specific, verifiable objectives. This is one of the most important functions of objectives in a business organisation, and we shall see in Chapter 6 that one of the key aspects of strategic management is to monitor the ongoing performance of the business by reference to its original objectives and the relevance of current strategy to the achievement of these.

This chapter continues by considering the forces which contribute to the determination of business goals, and this is followed by some examples of the resulting company objectives. We then examine some of the difficulties that arise in the analysis of business objectives such as the existence of multiple objectives, and the distinction between long-run and short-run objectives.

2.2 Determinants of Objectives

A number of groups of persons or institutions or circumstances are likely to influence the determination of the objectives of a business organisation. The profit objective – the annual rate of return on capital employed – is that most closely associated with the ordinary shareholders of the business. These shareholders have normally provided the largest proportion of the capital of most businesses; and in return for bearing the business and financial risk of the enterprise they receive, and are traditionally assumed to be exclusively interested in, the profits of the enterprise. These shareholders have a range of possible markets in which to invest their funds, and these alternative investments constitute the opportunity cost comparison for ordinary shareholders of their existing investments. Through the media of the stock exchange and the new issue market equity, shareholders, however imperfectly, impose a discipline upon businesses to achieve a return on capital employed which, with due allowance for risk and the transaction costs for the shareholders of shifting their investment, compares with the level of profitability elsewhere in the economy.[3] The category of 'personal' shareholders has admittedly declined in importance over the past two or three decades. The proportion of UK company ordinary shares held by 'persons, executors and trustees' declined from 65.8% in 1957 to 42.0% in 1973, while over the same period insurance companies increased their relative importance from 8.8% to 16.2%, and pension funds from 3.4% to 12.2%.[4] Figures published late in 1983 indicate that individual investors (persons, executors and trustees) now account for only 28% of equity shares. The proportion of these shares held by insurance companies rose from 16% in 1973 to 20% in 1981, while the proportion held by pension funds jumped from 12% in 1973 to 27% in 1981.[5] Nonetheless, while some of these institutional shareholders may have broader or longer-term investment goals, and while their representatives may have traditionally kept a low profile in corporate takeover battles, there is more recent evidence that they too are deeply concerned with the profit performance of the companies in which they invest their policyholders' funds, and that they are also on occasions willing to express publicly their dissatisfaction with poor company performance and to press for changes in business policy.[6]

Since the mid-1960s a number of 'theories of the firm' have emerged which base their analysis upon business goals other than profit maximisation. The need for these new theories is held to arise from the divorce between control and ownership in modern business, the bureaucratic complexity of the large firm, and also the demise of the structural market conditions relating to perfect competition which it is assumed forced businessmen to seek to maximise profitability. It is argued that a geographically scattered and technologically and financially uninformed group of shareholders is not in a position to make judgements regarding the goals or strategy of the company whose shares they hold. Attendance by shareholders at company annual general meetings is reportedly low – twenty-six shareholders for every 10,000 on the share register, representing about 1 per cent of equity capital according to one survey[7] – and in a firm of any size and organisational complexity it is unlikely that at such a metting even the broad goals or strategy of a business could be determined. By contrast, although in the vast majority of cases they account for only a minute proportion of the ordinary shares of the business, the board of directors is by default the body that is in the position to determine the goals and policy of the firm, relatively unsupervised by the shareholders.[8] In the U.K. this former group is in most cases almost entirely made up of senior managers of the company and is thus a board of management rather than a board of directors. The goals and strategy of the organisation are thus determined by the desires of management rather than of shareholders; and this may be expected to lead to the pursuit of goals for the firm such as size or growth which are associated with management incomes, or to an emphasis upon those aspects of business performance such as technological excellence which confer non-pecuniary but nonetheless attractive rewards upon managers.[9]

This does not mean for a moment that profitability is lost sight of altogether. Baumol's theory of the firm is based upon the assumption that managers desire to maximise the sales revenue of the business, on the grounds that this enhances management prestige and may also be associated with market dominance. Nonetheless Baumol specifically recognises that any desire by management to maximise sales revenue will be constrained by a requirement to earn a minimum level of profits necessary both in order to satisfy ordinary shareholders and other external providers of capital, and also to provide internal finance through the retention of some part of the profits.[10] Similarly, in Robin Marris's 'managerial' theory of the firm it is suggested that the annual rate of growth of gross assets is the major goal of management – premissed in this case largely upon the stimulation which the pursuit of this provides for senior management. Here too, however, and given that beyond a particular point there is a negative relationship between business growth and profitability, it is recognised that there are limits to the extent to which management will follow a policy of maximising the growth rate of the business if at some stage this results in a reduction in the level of profitability which in turn precipitates a decline in the share value of the firm and thus an increased likelihood of acquisition of the business by another group of managers.[11] Even those more complex theories of the firm that are based upon an extended analysis of manageral satisfactions in determining the goals of the organisation, or which are concerned with the emergence of a list of corporate goals sustained by a management team or coalition, lead not to the entire supplanting of the profitability objective of businesses but to its supplementation with company size, growth, market share or dominance, etc.[12] It is interesting in this context to note that research which has attempted to demonstrate a distinction between the profits/growth performance of shareholder-controlled as opposed to management-controlled businesses has not been able to show that managers in fact pursue radically different goals from those associated with equity shareholders.[13]

A further dimension to be considered at this stage in our analysis of business goals is the existence of certain broad constraints or restrictions which firms may find placed upon them or which they may voluntarily accept while pursuing their objectives. Thomas describes restrictive conditions placed upon the firm by outside agencies or circumstances as 'constraints', while internally adopted restrictions are termed 'responsibilities'.[14] Constraints upon the achievement of business goals may include finance, as in cases where firms in a particular size or risk category find difficulty in raising additional funds, or legislative restrictions on entry to individual industries such as the need to acquire licensed premises for the sale of alcoholic drinks or permission to engage in petrol retailing. Responsibilities also act as constraints in a broad sense but emanate from within the business itself. One of the most obvious responsibilities concerns personal independence. The desire to run one's own business, and thereby necessarily to be the dominant provider of equity capital, inevitably restricts the size of the organisation to one which can be personally supervised and financed. Such a constraint may obviously conflict with a desire for business growth, size or market share. Other responsibilities which may conflict with particular business goals or strategies include a recognition of one's importance as a local employer, a responsibility wherever possible to 'buy British', or a reluctance by a British firm for political, religious or ideological reasons to trade with certain other countries.

In summary, then, our perception of business objectives is that while the profit goal for large firms has probably been somewhat diluted and supplemented by additional objectives related to management satisfactions, it nonetheless remains very important. This is likely to be so inevitably during periods of general economic recession and in particularly competitive markets. Nor should one forget that although it has been suggested that business growth beyond a particular rate may involve a sacrifice of profitability, size and market dominance may in certain industries be conducive to profitability. US data in particular indicate a clear and significant relationship between market share and profitability. Over the period since the mid-1970s the data analysed by Buzzell and Wiersema, comparing businesses having market shares from less than 10 per cent to more than 40 per cent suggest that an increase in market share of 10 percentage points resulted in an increase in return on capital employed of 5 percentage points.[15] There is thus in some instances a close link between what is perceived to be the major goal of businesses – profitability – and those objectives such as growth and market dominance emphasised in the newer theories of the firm. Finally, it is also recognised that in considering their objectives firms accept certain restrictions which in some cases actually involve trading off one business objective against another: for example, growth and independence.

2.3   Business Objectives in Practice

A number of the above points are reflected in public statements of objectives, as the following extracts indicate.

Sir Charles Forte:[16]

> **I have always been ambitious to undertake projects which will earn money, because this is my principal job – to earn more money and in greater safety.**

Fisons Ltd:[17]

> **The objective is consistently to achieve profitable growth in real terms by increasing earnings per share and raising the return on capital employed ... Job satisfaction, employee participation,**

social responsibility and environmental concern are important matters in their own right and also as constraints against making financial objectives the only factor.

Scottish Amicable Life Assurance Society:[18]

One of the Society's most important corporate aims is to produce profits and to release these profits in the form of bonus additions to our with-profit policyholders to give them the best possible value for the money they have entrusted to us ... Our objectives then are to maximise the return from our invested assets and to minimise our unit costs.

Flymo Ltd:[19]

1. To expand in size, influence and profitability;
2. To strive to be just that bit professional than our competitors in the total package we present to the customer;
3. To remain in advance of all others world-wide in air-cushion mowers, petrol and electric;
4. To expand our range of products with other quality yard-care products (i.e. garden equipment), which can be marketed through our existing channels.

These examples of business aims indicate contrasting emphases, the relative importance of 'business' in comparison with broader social objectives or responsibilities, and the relationship that can be established between a primary set of aims and more detailed objectives which begin to constitute part of the strategy of the organisation. Sir Charles Forte's statement, although doubtless incomplete in so far as his philosophy of business is concerned, is in the traditional entrepreneurial mould. The objective of the business is to increase profitability, always providing that the level of risk does not rise above some intuitively set threshold level. In the case of Fisons, an organisation less personally identified with its chief executive than is Trust House Forte, certain wider responsibilities are explicitly recognised, but the major goal is nonetheless felt to be profitability, with the suggestion too of a growth goal. The statement by Scottish Amicable again recognises the obligation placed upon businesses by their capital providers to ensure the maximum return, and deliberately emphasises the cost side of the profit equation by explicitly referring to cost control as a business goal. The statement by Flymo offers the most comprehensive view of the aims of the business combined with part of the resulting intended strategy. The company has the clear objectives of increased size and profitability; it intends to achieve these within its existing defined market rather than by wider diversification; and the emphasis in marketing appears to be upon the quality and technology of the product rather than solely upon price.

A number of difficulties emerge in considering business objectives in practice. These concern the existence of multiple objectives, the role of partial objectives, and the question of the time period to be adopted in establishing objectives. Nearly all businesses pursue more than one objective at the same time. Growth and profitability are obvious ones (see Fisons and Flymo above), but implicitly profitability and risk reduction are almost always being considered simultaneously. Cyert and March suggest that their management coalitition has five objectives which are being pursued at the same time.[20] In the case of two objectives (for example, growth and profitability) a trade-off can easily be envisaged, providing we know the various possible combinations of the two parameters available and also the decision-maker's set of preferences. When the number of objectives to be pursued simultaneously is greater than two, then the most appealing solution is that of Cyert and March, who suggest that decision-makers attempt to achieve 'satisfactory' levels of performance in each goal area simultaneously, and emphasise one objective as opposed to another at any one time depending upon the actual performance relative to the 'satisficing' level. The target or aspiration levels for the various goal areas are set by reference to the past performance and anticipated market environment of the firm.

An alternative approach which is particularly appropriate for ongoing product-market operations, and which can be combined with the above, is to envisage firms as having a primary objective or objectives and secondary or contributive objectives. These secondary objectives may be especially useful if they can be followed on a day-to-day basis, in contrast to profitability, which either in respect of the business as a whole or an individual venture is something that can only be estimated in advance or computed after the event. One very obvious ongoing permanent contributive objective is cost efficiency. One management journalist wrote of Lord Weinstock's central corporate tenet that 'if you maintain efficiency at satisfactory levels and improve it continuously, the financial results should flow through in deeply satisfying quantities'; and quoted Lord Weinstock himself as saying 'the objective is to be efficient, not to be big. Growth is something that comes through efficiency'.[21] The choice of a particular subsidiary objective may be linked to the cost conditions of the business. For example, and as a matter of geometry, for a business that is characterised in the economist's short run by a high level of fixed costs relative to variable costs, or which experiences considerable economies of scale in the long run, sales revenue maximisation, which is something that can be immediately sought after, will contribute directly to profitability. On the other hand if a firm's costs are largely variable and there are few scale economies, then maximisation of the sales margin (that is, the gap for each unit of output between price and cost) is a more logical goal even if sales volume suffers. Thus it is perfectly logical for a business to have as its ultimate primary goal profitability or growth but to place emphasis in its strategy upon maximising sales revenue, increasing market share, expanding the price-cost margin or minimising costs. We would therefore identify as possible primary goals for the business variables such as profitability or growth and characteristics such as independence and personal satisfaction. Subsidiary or contributive goals would include maximisation of sales revenue, market share or sales margin, together with cost minimisation. In some cases the link between primary and secondary goals may be very direct. We have already referred to the relationship between sales revenue maximisation and profitability, and to the empirical research connecting market share and profitability (see note 15). In other cases the relationship may either be straightforward in so far as reasonable economy in costs will increse profits, or may involve a more complex relationship if significant cost reductions lead to an alteration to the product in the eyes of consumers.

Most business people would distinguish in some broad sense between the long term and the short term, recognising that certain forms of short-term behaviour such as reaping 'excessive' profits from a fortuitous market position need not necessarily be good for the business in the long term. Thus short-term profits may be sacrificed for long-term rewards; and one interpretation of the distinction made above between primary and contributive objectives is that the former are the long-term goals while the latter are shorter-term objectives. Ansoff, who considers that economic objectives largely in the form of return on capital employed exert a primary influence upon the firm, divides the time horizon for businesses into two parts: a proximate period of three to ten years over which forecasts can be made with an accuracy of plus or minus 20 per cent, and the long term, which is the period beyond ten years to the end of the firm's time horizon, which may be a very long period.[22] In Ansoff's view data are sufficient to use return on capital employed as the yardstick for investments within the proximate period of three to ten years. Within this period the firm thus seeks to maximise its profits by undertaking all investments covering its opportunity cost of capital set by reference to past experience and present returns in the product-market areas occupied by the firm, with due allowance being made for the different risk levels of various potential investments. Ansoff then turns to the long-term objectives of the business. These relate to the profitable survival of the business further into the future; and the danger is that by pursuing simple profit maximisation in the proximate period, longer-term needs may be ignored. Thus in Ansoff's view the business must move forward in the longer term on three fronts. First, it must expand the quality of its resources by continuing to invest in research and development, including staff development of both management and the remainder of the workforce in order to increase its depth of skills. Second, it must take steps to maintain its general efficiency relative to its product-market competitors. Measures of achievement in this area include growth, increased market share, etc., as well as indices of internal efficiency such as sales margins and capital turnover. Third, the business must pursue what Ansoff refers to as the long-term flexibility objective of avoiding undue dependence upon a narrow range of markets or customers or technologies, and also accumulate a cushion of financial reserves.

Thus some diversification of suppliers and customers, of product markets and technologies, together with the maintenance of a reserve of liquid resources must be pursued even if the adoption of such policies leads to reduced profitability in the proximate period. In this way Ansoff reconciles what is often an apparent conflict between short-term and long-term behaviour in businesses, although Ansoff appears to categorise growth and market share as longer-term goals, whereas we have suggested that pursuit of market share in the shorter term may be undertaken in order to increase longer-term profitability.

2.4 Conclusions

It was emphasised at the beginning of this chapter that the determination of business objectives was the first essential step in the strategic decision-making process. This chapter has outlined the form which these objectives may take and some of the problems in this area. These include the simultaneous existence of multiple objectives in businesses of all sizes, the need to distinguish between primary and secondary objectives, and the recognition of short-term and long-term objectives. It must be emphasised, however, that at this stage the business is not yet in a position to set its precise goals nor the broad strategy to be followed. In order to achieve this an analysis must be conducted of the product-market environment and resources of the business. The process of this analysis is covered in the following chapter, at the end of which the firm should be in a position to finalise its objectives and broad strategy.

References

1. W. R. Scott, 'Theory of Organizations', in R. E. L. Faris (ed.) *Handbook of Modern Sociology* (Chicago: Rand McNally, 1964) p. 488.
2. See H. Koontz and C. O'Donnell, *Principles of Management* (Tokyo: McGraw-Hill Kogakusha, 5th edn, 1972).
3. This discipline is ultimately imposed by dissatisfied shareholders refusing to supply a business with further capital or by selling their shares and thus depressing the market price and so raising the cost of equity capital for the firm. Shareholder dissatisfaction thus either cuts off the supply of new capital to unsucccessful businesses or provides them with capital only at a very high cost.
4. See the data in W. S. Howe, *Industrial Economics* (London: Macmillan, 1978) p. 18.
5. See *The Economist*, 16 November 1983, p. 86.

6. For the reaction of certain institutional shareholders to company policies, see 'The Man who Stopped a Tycoon in his Tracks', *Sunday Times*, 10 January 1982.
7. See K. Midgley, 'How Much Control Do Shareholders Exercise?' *Lloyds Bank Review*, October 1974, pp. 24–37.
8. For the largest firms in the UK the board of directors account in total for less than one-tenth of one per cent of the ordinary shares of the business. See data in J. R. Wildsmith, *Managerial Theories of the Firm* (Oxford: Martin Robertson, 1973) p. 4.
9. See G. Meeks and G. Whittington, 'Directors' Pay, Growth and Profitability', *Journal of Industrial Economics*, September 1975, Vol. XXIV, pp. 1–14; and A. Cosh, 'The Remuneration of Chief Executives in the United Kingdom', *Economic Journal*, March 1975, Vol. LXXXV, pp. 75–94.
10. See W. J. Baumol, *Business Behavior, Value and Growth* (New York: Harcourt Brace, revised edn, 1966).
11. See R. L. Marris, *The Economic Theory of 'Managerial' Capitalism* (London: Macmillan, 1964).
12. See, for example, O. E. Williamson, *The Economics of Discretionary Behaviour: Managerial Objectives in a Theory of the Firm* (London: Kershaw Publishing, 1974) p. 36; and R. M. Cyert and J. G. March, *A Behavioral Theory of the Firm* (New Jersey: Prentice-Hall, 1963) pp. 42–3.
13. See H. K. Radice, 'Control Type, Profitability and Growth in Large Firms: An Empirical Study', *Economic Journal*, September 1971, Vol. LXXXI, pp. 547–62; and P. Hall, 'Effect of Control Type on the Performance of the Firm in the UK', *Journal of Industrial Economics*, June 1975, Vol. XXIII, pp. 257–71.
14. See R. E. Thomas, *Business Policy* (Oxford: Philip Allan, 1977) Ch. 4.
15. See R. D. Buzzell and F. D. Wiersema, 'Successful Share-building Strategies', *Harvard Business Review*, January–February 1981, pp. 135–7.
16. Quoted in R. Heller, 'Lessons of the Entrepreneur', *Management Today*, April 1981, p. 55.
17. Quotation from *Financial Times*, 12 April 1977, reproduced in R. Oldcorn, *Management: A Fresh Approach* (London: Pan Books, 1982) p. 50.
18. Scottish Amicable Life Assurance Society, *Results '82*.
19. Quoted in T. Lester, 'How Flymo Flew Up', *Management Today*, January 1981, pp. 59–61.
20. These are production, inventory, sales, market share and profit. See Cyert and J. G. March, *A Behavioral Theory of the Firm*, pp. 40–3.
21. See Heller, 'Lessons of the Entrepreneur', pp. 56–7.
22. See Ansoff, *Corporate Strategy* (Harmondsworth: Penguin, 1968) Ch. 4.

Assessment of the Business Environment and Resources

3

> The advocates of systematic corporate planning base their case on the view that the determination of the future can be improved by a systematic analytical approach which reviews the business as a whole in relation to its environment. — B. W. Denning (ed.), *Corporate Planning* (London: McGraw-Hill, 1971) p. 4.

3.1 Introduction

In the previous chapter we studied corporate objectives: the range of these, the forces which determine business objectives, and how objectives might vary with the time dimension adopted. This process of objective-setting constitutes the first step in the strategic decision-making sequence (see Table 1.2 on p. 8), and as a result of this process the firm arrives at an understanding of its short- and long-term goals. The objectives set by an organisation naturally have a major influence upon the strategy it chooses to follow. However, unless the business has expressed its financial objectives in the context of specific product-market areas in which it intends to operate, these objectives will merely be end results which the business wishes to achieve, and therefore will constitute only the first step in the strategic process. To narrow the focus of strategy further it is necessary for the firm to identify potential markets in which its goals may be achieved. Moreover an assessment by the firm of its environment relative particularly to its current and potential resources may well lead to some modification of the business objectives or goals themselves. Thus in Ansoff's words, 'While the management at the outset will have some ideas about the value of proximate ROI it wishes to achieve, before the final values are selected it will have to modify the original aspirations in the light of the firm's capabilities and of available opportunities'.[1]

The next step in the strategic decision-making process thus involves the business in conducting an assessment of the environment in which it operates together with an audit of its own resources. The former process is referred to as the assessment of the *external* environment of the business leading to the identification of opportunities and threats for the organisation, while the latter involves an *internal* assessment of the business itself in terms of its particular strengths and weaknesses. This next step in the strategy-making process is necessary in order to carry the business forward from its broad objectives to the selection of a particular strategy; and providing that the external and internal business assessments discussed in this chapter do not contribute to a significant revision of corporate goals, these assessments should lead directly to a more refined choice of strategy in respect of individual product-market areas. The discussion of environmental and company assessments in this chapter is therefore followed in Chapter 4 by an analysis of the various possible strategies which firms may choose; this in turn is followed in Chapter 5 by a discussion of the techniques that may be used to evaluate possible strategies on the basis of these assessments.

The relationship between the internal and external appraisals (strengths and weaknesses, opportunities and threats – SWOT) and the subsequent stages in the total strategy-making process can be seen in Figure 3.1.

Figure 3.1 emphasises the way in which, given a set of broad corporate objectives, the external and internal appraisals provide a basis for subsequent evaluation of a range of possible strategies with a view to arriving at a specific corporate strategy. The remainder of this chapter examines the constituent parts of the external and internal appraisals of the firm, and brings these together in order to see how SWOT analysis can be used in helping to formulate strategy.

**Figure 3.1
Strategic Planning Flowchart**

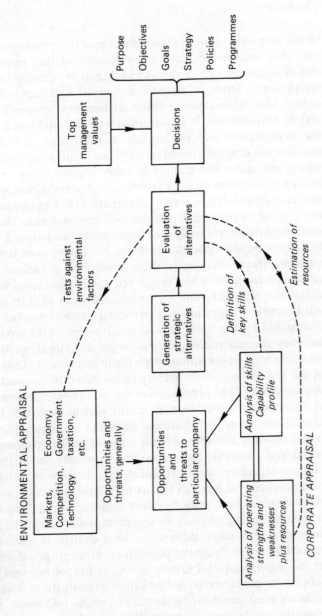

Source: B. W. Denning (ed.), *Corporate Planning* (London: McGraw-Hill, 1971) p. 8.

3.2   The External Environment: Opportunities and Threats

In this section we consider the definition of the environment of the business, analyse the various components of that environment, and examine how opportunities and threats are derived from these components. Strategic analysis as defined in Chapter 1 is concerned with the structuring of the relationship between a business and its environment. It is concerned with the interaction between the organisation and the outside world. Paine and Anderson describe the firm's environment as 'those inputs to an organization which are under the control of *other* organizations or interest groups or are influenced by interaction of several groups, such as the 'economy'.[2] These authors divide the firm's environment into the general environment and the task environment. The former general environment comprises those conditions having a broader, less direct impact upon the business. Normally, even if there are quite significant changes in these conditions the impact of such changes is likely to be less keenly felt and in most cases with some delay, during which time the organisation can plan its response. All businesses operating in a particular product-market area are confronted by the same general environment. This environment includes the macroeconomic, demographic, legal, political and social/cultural world within which the firm operates. Thus changes in the level of economic activity (gross domestic product), in the age structure of the population or the trend towards urbanisation, in the laws relating to business activity such as those which impose restrictions upon such business strategies as acquisition, in the broad political attitudes towards business in the economy, in the social and economic role of women in society, or in the public attitude regarding the acceptability or otherwise of certain business practices, all have an impact upon business strategy-making. An individual firm, may therefore find itself in making strategic decisions, having to react to a general reduction in the level of consumer disposable income, or to a change in the size of a particular age group in the population. Strategic possibilities such as the acquisition of a firm in the same line of business may be subject to government restriction or investigation; and private industry must generally be aware of policial and social attitudes towards the business community as a whole or to individual business practices such as 'golden handshakes'.

Normally of much more direct or immediately relevance to strategic decision-making for an individual firm is the task environment. Although this aspect of the business environment is normally better understood by a firm, and is possibly more predictable than the general environment, the immediate impact which changes in task environment factors can have upon a firm tends to make this a more obvious source of threat or opportunity. The principal dimensions of the task environment are set out in Table 3.1 below.[3]

Table 3.1
Key Dimensions of the Task Environment

Dimension	Factors
Demand	Size and growth of existing markets Number and size distribution of customers Physical distribution channels Nature of competition in markets, e.g. importance of price and non-price competition
Market Structure	Number and size distribution of competitors and suppliers Barriers to entry and exit in the market Product characteristics, e.g. differentiation
Technology	Level of technology and likely changes Cost structure, including economies of scale Dependence upon particular raw materials or labour
Government	Impact of particular legislation on the industry relating to production or consumption Role of government as supplier, competitor or customer.

The task environment has a major impact upon strategy formulation in any organisation. The degree of competition faced by the firm – arising from the 'demand' and 'market structure' variables – will determine not only the current profitability but also the room for strategic manoeuvre by the firm in the market. Low levels of demand and modest growth rates will constitute threats in a market and will intensify competition. Furthermore the structure or composition of both customers and other sellers will also affect the degree of competitiveness in the market and the appropriateness or otherwise of particular strategies. Barriers to entry in respect of a market will, according to their extent and nature, afford existing sellers some degree of protection from new-entrant competition, while at the same time posing a threat to firms which wish to compete in that sector. One of the most important sets of environmental variables is the nature of competition in any particular market, deriving from the nature of the product and customers' perception of it. This variable is likely to exert a major influence upon competitors' choices of individual strategies. Broadly speaking, firms operating under market conditions approaching the economist's 'perfect competition', where there are a large number of producers, where barriers to the entry of additional suppliers are low, and where customers in the market regard the products offered by competing sellers as close substitutes, will generally experience low levels of profitability and limited room for strategic manoeuvre, especially if they are confronted by a limited number of large customers. By contrast, firms operating in markets comprising a small group of sellers (oligopoly), which are protected by significant entry barriers and which sell highly differentiated products to a large number of small buyers, will generally have more strategic opportunities for establishing and maintaining a higher level of profitability.

The technology and cost structure in an industry may be taken largely as given by most individual firms in the market. They may strongly influence part of the strategy of firms, for example through market entry or current pricing policies being conditioned by the extent of economies of scale in production or other areas of the business. Firms may, however, use technological change as a means of competing against other sellers in the market. Finally, in addition to the impact which general legislation and government activity can have upon businesses, the task environment of an individual firm can be significantly influenced by more particular government activities. Legislative limitations on cigarette advertising, or the role of the government as a major purchaser of industrial gases for steel-making, are examples of the direct impact upon manufacturers of specific government action in their markets. Changes in tax or hire-purchase regulations will also have a direct impact upon firms in the industries affected; and in the case of the petroleum revenue tax and royalites payable to the government by oil companies, the government itself is aware that changes in these have a significant influence on exploration and development decisions.

If we take as an example of the impact of the task environment upon business strategy the case of corporate growth, then it is clear that expansion by the firm in its present market will crucially depend upon the growth rate of that market itself (which may be influenced by government macroeconomic policies), the existence of individual market segments which can be created or exploited, the possibilities for price and technological competition in the market by which the firm may attempt to increase its market share, the general strength of the firm's present competitors, and the financial and legislative ease with which other sellers in the market may be acquired. If the firm wishes to consider expanding into other market areas, then these same factors will have to be considered in respect of each of the potential markets it may consider entering.

There is some evidence to suggest that firms which carry out environmental analysis enjoy enhanced financial performance.[4] How therefore can businesses benefit from this process? First, a knowledge and understanding of its environment by a firm is likely itself to lead to more effective strategic decision-making by permitting *proactive* strategy based upon forecast scenarios for the business. For most organisations this involves adapting one's strategy to the environment: for example, by moving to different energy sources in anticipation of a rise in the cost of a particular fuel, or by diversifying away from a market that is dependent upon an age sector of the population which is known to be declining. For some firms, however, it is possible to envisage adapting the environment to one's strategy. This is much less likely to be the case in respect of the general environment. However, dimensions of the task environment such as the structure of the market (including the number of independent sellers, relationships with customers, and product characteristics) can be modified to the advantage of an individual firm. This could most obviously be achieved through the acquisition of competitors, suppliers or customers, or through the creation of market entry barriers by means of product differentiation.

In addition to this broader understanding of one's market to which envrionmental analyses should lead there is the issue of the identification of what Ohmae refers to as the key factors for success in a market.[5] Competitive success in a market involves identifying customers, understanding the basis upon which they buy the product, and attempting to provide buyers with the product in a better way than competitors. In some markets the basis of competition is price. But in others service to the customer, technological expertise or marketing skills play very significant competitive roles, and will therefore figure largely in strategic decision-making. In particular the results of the key factors for success analysis will strongly influence the way in which a business assesses its own strengths and weaknesses. A knowledge and understanding of its environment should thus increase the quality of strategic decision-making by virtue of the consideration of a full range of relevant factors well before the actual need to make a final decision. This in turn should lead to a greater chance of the organisation achieving its strategic goals.

Second, it is on the basis of environmental analysis that one identifies the threats and opportunities facing the business. That is to say, management must analyse the environment to identify those factors that will assist the firm in achieving its objectives (opportunities) and those which constitute a barrier to the achievement of objectives (threats). It is here that the exercise of the management skills of insight and foresight is required, for as Denning has commented, 'to a great extent the question of whether some factor is an opportunity or a threat is often as much a function of the perception and the attitude of the manager as it is of the factor itself'.[6] For example, the increase in the share of the grocery distribution market accounted for by multiple supermarket organisations may be seen by a food processor hitherto dependent upon 'corner shops' as either a threat to its existing level of sales through traditional outlets or an opportunity to reach a much greater potential audience by adapting its distribution channels to reflect changes in the market.

Third, there is the issue of what Porter refers to as 'environmental fit'.[7] By this is meant not only that strategy-makers should recognise trends in the environment and identify opportunities and threats, but that the strategy of the organisation should be specifically directed to exploiting environmental opportunities and to blocking threats. New markets which can be satisfied by using a firm's existing production facilities or technology should be exploited, while advances by competitors in terms of reduced production costs or the adoption of new distribution channels must either be matched by similar advances or counteracted by, for example, increased product differentiation designed to retain existing customers.

The purpose of environmental analysis is thus to maximise the competitive position of the firm; for as Porter has put it, 'intensive competition is neither coincidence nor bad luck'.[8] Environmental analysis, through an examination of all the relevant factors in a market (and indeed in potential markets) with a view to optimising the position of the firm, should lead to a greater understanding by a business of its markets, and an enhanced capacity to react to this through anticipatory strategy-making. Such analysis should identify opportunities and threats faced by the firm, and this in turn should lead to positive steps being taken to exploit opportunities and combat threats.

How successful such environmental analysis can be expected to be depends very much upon the characteristics of the environment itself. Among the most important dimensions of the environment in this context are its complexity, the rate of change in the environment, and the amount and cost of information available.[9] Complexity as a characteristic of the environment refers to the number of variables in the environment. This is likely, for exmaple, to be lower in mature product markets served by traditional technologies than in the case of newer industries. Again there is likely to be a similar contrast between the rates of change or dynamism of such markets. In mature markets the identity of suppliers and customers, and the cost and production conditions will normally have remained relatively unchanged for a number of years. Thus in addition to its reduced complexity such an environment is also likely to be relatively stable and predictable in contrast to one which, even if the number of variables is quite small, may be subject to rapid and unpredictable change in terms of customers, competitors or technologies. Finally, the extent to which environmental analysis may be carried out depends upon the cost and availability of information. Such information on the environment can come from a range of sources varying in accuracy and expense. For convenience these sources and their characteristics are summarised in Appendix Table 3.A1 on pp. 50–1. The situation with regard to information on the business environment may not only determine how much strategic analysis is done but also tip the competitive balance in this respect in favour of larger organisations which can more easily afford the expense of acquiring the necessary information.

As a particular example of environmental analysis, consider the case of the UK confectionery industry.[10] The general environment of this industry at the present time is one of low growth of consumer disposable incomes, and consequently restricted discretionary expenditure on confectionery. An ageing population is also likely to depress confectionery sales, as is the trend towards greater concern with general health and dental hygiene. Macroeconomic or government forces influence the industry in so far as the major ingredient of chocolate confectionery is imported cocoa, the sterling cost of which is determined by the external value of our currency. Furthermore, the imposition and changes in the level of VAT have also affected confectionery sales. The more immediate or task environment of the industry is that of a market characterised by low growth and dominated by three large suppliers accompanied by a considerable 'tail' of smaller firms. Confectionery manufacturers' sales of 766,960 tonnes in 1982 were better than those of the previous two years, but were considerably down from 840,690 tonnes achieved in 1973. Thus although UK confectionery consumption at 8 ozs per head per week was until recently the highest in the world, this has changed little over the past twenty-five years, and the industry generally is faced with poor growth prospects. Two major producers in the market are Rowntree-Mackintosh, with UK confectionery sales in 1983 of around £370 million out of a global turnover of £952 million, and Cadbury-Schweppes, whose total 1983 UK sales of confectionery were £304 million from a world-wide turnover of £1,703 million. The other major supplier is Mars, a firm about whose market position much less is known because of its private company status. Thus although there are more than 200 confectionery manufacturers in this country the three major suppliers mentioned above are estimated by trade sources to have a combined market share of about 80 per cent, with each of the dominant producers having around 25 per cent of the market. The industry has traditionally been characterised by high levels of advertising and promotional expenditure. It is estimated that the proportion of manufacturers' costs accounted for by such expenditure is around 15 per cent, and in 1978 the actual expenditure on press and television advertising by the industry was only marginally short of £35 million. This advertising and promotional expenditure has contributed to the very strong product differentiation in the market, and must constitute a considerable barrier to the entry of new suppliers. The industry also places additional financial demands upon constituent firms by virtue of the increasingly sophisticated capital-intensive technology now available, and the seasonal nature of sales. The major input into chocolate confectionery is of course cocoa, whose price has risen considerably over the past decade and is also subject to considerable fluctuation, thus emphasising the importance of purchasing skills in this area. Distribution of confectionery is through a total of some 250,000 retail outlets, although multiple grocers and supermarkets now account for an increasing share of this market at the expense of the more specialist confectioner-tobacconist-newsagent outlets. In common with other food processors there is concern among confectionery manufacturers that the power of such large-scale food distributors in terms of the margins and additional discounts which they are able to extract from manufacturers is detrimental to the profitability of the latter.

This brief sketch of one market indicates the range of general and task environment features that have an impact upon strategic decision-making in the industry. Any firm considering entry into the confectionery market or the strategy which it should adopt in continuing to operate in this area must consider these environmental features of the industry in the context of its corporate goals and in relation to the resources of the business. It is to a consideration of the latter that we now turn.

3.3   The Internal Business Audit: Strengths and Weaknesses

No business can develop a strategy simply on the basis of identifying market opportunities. However attractive an existing or prospective market may appear to be, the firm's strategy must take account of the particular resources or competence of the organisation. Strategy must therefore emerge from the combined assessment of market attractiveness and business strengths. Thus although the exercise may well be in part a subjective one, the second stage of the total analysis necessary for strategic decision-making comprises the internal audit of the business: the analysis by the organisation of its own resources and capabilities. The purpose of this analysis is to determine the competitive advantage of the business *vis-à-vis* its current and prospective general and task environments, and particularly in relation to its present and potential competitors. The data in Table 3.2 suggest a framework within which this analysis may be conducted.[11]

The material in Table 3.2 provides a framework within which an organisation can appraise itself. Three aspects of the internal audit should be stressed. First, in considering the external appraisal of the business the point was made that what were seen as opportunities or threats was to some extent dependent upon management's perception of the situation. Correspondingly, in respect of the internal audit one can only consider a particular feature to be a strength or a weakness in relation to other factors. These include principally the present product-market environment of the business and its perception of its broad strategy. Obviously a financial structure or cash position for the business which in one industry is wastefully liquid may in another constitute prudent financial management. Similarly, the appropriateness of particular distribution networks, production capabilities or organisation structures will be dependent upon the chosen product market. The company can thus only identify its strengths and weaknesses relative to an individual product-market area.

This relative aspect of the internal appraisal of the business can be demonstrated in the context of broad strategies. Porter, in his analysis of competition, speaks of three generic strategies or broad policies which businesses may adopt in attempting to optimise their position in the market.[12] These strategies are: (1) overall cost leadership, under which a firm places primary emphasis on attain-

Table 3.2
Analysis of Business Resources and Competence

Key Areas	Dimensions
Product-Market	Share of existing markets
	Range of products
	Position of products in product life-cycle
	Dependence upon key products for sales/ profits/cash flow
	Distribution network
	Marketing and market research competence
Production	Number, size, location, age and capacity of plants
	Specialisation/versatility of equipment
	Production cost levels
	Cost and availability of raw materials
	Production control systems
Finance	Present asset structure
	Present capital structure – gearing ratio, etc.
	Access to additional equity and debt finance
	Pattern of cash flow
	Procedures for financial management
Technology	Up-to-dateness of production methods and products
	Research and development spending and efficiency
Organisation and Human Resources	Organisation structure – form and appropriateness
	Management style
	Management succession
	Staff development
	Wage and salary levels
	Management-trade union relations

ing the lowest cost position in the market; (2) differentiation, by which is meant emphasising the uniqueness of the product which is marketed on an industry-wide basis; and (3) focus, which is a strategy that emphasises the attainment of a superior position in a particular market segment. The choice of one of these strategies will depend upon the firm's perception of the environment (the existence of individual segments or niches in the market) and of the basis of successful competition (price or product differentiation). Having adopted a particular generic strategy, the firm will appraise its resources in that context. For a firm that is following a broad cost leadership policy the emphasis will be upon a narrow range of products and the achievement of full economies of scale in specialist plants. In this instance the maintenance of a range of products with innovative and versatile production equipment capable of meeting the needs of a wide range of customers would therefore be incompatible with the broad strategy. By contrast, for the organisation following a policy of differentiation, emphasis upon low-cost operations and economy of distribution network costs or advertising would be quite wrong, and in the context of such a policy would be inappropriate. Market segmentation or focus involves identifying a particular customer or product type or geographical area within a market and devoting one's resources to serving this segment. For such a policy to succeed the required strengths are in the areas of market research, a particular geographical location of plants, or a particular standard of distribution network. Producing a range of products on a national basis would in this case be correspondingly inappropriate. In this way, therefore, the identification of a very broad strategy can be helpful in assessing the organisation's strengths and weaknesses.

As an example of the adoption of one of these broad strategies the *Financial Times* recently reported the success of John Deere in pulling itself from third to first place in the American agricultural equipment market. Deere attacked this market nationally on the basis of product and production technology (six-cylinder engines for harvesters, and a high level of electronically controlled production), consequent low-cost production, and a well organised dealer organisation giving farmers speed and efficiency in delivery, parts and servicing. This strategy obviously arose from Deere's perception of the environment of this market and the key competitive factors. These in turn dictated a particular strategy, and thus the firm's identification of strengths and weaknesses.[13]

The second point regarding the internal audit, and correspond-ing to our earlier emphasis upon 'fit', is that a firm should consciously direct its strengths towards exploiting market opportu-nities and blocking threats, while at the same time minimising exposure of its weaknesses. In this way the combined analysis of strengths and weaknesses with opportunities and threats can lead to the identification of quite specific strategies. For example, strategies which align strengths and opportunities may be referred to as exploitative or developmental. Those which direct strengths to threats may be termed blocking strategies. Finally, a business may use its strengths to repair perceived weaknesses. This linking of strengths and weaknesses, opportunities and threats (SWOT) provides the basis for a comprehensive analysis by a business of its environment and competence. For example, a firm that has a developed competence in market research (strength) should seek out those parts of the market (geographic or customer type) which are not presently being catered for by its competitors (correspond-ing opportunity). This market research strength could also be used to repair the perceived weakness of an existing dependence upon a narrow range of customers. An organisation with low production costs can, on the basis of an appropriate pricing strategy, use this strength to increase market share, while a firm that is in a strong financial position can use this strength to achieve the same goal by the acquisition route, always provided that there are no general environment barriers to adopting this latter strategy. If such barriers exist then the same firm may have to use its financial strength to improve its production or technology performance as a means of achieving the original goal of increased market share. Finally, for a business that is weak so far as breadth of distribution network, production cost levels or research and development are concerned, strategies should be adopted which allow it to concentrate upon a restricted range of customers who are less price conscious and whose requirement is for a service which does not imply a high level of technological sophistication.

A third aspect of the internal audit of the business is that firms should use this approach to assess their position relative to their competitors. That is, the organisation's resources should be assessed not only in some absolute sense or against the needs of its present markets, but also relative to those of its present and potential competitors. This involves the firm in carrying out an 'internal' audit of its fellow suppliers in the market in order to pit its strengths against their weaknesses, to avoid a confrontation along a 'strong' dimension of a competitor, and to recognise areas in which one is most exposed to one's competitors. Competitor analysis is itself a potentially major area of strategic analysis.[14] But to take a simple example, while a business which enjoys low production cost levels could envisage increasing its market share by reducing prices against a competitor which did not possess this characteristic, it would be unwise to adopt such an approach against an equally low-cost competitor, particularly in the context of a relatively stagnant market in which price levels are not a major determinant of either individual market share or aggregate demand. In a typically oligopolistic market the adoption of such a price-cutting strategy might simply result in a round of price reductions which left all sellers with unchanged market shares in a very slightly expanded market characterised by significantly reduced profit margins for all. Market share under such conditions may rather be increased by more effective advertising, or the establishment of a technological lead with respect to the product itself.

3.4   Combined Analysis of Environment and Resources

Environmental and resource analysis is a vital second stage in strategic decision-making following the broad choice of objectives. Success in using the SWOT approach involves going beyond a mere listing of the pros and cons of a particular market for the firm, and combining the dimensions listed in Tables 3.1 and 3.2 to identify appropriate strategies for the business. At the risk of simply producing another similar list, Table 3.3 contains a number of strategic pointers derived from our analysis so far.

In case the list of points in Table 3.3 should seem too obvious, consider the case of Rolls Royce and the events in the aero-engine market leading up to the collapse of this firm in 1971.[15] In the mid-1960s Rolls Royce foresaw enormous market growth for very large jet engines for wide-bodied aircraft, especially in comparison with the projected severe decline in demand for Rolls's existing smaller engines. Thus despite Rolls's admitted technological lag behind its American competitors in this area, the company embarked in 1967 on the development of a new large jet engine –

Table 3.3
Strategies Deriving from Analysis of the Business Environment and Resources

1. Analyse the environment to identify the key factors for market success.

2. Use existing business strengths to exploit market opportunities.

3. Try to create new opportunities from strengths.

4. Use strengths to counteract threats and repair weaknesses

5. Avoid competition in 'threatened' markets or along 'weak' resource dimensions.

6. Assess competitors:
   (a) capitalise upon competitor's weaknesses.
   (b) avoid competing against rival's strengths.

the RB211. What Rolls ignored was the fact that the market was predominantly an American one, and that its American aero-engine competitors were not only much larger, but had a technological advantage. This advantage was supplemented by a US government attitude which encouraged American airlines to adopt a 'buy American' policy in this market, and also by massive support from the US government to aero-engine firms related to defence contracts. In addition Rolls significantly underestimated development costs, which were initially put at £60 million but which eventually totalled more than £200 million. We would argue that the events that led Rolls Royce to receivership early in 1971 stemmed from a poor initial strategic decision. Market opportunities were taken up with a lack of apparent regard to the threats (the attitude of the US government, the power of competitors, etc.) or the relative weakness of Rolls itself in terms of technological expertise, cost control, size and financial resources. In other words, Rolls attempted to operate in a market which, although admittedly attractive in global terms, was in all of the circumstances inappropriate.

To date the 1980s group equivalent of the Rolls Royce affair seems to be the notable lack of success which the British clearing banks have had in the US retail banking market. Excessive prices paid for acquisitions, the harshly competitive impact on the American banking market of government deregulation and the entry of stores and finance houses into retail banking, and the need to spend additional sums of money on banking automation, have combined to produce large capital losses and minimal returns among the 'big four' UK commercial banks. Here the evidence of serious strategic errors is not so obvious. Nevertheless, the competitive environment – both in its form and intensity – would appear to have been misjudged by the UK entrants into this market to the disadvantage of their shareholders.[16]

As a final example consider the competitive strategies adopted by the two firms dominating the US intercity bus market. In the late 1970s Greyhound and Trailways together accounted for 75 per cent of this market, in which the number of scheduled passengers had declined from 200 million in 1967 to 125 million in 1978. The buses are caught between airline competition on longer routes and increased ownership of motor cars on shorter runs. In the former market the airlines could offer in 1978 a one-way ticket from Chicago to Miami for $99 for a two-and-a-half-hour flight, while the bus ticket price was $69 for a journey time of a day and a half. Faced with a declining market where price elasticity of demand between competing transport systems is likely to be minimal, but where consumers are equally likely to be sensitive to price differences between rival bus companies, Greyhound and Trailways (both of whom are subsidiaries of large conglomerate parents) entered in the late 1970s into what the American business magazine *Fortune* described as a 'fierce and profitless shootout over passenger fares'.[17] Greyhound, by far the larger of the two rivals, commenced a price war on long-distance journeys which did nothing but increase the problems of the two operators. Instead of isolating the total market into segments according to length of journey and examining each environment in terms of growth and competitiveness; instead of asking whether the key factor for success was price and not better depot management, more convenient schedules and more comfortable buses; and instead of ancitipating one's competitor's response to an initial price reduction and calculating whether one could afford to compete in this dimension, a personalised price war combined with acrimonious disputes regarding the accuracy of promotional claims was embarked upon in which these rivals competed in a way which was strategically inept, which reduced their contribution to their corporate parents' earnings, and cost one chief executive officer his job.

These three examples indicate the consequences of poor strategic analysis at the level of considering the importance of the environment of the market, the key factors for competitive success, and the related strengths and weaknesses in determining the strategic approach to be adopted. It is almost certain that in all three cases a better performance outcome could have been achieved by a consideration of these variables.

There is evidence to suggest that although a number of companies use the analysis of market conditions and business resources as a contribution to strategic decision-making, certain difficulties arise in its practical implementation. Stevenson's research, for example, indicated a number of problems.[18] First, businessmen appear to neglect certain fundamental data such as market share, distribution channels or trade union relations in carrying out their audit. These areas are quite clearly included in our Table 3.2 above; and their ommission by Stevenson's business respondents strongly indicates the value of such a checklist and also the need for business people to take a broad view of the possible strengths and weaknesses of their organisation. Second, although it may be considered to be appropriate for the most senior managers (presidents and board chairmen in Stevenson's terminology) to be more concerned with certain areas of company strengths and weaknesses compared with their subordinate colleagues, there does appear to be an over-emphasis by senior corporate strategy-makers upon the organisational and personnel aspects of this analysis as compared with marketing and technical features. Another interesting point to emerge from this study is the positive association between optimism and level in the corporate hierarchy in considering business strengths and weaknesses. Senior managers generally tended to perceive the range of company attributes as strengths, whereas these same attributes appear to have been regarded more critically by managers at a lower level in the organisation. Third, managers varied in the use made of criteria by which an attribute was judged a strength or weakness. Historical, competitive and normative bases (e.g. consultants' opinions) bases were adopted. Concern may be expressed as to whether the right approach is always used (for example, there appeared to be an almost total neglect of competitive criteria for some attributes), or whether the use of historical or budget criteria are not likely to lead to complacency on the part of management by ignoring standards capable of being achieved elsewhere. These and other behavioural difficulties, such as the adoption by all managers of a sufficiently objective approach to the appraisal, suggest that considerable progress has yet to be made in using this approach in formulating corporate strategy.

3.5   Conclusions

SWOT analysis is basically an exercise in identification and analysis. Management should use the technique in order to identify the key features of their environment (both general and task) which determine business success, and likewise develop an awareness of the fundamental internal strengths and weaknesses of the organisation which not only influence the current position of the business but also, at least in the short term, dictate the strategies open to the firm. The application of SWOT analysis to competitors as well as oneself should indicate to a business its relative position in the market and again direct the firm towards appropriate strategies.

SWOT analysis itself provides no formal set of rules for strategic success. Certain general guidelines may nonetheless be derived from it. The first is to recognise the particular characteristics of an individual market. Is overall demand static? How expensive is it going to be to keep up with technological developments? How long is it likely to take to build up market share? Is one's market performance going to depend upon price competition or relative technical expertise? The answers to these questions derive from the external appraisal of the business environment. They determine correspondingly the technological, financial and other strengths that are required for success in any particular market.

Second, the latter part of the SWOT analysis highlights the basis of one's own present success, and one's competitiveness *vis-à-vis* market rivals. Consolidation of one's own strengths, exploitation of competitor's weaknesses, and avoidance of 'head on' confrontation with other sellers are all individual strategies which derive from SWOT analysis.

The third point to emerge from the material in this chapter is that the analysis of markets and competitors may lead a business to revise its objectives, and in particular the targets which it can hope to achieve in terms of profitability or growth. Thus there is a feedback between Stage 2 of the corporate strategic decision-making process analysed in this chapter and the broad objectives set at Stage 1 which were discussed in Chapter 2.

On the basis of this refined set of objectives and with a greater awareness of the significant characteristics of its markets and its own resources the firm is now able to consider the range of strategic possibilities open to it. These are the topic of Chapter 4.

Appendix Table 3.A1
Sources and Techniques for Environmental Analysis

	Sources of Information	Techniques
Economic forecasts national economy sector forecasts	(i) Government and private forecasts	(a) Critical appreciation of published forecasts
		(b) Development of models or relationships for sector forecasts
	(ii) Industry association, government, private forecasts	(c) Input-output analysis
	(iii) Market research	(d) Large number of quantitative techniques
Technological forecasts	(i) Technical intelligence service reports	(a) Demand and conditional demand analyses
	(ii) Technical market research	(b) Opportunity identification techniques
	(iii) Research into competitors' developments	(c) Theoretical limits testing
		(d) Parameter analysis
		(e) Various systems analysis methods

		(f) Discipline reviews
		(g) Expert opinion
Sociological fore-casts	Wide variety of sources of data, including government reports, educational fore-casts, population forecasts, regional forecasts, skilled labour forecasts, institutional changes, etc.	(a) National models such as built by Battelle (unlikely to be done in any one corporation)
		(b) Expert opinion
Political forecasts	Political intelligence services and government reports	Expert opinion
Forecasting com-petitors' actions	Any intelligence about com-petitors	Any relevant technique to give information from intelli-gence

Source: B. W. Denning, 'Strategic Environmental Appraisal', *Long Range Planning*, March 1973, p. 26.

References

1. H. I. Ansoff, *Corporate Strategy* (Harmondsworth: Penguin, 1968) p. 51.
2. F. T. Paine and C. R. Anderson, *Strategic Management* (New York: Dryden Press, 1983) p. 16.
3. This table is based upon B. W. Denning, *Corporate Planning* (London: McGraw-Hill, 1971) p. 10.
4. See P. H. Grinyer and D. Norburn, 'Strategic Planning in 21 U.K. Companies', *Long Range Planning,* August 1974, p. 80.
5. See K. Ohmae, *The Mind of the Strategist* (Harmondsworth: Penguin, 1982) Ch. 3.
6. Denning, *Corporate Planning,* p. 11.
7. See M. E. Porter, *Competitive Strategy* (New York: Free Press, 1980) p. xix.
8. M. E. Porter, 'How Competitive Forces Shape Strategy', *Harvard Business Review,* March–April 1979, p. 137.
9. See Paine and Anderson, *Strategic Management,* pp. 39–40.
10. This analysis is based upon data contained in the annual report and other publications of The Cocoa, Chocolate and Confectionery Alliance and upon the essay by the author 'Competition and Performance in Food Manufacturing' in J. Burns *et al.* (eds), *The Food Industry* (London: Heinemann, 1983) pp. 101–26.
11. This table summarises the analysis in D. F. Harvey, *Business Policy and Strategic Management* (Columbus, Ohio: Merrill Publishing, 1982) pp. 113–17.
12. See Porter, *Competitive Strategy,* Ch. 2.
13. See 'Deere Ploughs a Lone Furrow', *Financial Times,* 20 January 1984.
14. Porter, *Competitive Strategy,* Ch. 3.
15. See J. Argenti, *Corporate Collapse: The Causes and Symptoms* (Maidenhead: McGraw-Hill, 1976) Ch. 5.
16. See 'Over There and Overdrawn', *Sunday Times,* 4 March 1984.
17. See 'The Bus Lines are on the Road to Nowhere', *Fortune,* 31 December 1978, pp. 58–63, from which the details of this case are taken.
18. See H. H. Stevenson, 'Defining Corporate Strengths and Weaknesses', *Sloan Management Review,* Spring 1976, pp. 51–68.

Strategic Possibilities 4

> Any business has one or more activities, whether the supply of physical artifacts or services . . . and these may be directed at one or more identifiably separate markets. — R. E. Thomas, *Business Policy* (Oxford: Philip Allan, 2nd edn, 1983) p. 159.

4.1 Introduction

In Chapter 2 we discussed corporate objectives, and in Chaper 3 the analysis of the external environment of the business and the assessment of the firm's resources. When a firm has completed this analysis it should have developed a clear idea of its financial objectives, refined if necessary on the basis of any feedback into the process of determining these objectives from the environment and business resource assessments. The business should also at this stage have a full understanding of the product-market areas open to it on the basis of its unique capabilities. The firm is thus now in a position to move towards a decision on the choice of strategy to be adopted in achieving its goals. The purpose of this chapter is to indicate the range of strategic possibilities open to businesses. A broad description of these is offered here while some individual strategies are analysed in greater detail in Part II of this text (Chapters 7–12). On the basis of our description of individual strategies and its market circumstances, the firm should then be able to match its strategy to the market conditions; and techniques for achieving this are examined in Chapter 5.

4.2 The Range of Strategies

The purpose of a selected strategy is to take the firm from its present position in the market towards the goals it has identified for itself. The strategy will be chosen on the basis of the business goals and the market conditions/business resources situation obtaining at the time. In some cases the choice of strategy is fairly straightforward. If a business has adopted growth as its major goal then an aggressive growth strategy is obviously appropriate. However, when the business goal is profitability, then a whole range of strategies ought to be considered in the context of the product-market and resource conditions. In practice, of course, firms are not always able or willing to spend unlimited resources on strategic decision-making, for this activity has a cost to the firm in terms of financial resources and the loss of time in putting the strategy into operation. It is also undoubtedly true that businesses find it difficult to change strategic direction quickly; and future strategy is often heavily influenced by the past. Our view, however, is that wherever possible businesses should ensure that their strategic decision-making is carried out in such a manner as to allow for consideration of a full range of options, and that this is done sufficiently far ahead of events for a genuinely proactive strategy to emerge rather than simply a crisis reaction.

Table 4.1 indicates the broad types of strategy that are available to firms, together with possible goals and constraints associated with these. Each strategy is then discussed in turn.

4.3 Expansion Strategies

Growth within existing markets

We have already noted in our discussion of business objectives the important role of growth in modern theories of the firm. Bearing in mind the dominance in business decision-making of managers rather than equity shareholders, Marris has presented a convincing

Table 4.1
Strategic Possibilities

Strategy	Goals	Constraints
Expansion		
Growth within existing markets	growth profits	competition in market; growth rate of market
Related diversification	growth profits diversity	availability of 'adjacent' markets or technologies; transfer of management skills
Unrelated diversification	growth diversity	transfer of management skills; control of operations
Vertical integration	growth control	transfer of management skills; co-ordination of outputs
Status quo	?	characteristics of existing market
Contraction		
Strategic shrinking	reduced commitment to particular market	rate of market contraction; reaction of competitors
Divestment	immediate exit from market	ability to dispose of operations
	release of resources	

case for growth being a major business objective. In one American study, for example, it was found that among a sample of firms drawn from the *Fortune* 500 companies, more than 50 per cent of senior business executives had growth as a primary strategy.[1] In addition to the general attractions of growth already suggested, the strategy of expansion within existing markets has considerable appeal to management for a number of reasons. First, providing the market conditions are appropriate, this is a strategy that involves the minimum degree of risk for management. The firm is in this case seeking growth by doing 'more of what it is doing already', as Edwards and Townsend put it.[2] Thomas suggests that given the management difficulties involved even in expansion through related diversification, growth within a single market will appeal to those managers who wish to stick to their product-market lasts.[3] Thus expansion of activity within one's own market, by obviating the need to accommodate to new customers, products or technologies, is a particularly attractive direction of corporate growth.

Second, there are advantages from growth within a single market arising from market power and cost reductions. We have already noted in Chapter 2 the US evidence relating to the positive association between market share and profitability (see Chapter 2, note 15). If, by expanding within its existing market area at a rate that is greater than that of the market as a whole, a firm enjoys increased market share along with growth, then experience suggests that profitability is likely to increase. This may be a further incentive to home-based expansion as opposed to those growth strategies which take the firm away from its existing product-market area. Additionally, horizontal expansion may confer on the business reductions in unit costs arising from economies of scale and the effects of moving down the learning or experience curve. Economies of scale result in unit costs falling as the scale of output rises when output can be increased proportionately faster than inputs. This may happen for a variety of reasons, including the benefits of specialisation and division of labour, access to scale economies in purchasing of inputs, or spreading certain fixed costs over a greater output.[4] The point is that most of such economies would appear to occur at the plant level and relate to expansion of output of a limited range of goods rather than to the scale of a multi-product enterprise as a whole. The concept of the learning curve – popularised in this context by the Boston Consulting Group – suggests that as *cumulative* output rises then unit costs fall. The Boston Consulting Group data indicate that, typically, unit costs decline 20–30 per cent in real terms each time accumulated production is doubled. This is held to arise from productivity improvements associated with technical change, more efficient factor combinations, and modification and redesign of the product, which have the effect of reducing costs.[5]

Although it has been suggested that it would be simplistic to assume that the benefits of scale economies or learning effects accrue to an organisation without any managerial effort, or that there may not be offsetting problems in such areas as industrial relations or management co-ordination attaching to increased scale at the plant or firm level, these factors nonetheless exert a strong influence in favour of horizontal expansion as a corporate strategy, providing the market conditions are appropriate.

Related diversification

This strategy, known in the American literature as concentric diversification, is one possible reaction to the major problem attaching to horizontal expansion – that is, the difficulty of securing continued expansion in a market which itself is not growing rapidly or where competitors are also following a strategy of horizontal growth. The problem of growth under these conditions arises from the need to expand by way of price or product competition – a problem which, as we shall see in Chapter 10, may not be entirely overcome by acquiring competitors. Related diversification allows a business to escape from a possible internecine war with existing competitors while minimising product-market adjustment costs in terms of having to adopt new technologies, etc. Firms may thereby increase rates of return by moving into related markets offering better prospects than existing ones, and also achieve a greater spread of interests and reduced exposure of profitability to the fortunes of an individual market.

Firms pursuing this type of strategy may broadly exploit their existing technology in new product-market areas, seek new markets for existing products, or capitalise upon existing distribution systems to increase their range of products. Dunlop, for example, has branched out from its original pneumatic tyres to producing a range of products such as sports goods which use polymer technology, and has also diversified into other engineering areas related to wheels, brakes and hoses.[6] More recently ICI has announced that it is seeking to use its technological expertise in order both to broaden its market base and reduce its exposure to the cyclical nature of some of its chemical business by expanding its drug and agrochemicals divisions.[7] In the author's research on the traditional jute industry based in Dundee an interesting dichotomy was found between those firms which followed a policy of diversifying by changing their technological base from that of jute to polypropylene to continue to serve the same markets (predominantly tufted carpet primary backing) and those which both in jute and polypropylene tried to find new markets for existing products. Firms which adapted jute from floorcovering to wallcovering, or which added civil engineering and other end uses to the floorcovering markets for polypropylene, were adopting a limited diversification policy of seeking new end uses for existing products as a means of expanding overall demand and reducing dependence upon a single market area within a given technology.[8] Finally, Thomas gives an example of the major oil companies diversifying their product range through taking advantage of their existing motor service station operations or connections to provide a wider range of motor accessories and replacement components.[9] In this case again the intention is to increase sales and at the same time reduce dependence upon a single product area (petrol and oil) through building upon existing market knowledge and distribution facilities.

A firm adopting a strategy of related diversification in order to achieve growth is seeking to capitalise upon an existing strength – technological or marketing – in order to expand without a dramatic change in its activities. If such new ventures offer increased growth or profit opportunities combined with some technical or marketing commonality with the firm's existing activities, then this growth path will be particularly attractive to management.

Unrelated diversification

Expansion by a business into market areas that are not related to its existing products or services in terms of technology, distribution channels or end use is referred to as unrelated or conglomerate diversification. The rationale for such an expansion path is financial rather than industrial, although just where 'industrial' logic ends and 'financial' logic commences is difficult to judge. Unrelated diversification obviously releases the firm from any constraints upon the chosen market in which to expand; but by the same token the effort required of management to comprehend and control far-flung market interests is much greater. In practice, however, for some businesses with a fairly restricted technological or market base any diversification is almost bound to be conglomerate rather than concentric, and it is argued by some that although operating economies of scale are by definition not available to widely diversified businesses, conglomerate expansion may nonetheless give rise to economies of scale or synergy in the areas of finance or marketing.[10] In fact conglomerate businesses tend to require to be managed on a completely different basis from that of firms with a narrower product range, and this is a point to which we shall return in Chapter 9. Because of the way in which unrelated diversification releases growth-oriented businesses from the restrictions of their existing markets, and must also reduce the overall business risk of the enterprise, this strategy became extremely popular in the 1960s and 1970s. Although we shall see in Chapters 9 and 10 that some of this popularity has since waned, the policy nonetheless deserves consideration by expansionist management.

Vertical integration

This strategy is considered in more detail in Chapter 8; while here we present a broad outline of its strategic features. Vertical integration involves the firm in moving backward or forward along the path followed by a product from raw material to being placed in the hands of the final consumer. For an individual business vertical integration therefore involves, in Edwards and Townsend's words, either 'making what was bought' or 'reaching forward toward the ultimate customer'.[11] The former strategy is referred to as backward vertical integration, while the latter is referred to as forward vertical integration.

As a strategy vertical integration has the attraction, from the point of view of management, of not involving entry into altogether new markets while at the same time expanding output and also exerting greater control over a market in terms of participating in an increased number of stages in the production/distribution chain. Thus backward vertical integration is often undertaken in order to ensure adequate supplies of raw materials in terms either of quantity or quality. These factors probably explain the acquisition in the 1960s by the motor car assembly firms of previously independent car body manufacturers, and also the investment by petroleum companies in oil exploration and production. On the other hand, forward vertical integration is often observed in declining markets as manufacturers seek to buy up customers for their products under increasingly competitive conditions, or in response to institutional restrictions which encourage manufacturers to gain control of retail outlets. Thus during the period of falling bread consumption in this country since the mid-1950s there was a steady acquisition of independent bakeries by the major flour millers in an attempt to capture outlets for their product.[12] A similar policy was followed by Courtaulds during this period as demand for the older type of synthetic fibres fell off.[13] In the cases of beer sales to public houses and also petrol sales, licensing restrictions have encouraged brewers and petroleum companies either to acquire retail outlets or establish 'tied sales' arrangements in order to provide greater stability of sales in industries where there are high fixed costs of manufacture.

As we shall see in Chapter 8, vertical integration as a strategy for growth or increased security is not without its limitations or dangers. For example, such a strategy in no way reduces the dependence of the firm upon a single market, while at the same time the ability on the part of management to operate successfully at different stages in the same market is not something that can be taken for granted. This strategy nonetheless deserves consideration as a means of achieving business growth without the major adjustments involved in moving across product-market boundaries.

4.4 Status Quo

Although most business people and business writers would share Harvey's view that 'to stand still in a dynamic environment is to move backward', a positive decision to retain the business in its present market position is nonetheless a perfectly logical one.[14] A business which in its present product-market area and with its current scale of operations is earning a satisfactory return on capital and which is therefore experiencing no significant gap between current performance and aspiration levels, is faced with no obvious requirement for a dynamic strategy. Furthermore, management may either prefer to avoid any of the risks associated with expansion of the business, or may in the case of owner-managers accept the constraint of limited availability of additional finance, which would also tend to favour remaining at the present scale of operations. If in addition to these factors the market environment in which the firm is currently operating appears to be stable at a reasonable level of demand, this may reinforce the case for a status quo strategy.

Thomas, however, echoing the sentiments of Harvey, argues that beyond a very limited period a status quo policy is inappropriate, and suggests that 'much of the crop of (business) failures in recent years has been due to complacent adherence to such untenable positions'.[15] The major error in a status quo policy is the neglect this will give rise to of assessing the environment and resources of the firm, and in particular the changes which may occur in these factors. Analysis of the present environment of the firm may reveal a number of features which, even if they do not constitute present threats to the business, may well become so in time. How aware is the business of the market position of its customers in their product areas? Should the firm remain dependent upon its existing products and/or customers? Who are the firm's existing and potential competitors in its present product areas? What is the basis of competition in the market, and what are the distinctive competences of the firm *vis-à-vis* its market rivals? What is the state of technology with regard to the firm's existing products and production processes, and what are the trends in these areas? A business may be performing quite satisfactorily without realising the dangers of its present situation. These include the danger of the collapse of one of its major customers, of a rapid reduction in demand for the product, the appearance of new competition from another industry, or a rapid escalation in the rate of technological progress in the market with accompanying financial demands upon firms. A complacent acceptance of the status quo puts the firm at risk both in the long term and the short term. In particular, a failure to analyse its environment and resources means that action which could quite easily be taken by the firm now to assure its future may be overlooked. Steps should thus be taken currently on the basis of SWOT analysis to consider each of the questions put above. To take one example, recognition that demand for the firm's product has reached its peak of expansion and is unlikely to grow further should lead to the adoption of a 'harvesting' strategy. That is, investment in this product area will be cut back and prices set to maximise cash flow. Equally important, this cash flow must be used to invest in alternative product areas that are appropriate to the particular competence of the business and which will provide it with adequate returns in the future, bearing in mind that there may be a considerable time lag while such returns build up. The author's research suggests that this failure sufficiently to anticipate the falling off in demand for existing products and to build up replacement markets is a major cause of poor performance, especially among small and medium-sized businesses.

Maintenance by an organisation of the status quo with regard to its product-market position is an understandable policy. Adequate returns may be being generated, and there may not only be significant risks involved in any major change in strategic direction but also considerable barriers in the form of finance or managerial expertise. Sound corporate strategy, however, demands a continued questioning of the advisability of the status quo position, thorough and continuing assessment of the environment and resources of the business, and a preparedness to react quickly to any need for adjustment.

4.5 Contraction

There is a range of circumstances in which it is appropriate for a business to follow a policy of reducing either its commitment to a particular market or the overall scale of its operations. Thus although long-term contraction in the size of the organisation may often correctly be interpreted as a sign of business failure, there are situations in which a reduction in the scale of some operations may be part of a sensible adjustment by the business to changing market conditions.

Broadly speaking, there are two sets of circumstances in which the whole or part of a business's operations may be deliberately reduced in scale or abandoned. The first occurs when a firm is withdrawing from a declining market, in which case we would expect to find the resources so released being reinvested in new product-market areas to take the place of those which are being phased out. This, to borrow one of Harrigan's expressions relating to 'endgame' strategies, we may call *strategic shrinking*.[16] The other contraction situation is the rather more dramatic one in which a major strategic repositioning of the business is required. Here a change in either the general or task environment may have revealed weaknesses in the present position of the business or its pattern of interests, and a sometimes drastic reappraisal of a part of the firm's activities is required, with large-scale liquidation of some investments and a restructuring of the organisation. This we shall call *divestment*. The strategies of strategic shrinking and divestment should be regarded as the opposite ends of a spectrum in the degree of forward planning, speed and scale which may have to be adopted by the firm in undertaking contracting strategies.

Strategic shrinking is the planned and orderly withdrawal from what a firm has perceived to be a declining market. Under these circumstances existing firms in the market will either gradually withdraw from the whole market over a period of time, withdraw from particular market segments if these exist, or make a decision to pull out of the market completely at an early stage in its decline. In each case the decision should be the result of a proactive strategy, and the financial and other resources released will be carefully reinvested in product-market areas which will provide replacement growth or profitability for the area which has been left.

Contrast this with the summary of a recent phase of divestment activity in the USA. Referring to what he termed a 'disinvestment boom', Thackray suggested that 'Seldom before in history have so many corporations restructured their firms' products and services and redeployed their assets in such far-ranging ways. Often, the sell-offs represent a 100% reversal from past philosophies and goals.'[17] The scale and suddenness with which this appears to have taken place presents us with a quite different scenario from that of strategic shrinking. We shall examine some aspects of divestment in more detail in Chapter 11. At present we may note that the strategy appears to be the product of excessive diversification in the past, unrealistic prices paid for diversifying interests, and a general environment combining historically high rates of interest (penalising highly geared businesses) and low rates of economic growth. Thus the more common picture here is that of a business selling off a whole section of the organisation very often obtained through acquisition in the not so distant past, and using the finance thus raised partly to reduce the level of borrowing, with the remainder being put back into the firm's traditional product-market areas.

4.6   Conclusions

The purpose of this chapter has been to identify the broad strategic possibilities open to the firm. For a single-product business one particular strategy will be adopted which is considered to be the most appropriate at the time. For a multi-product firm a range of individual strategies will be adopted, each one of which is appropriate to a particular product-market area; and the way in which these individual product strategies should be combined is considered in Chapter 5 below. The chosen strategy for the firm will depend upon four factors: the goals which the organisation is pursuing, the current performance of the firm relative to its expectations, the balance of threats and opportunities in any individual product-market area, and the overall strength or weakness of the business in the market. A firm which is in a strong position in a growth market and which has unrealised growth ambitions is likely to follow an aggressive expansion strategy within its existing market. On the other hand a firm which also has growth ambitions but which, although in a strong position, presently operates in a market in which demand is falling, will pursue one of the strategies within the area of strategic shrinking and use the funds released to invest for growth in a market area which is likely to satisfy its aspirations and which is appropriate to the particular competences of the firm. There is a set of techniques that can be used to help strategists arrive at improved decisions by combining these various aspects, and it is to these that we now turn in Chapter 5.

References

1. See W. Glueck, *Business Policy and Strategic Management* (New York: McGraw-Hill, 1980) p. 290.
2. R. S. Edwards and H. Townsend, *Business Enterprise* (London: Macmillan, 1958) p. 45.
3. R. E. Thomas, *Business Policy* (Oxford: Philip Allan, 2nd edn, 1983) p. 167.
4. See the evidence on this and on learning curves in *A Review of Monopolies and Mergers Policy* (London: HMSO, 1978, Cmnd 7198) Annex c.
5. See B. Hedley, 'A Fundamental Approach to Strategy Development', *Long Range Planning*, December 1976, p. 3.
6. Edwards and Townsend, *Business Enterprise*, p. 55.
7. See 'Has ICI got its chemistry right?', *Sunday Times*, 31 July 1983.
8. See W. S. Howe, *The Dundee Textiles Industry* (Aberdeen: Aberdeen University Press, 1982) Ch. 3.
9. Thomas, *Business Policy*, pp. 174–5.
10. H. H. Lynch, *Financial Performance of Conglomerates* (Boston: Harvard Business School Division of Research, 1971) p. 5.
11. Edwards and Townsend, *Business Enterprise*, pp. 55–8.
12. W. P. J. Maunder, *The Bread Industry in the United Kingdom* (Nottingham: Universities of Nottingham and Loughborough, 1970) p. 79.
13. See Monopolies Commission, *Man-made Cellulosic Fibres* (London: HMSO, 1968 HCP 130) Ch. 4.
14. J. Harvey, *Business Policy and Strategic Management* (Columbus, Ohio: Merrill Publishing, 1982) p. 133.
15. Thomas, *Business Policy*, pp. 159–60.
16. See K. R. Harrigan, *Strategies for Declining Businesses* (Lexington: D. C. Heath, 1980) pp. 16–17.
17. J. Thackray, 'The Disinvestment Boom', *Management Today*, January 1982, p. 46.

Strategic Comparisons 5

In diversified business organizations one of the main functions of the management is to decide how money, materials and skilled manpower should be provided and allocated between different business sectors in order to ensure the survival and healthy growth of the whole. — S. J. Q. Robinson *et al.* 'The Directional Policy Matrix', *Long Range Planning*, June 1978, p. 8.

5.1 Introduction

In the previous chapter we outlined a number of possible business strategies, and in the concluding section suggested that the choice of individual strategy would depend upon the goals of the organisation, the extent to which the firm's present aspirations were being achieved, the overall strength of the business, and the conditions in the product-market areas in which the company operates. In this chapter we shall systematise some of these considerations in order to indicate how management should choose the right strategy for an individual product area or strategic business unit. The same approach is also used to indicate how multi-product firms should structure their various product interests in the form of a portfolio. The purpose of these techniques is thus to match the joint assessment of the environmental and business resources analysis set out in Chapter 3 with the strategic possibilities discussed in Chapter 4.

5.2 The Boston Consulting Group Matrix

The basic model

One of the most widely accepted bases for making strategic decisions relating to individual product areas and for allocating resources across the business is the Boston Consulting Group Matrix.[1] In order to summarise the factors involved in making strategic decisions, the BCG matrix focuses on two variables: the rate of growth of the product-market area, and the market share in that area held by the firm relative to that of its largest competitor. The former measure is adopted as a global indicator of the attractiveness of the market, while the latter variable summarises the overall strength of the firm in that product-market area relative to its competitors. Growth is chosen as a measure of market attractiveness because of the opportunity that market growth gives for individual business expansion. Furthermore, not only are competitors in expanding markets less likely to resent each other's growth so long as each does not have to accept a reduction in output, but expanding markets are also generally less competitive than contracting ones. The relative market share possessed by a firm is not only a measure of the success of an individual business in competition with other sellers but also indicates the extent of likely benefits to the firm in terms of the increased profitability arising from the lower unit costs and enhanced market power associated with dominant market share. Figure 5.1 illustrates the BCG matrix.

This matrix can be used at three levels. First, for each stage at which an individual product-market is perceived to be in terms of market growth and the firm's relative strengths (market share), the matrix indicates the particular strategy that should be adopted. These strategies are summarised in the terms 'Question Mark', 'Star', 'Cash Cow', and 'Dog', and are analysed as follows.

High growth/low market share (Question Mark). Products in this category can enjoy a high rate of growth on the basis of the high market growth rate, but the firm's present market share is low. Thus at this stage the firm experiences a competitive disadvantage associated with low market share and a smaller scale of operations than its major competitors combined with the need for large cash

Figure 5.1
The Boston Consulting Group Matrix

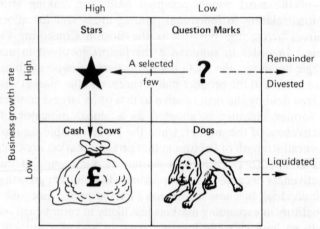

Source: B. Hedley, 'Strategy and the "Business Portfolio"', *Long Range Planning*, February 1977, p. 10.

injections if it is to keep pace with the overall market growth. Management in this situation must make a decision either to invest heavily in the product in order to gain the advantages of a Star position of high market share combined with growth, or to divest from the market altogether to avoid eventually finding oneself in the doubly disadvantageous position of low market share and low growth (Dog) from which one would also ultimately want to divest.

High growth/high market share (Star). Products in this market position confer on the firm the market power arising from high market share, and also the cost advantages associated with increased scale and growth. In such circumstances profitability is likely to be high, but at the same time cash flow requirements will also be great because of the high market growth rate. The strategy for products in this sector is to continue to invest to retain market leadership in order to benefit from the subsequent stage in the normal development of the product market.

Low growth/high market share (Cash Cow). As the product market itself reaches maturity or the plateau of the product life-cycle, Star products become Cash Cows. At this stage not only should the profitability associated with market leadership continue, but because of the relative absence of new investment requirements cash flow should be strongly positive. As Hedley of the BCG puts it, 'Cash Cows pay the dividends and interest, provide the debt capacity, pay for the company overhead and provide the cash for investment elsewhere in the company's portfolio of businesses. They are the foundation on which the company rests'.[2] Firms should resist the temptation at this stage to over-invest in such markets through proliferation of brands,etc., although in order to retain market leadership some investment in promotion and technology may be necessary.

Low growth/low market share (Dog). Market areas in which the firm is not one of the leaders and in which the market as a whole is not expanding fall into this category. The firm in these circumstances suffers from the twin disadvantages of operating at a low level of output, and thus in all likelihood at a cost disadvantage in comparison with the market leader, combined with minimal growth in the market. In these circumstances the firm should follow one of the contraction strategies outlined in Chapter 4: strategic shrinking or divestment.

So far we have looked at the way in which the BCG matrix can be used to indicate strategies for products falling into one of the four individual categories identified in the matrix. Yet even in discussing these it was implied that there was a logical progression of products from one quadrant of the growth-share matrix to the next arising in part from the product life-cycle itself: from Question Mark to Star through Cash Cow to Dog.[3] Thus a product in the high growth/low market share category which the firm chooses to develop rather than divest will be moved into the Star position as the necessary investment is made to increase market share even as the market continues to expand. The impact of the product life-cycle, as the rate of growth of the market itself begins to slow down, will take the firm's product from the Star category of high share/high growth into the Cash Cow position of dominant market share combined with reduced growth so long as the firm makes sufficient investment to maintain its market position. At this stage the firm may either maintain its market leadership and enjoy the cash flow associated with this, or forsake this position and allow the product to enter the Dog category of low market share combined with low growth. Once this last position has been reached, a specific policy of contraction will be adopted through divestment. Thus an understanding of the implications of the growth-share matrix combined with a recognition of the product life-cycle concept leads to an appreciation of the path which a single product is likely to follow over its life and of the strategy appropriate to the product at each phase.

The third aspect of the BCG matrix to be emphasised is its implications for a firm's product portfolio, that is, for the strategic relationships between the individual products of a multi-product firm. Although there will be characteristics of these products other than their respective cash flows which relate them, this is the connection that is emphasised in the growth-share matrix. This is illustrated in Figure 5.2, where the net cash generated and the direction of cash flows within the matrix are indicated.

Figure 5.2 illustrates the way in which Question Mark (problem child) and Star products require large net cash injections in order to sustain growth and achieve or maintain market dominance, while Cash Cow and Dog products release cash either as a result of the high profits-low investment profile of the former or the application to the latter of contraction strategies which release resources.

This pattern of cash flows arising from the growth-share matrix is perhaps the most relevant feature of the model for multi-product firms. But for all businesses there are important implications. First, firms should avoid an incorrect cash flow pattern within any of the quadrants of the matrix – for example, through permitting a net cash deficit to occur in respect of Cash Cows through over-investment. Second, firms can minimise their net new cash requirements by ensuring where possible a matching of the net cash generation by Cash Cow and Dog products with the investment

Figure 5.2
Cash Pattern and Flows within the Growth-Share Matrix

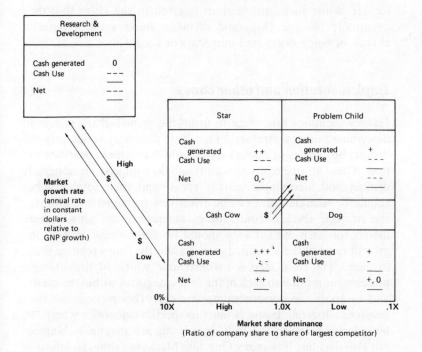

Source: G. S. Day, 'Diagnosing the Product Portfolio', *Journal of Marketing,* April 1977, p. 32.

requirements of Question Marks and Stars. This is the essence of the portfolio approach of the growth-share matrix. Finally, the adoption of this portfolio approach highlights the crudity of applying business goals equally to all product-market areas or strategic business units regardless of their stage of development.

For example, profitability, cash flow or growth targets which all product areas of the firm's activity are expected to reach may be quite easily achieved by Cash Cow products but not necessarily by Question Marks. This may lead to further (over)investment in the former, while such little support is given to the latter that they eventually become Dogs and certainly stand a much reduced chance of being developed into Stars or Cash Cows.

Implementation and other issues

Harvey identifies four steps in using the growth-share matrix to determine business strategy.[4] First, it is necessary to identify the distinct businesses or market sectors which together constitute the firm. These strategic business units should comprise economically distinct and identifiable market areas, and their total number should be such that they can be effectively managed as a group at the strategic level. Second, the parameters of the growth-share matrix for each market area should be determined: that is, the growth rates of the identified markets and the firm's relative share of each. The third step is to determine which of the strategic business units fall into each of the four categories within the matrix and to apply the corresponding strategy. This process not only involves allocating business units to specific categories where the boundaries between the BCG quadrants are inevitably blurred, but also deciding how many Question Marks the firm can afford to invest in given the resources available to it. At this stage it will be necessary to distinguish between those current Question Marks which should be moved into Star positions and those which must be divested. As a final step in an ongoing process, Harvey emphasises the need for a continuing strategic review of each business unit in the light of changes in the general and task environments, including particularly the reaction by competitors to one's own initial strategy.

   A number of problems arise in using the BCG matrix as a basis for strategic decision-making. Some of these are purely practical or arise from using a basically simple tool in a complex situation. On the other hand there are one or two fundamental flaws which invalidate the use of the matrix in certain situations. At the practical level there is the problem of identifying the market and measuring market share for the product that is being considered. The analyst should adopt a definition of the market which embraces all products identified by consumers as substitutes. He or she must also remember that the boundaries of this market will change as new substitute products appear or as the nature of market segments changes.

The BCG matrix is designed to be a guide in strategic decision-making, and as such must be used in conjunction with managerial judgement. Inevitably the matrix is too simple to allow for every nuance of market conditions. No account is taken, for example, of the different risks attaching to individual product interests, or of the need to balance risks as opposed to cash flows in the product portfolio. A firm's products may be related in other ways, too, which are not recognised in the matrix approach. Sometimes a firm will be prepared to lose money in one product area if this leads to increased sales and profits in another. Or, more generally, a firm will carry a range of products as part of its sales policy without expecting to earn the same return on each line. It is difficult to see how the BCG matrix can be applied to these situations.

One further danger is that because of its brevity and apparent precision, the growth-share matrix will be taken to prescribe common strategies for market situations which although broadly similar have different characteristics and thus require separate approaches. In their analysis of 'endgame' strategies, for example, i.e. situations in which a market is in long-term decline, Harrigan and Porter identify a wide range of variables that will dictate different approaches by the firms involved.[5] In choosing an individual strategy Harrigan and Porter suggest that account should be taken of the certainty of market decline in the eyes of competitors, the likely rate and pattern of decline, the structure of remaining pockets of demand in the market, the barriers to exit from the market for all participants, and the volatility of the market situation in terms of the behaviour of manufacturers, distributors and final consumers. On the basis of this analysis these two authors suggest that in addition to the more obvious strategies of divestment, two other possibilities of leadership or niche should be considered in the endgame situation. The leadership strategy involves the firm's attaining a dominant, low-cost position in the market, often by acquiring competitors or adopting aggressive pricing policies. In effect such a strategy is an attempt by the firm to retain a Cash Cow position in what would otherwise be a Dog situation, although it may merely be a prelude to a more tradition-al exit strategy by the business. As an alternative firms may concurrently follow a policy of divestment in respect of most of their interests in a market while also holding on to a profitable niche in the form of a premium-price market segment. Both of these strategies of leadership and niche are more sophisticated variants which may be adopted by firms operating in declining markets, and the conditions appropriate to them are not revealed by the simple growth-share matrix alone.

Two very basic assumptions that are central to the growth-share matrix analysis are the traditional product life-cycle pattern of sales in a market and the benefits to a firm of high market share. If these assumptions do not apply in an individual market then the BCG matrix analysis is not valid. The product life-cycle concept assumes in particular that there is an extended plateau phase of sales in respect of any product. This is the phase in the life of the product when it can be regarded as a Cash Cow by the firm which has achieved a dominant market position. If, however, this phase is likely to be short-lived, then the whole policy of investing in Question Mark and Star products in the anticipation of a financial return from Cash Cows is misplaced.[6]

Perhaps the most damaging criticism of the BCG model is the excessive emphasis it places upon the value of market share and the policy implications that arise from this. The model sets considerable store upon firms investing resources in order to move products from Question Mark to Star and Cash Cow positions in the matrix. Correspondingly firms are advised to divest from Dog positions where they no longer enjoy high market share. There is admittedly some persuasive US evidence linking return on invest-ment and market share at the business product level.[7] By defini-tion, however, a product market can have only one leader; and economic circumstances at the present time dictate that most markets are growing only slowly. Most firms are therefore operat-ing in Dog situations. Yet to take only two examples, in the confectionery market smaller producers such as Terry and Needler survive along with Cadbury-Schweppes and Rowntree Mackin-tosh, while in carpets Readicut International and Carpets Interna-tional (each with sales currently in excess of £100 million annually) face competition from smaller firms such as Hugh McKay, BMK and Brintons. Nor do industrial economics studies suggest that size or monopoly power confer enhanced profitability or growth upon industry giants.[8] American case histories have shown in fact that by following appropriate strategies, firms with low market shares can enjoy profit and growth rates higher than their dominant market rivals.[9] These strategies involve the identification of segments in the market neglected by competitors or in which smaller firms possess greater relative strengths, the efficient use of product development and research expenditures to fit products into particular market segments, and the avoidance of the more grandiose diversification policies followed by larger rivals.

As an example of the adoption of such strategies, *Management Today* recently highlighted the success of the US Ball Corporation.[10] Around 70% of Ball's output is accounted for by its 8–9% share of the two-piece beer and beverage can market in the USA and 15% of the food glass jar market. In neither case is the total market expanding, and at the time of writing excess capacity in the markets was 15–20% in glass containers and as high as 30% in metal containers. Yet Ball almost doubled both sales and profits in the five years to 1982, with a return on shareholder equity over that period of between 15% and 17%. Ball's success has derived from three factors. First, it has avoided highly competitive markets such as food cans, and has concentrated instead upon a narrower range of products which it has identified as appropriate market segments. In these it produces only two sizes of two-piece cans, and concentrates its glass jar production on wide-mouthed food jars. Second, and based upon this narrow product range, the firm has set itself the target of being a low-cost producer. Third, the firm has avoided other than a limited degree of diversification. By following policies very much along the lines of those advocated by Hamermesh *et al.* (see note 9) Ball has achieved growth and profitability within the context of a static market and a low market share, which is quite contrary to the implications of the BCG model.

The existence of some of these complications, together with certain reservations regarding the applicability of the growth-share matrix concepts in making strategic choices, suggests that there is scope for a more comprehensive situational approach to determining strategy for individual business units, and this is considered below in terms of the Shell matrix.

5.3 The Shell Directional Policy Matrix

Corporate planners at the Shell Transport & Trading Co. – regarded by some as having one of the best planning systems in the world[11] – have put forward a development of the BCG matrix which takes account of a wider variety of circumstances relating to the firm and its market environment.[12] The Shell matrix takes fuller account of qualitative assessments as well as quantitative variables. A version of the Shell DPM with the strategy guides is shown in Figure 5.3.

The 'Prospects for market sector profitability' dimension in Figure 5.3, which corresponds to the simpler market growth-rate axis of the BCG matrix, includes for firms in the chemical industry market growth, market quality, industry feedstock situation, and environmental aspects. For other markets a correspondingly manageable list of characteristics can be devised; and each product-market sector is rated attractive, average or unattractive on the basis of comparison with other sectors. The richness of detail incorporated into the Shell DPM compared with the growth-share matrix may be seen by reference to the market quality dimension. Robinson *et al.* (see note 12) list ten components of this, including level and stability of profits together with sensitivity of margins to changes in capacity, number and size distribution of suppliers and competitors, and the risk of product substitution. The quality of the market is rated along the satisfactory/unsatisfactory spectrum, according to management's interpretation of these factors. On the vertical axis of the Shell matrix, and corresponding to market share in the BCG analysis, company competitiveness for firms in the petrochemical sector is assessed by three criteria: market position, production capability, and product research and development. The firm is scored in these terms relative to significant competitors, and the overall assessment is obtained by taking an unweighted average of the company competitiveness scores in respect of each of the criteria.

The outcome of the DPM analysis is a 3 × 3 matrix, illustrated in Figure 5.4. The diagram indicates the way in which the Shell matrix can be used by a firm not only to analyse its own portfolio of product-market interests but also to include reference to its competitors. Thus in Figure 5.4, A, B and C are competitors each of whom regards the product-market being considered as equally

Figure 5.3
The Shell Directional Policy Matrix

Prospects for market sector profitability

		Unattractive	Average	Attractive
Company's competitive position	Weak	Disinvest	Phased withdrawal Proceed with Care	Double or quit
	Average	Phased withdrawal	Proceed with Care	Try harder
	Strong	Cash generator	Growth Leader	Leader

Double or quit

Tomorrow's breadwinners among today's R & D projects may come from this area. Putting the strategy simply, those with the best prospects should be selected for full backing and development. The rest should be abandoned.

Try harder

The implication is that the product can be moved towards the leadership box by judicious application of resources. In these circumstances the company may wish to make available resources in excess of what the product can generate for itself.

Leader

The strategy should be to maintain this position. At certain stages this may imply a need for resources to expand capacity with a cash need which need not be met entirely from funds generated by the product, although earnings should be above average.

Growth

Investment should be made to allow the product to grow with the market. Generally, the product will generate sufficient cash to be self-financing, and should not be making demands on other corporate cash resources.

Cash generator

A typical situation in this matrix area is when the company has a product which is moving towards the end of its life-cycle, and is being replaced in the market by other products. No finance should be allowed for expansion, and the business, so long as it is profitable, should be used as a source of cash for other areas. Every effort should be made to maximize profits since this type of activity has no long term future.

Proceed with care

In this position, some investment may be justified but major investments should be made with extreme caution.

Phased withdrawal

A product with an average to weak position with low unattractive market prospects, or a weak position with average market prospects is unlikely to be earning any significant amounts to cash. The indicated strategy is to realize the value of the assets on a controlled basis to make the resources available for redeployment elsewhere.

Disinvestment

Products falling in this area will probably be losing money – not necessarily every year, but losses in bad years will outweigh the gains in good years. It is unlikely that any activity will surprise management by falling within this area since its poor performance should already be known.

Source: D. E. Hussey, 'Portfolio Analysis: Practical Experience with the Directional Policy Matrix', *Long Range Planning*, August 1978, pp. 3–4.

attractive, although this need not necessarily be the shared perception by each participant in a market. A, B and C are ranked in terms of their relative competitiveness in this particular market, and this suggests a more complex possible interpretation of the Shell matrix. The strategy to be adopted by a firm in respect of one of its products which is in a particular position in the matrix will depend not only upon that position but also upon the positions in the matrix occupied by the firm's other products *and* the positions held by other producers of the products. Thus for a firm having one of its products in the 'Try harder' position in Figure 5.4, the strategy to be adopted will depend upon the location of its other product-market interests in the matrix and also the relative position of all other producers of this product. Whether the firm decides to try to move the product into a 'Leader' position will depend upon the balance among the remainder of its products of 'Cash generation' and 'Double or quit' situations and also the prospects of catching up with the existing market leader.

The Shell matrix has been widely adopted in practical business situations. It combines a broader range of variables than the BCG matrix, yet involves terminology such as market growth, profitability, ease of entry, supply position, etc. which is familiar to management. Its prescriptions are more varied than those of the growth-share matrix, and the Shell matrix is not so obviously dependent in its analysis upon the more questionable link between market share and profitability.

5.4 Conclusions

In Chapter 4 we examined a range of broad strategies open to businesses. These strategies were categorised in terms of the degree of expansion or contraction involved, and also of the goals they were designed to allow the firm to achieve. In this chapter we have taken the analysis a stage further and emphasised three features. First, the strategy adopted by a firm in respect of a product must be related to the relevant market conditions and to the relative competitiveness of the firm in that market. In a sense this is simply to say that strategy must reflect the general and task environments in which the firm operates and the unique relative competence of the business – that is, the opportunities and threats

Figure 5.4
The Shell Matrix Strategic Analysis

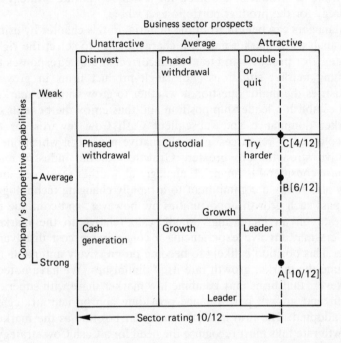

Source: S. J. Q. Robinson *et al.*, 'The Directional Policy Matrix –
Tool for Strategic Planning', *Long Range Planning*, June
1978, p. 13.

and strengths and weaknesses discussed in Chapter 3. The BCG
and Shell matrices analysed in this chapter thus formalise and
summarise that earlier discussion. Second, however, these matrices emphasise for single- or multi-product firms the stages of
development through which product markets go and the cash-flow
characteristics (as one particular feature) exhibited by products at
different stages in their market development. Thus the strategy
appropriate for a product will change as the product moves
through its life-cycle, and the strategy applied to it must be

correspondingly dynamic. Third, for multi-product firms the analyses in this chapter have emphasised, in terms of the relative cash-flow characteristics of the individual components of their portfolio of products, the need for a truly corporate strategy: a strategy for the product portfolio as a whole.

Managers can benefit from the material in this chapter by using the analysis of market and firm characteristics to select the right strategy for products and to avoid incorrect strategic responses to existing market situations. For single-product firms in growth industries the major question is whether to grow with the market and establish a leadership position and thus enjoy the benefits of market dominance and subsequent Cash Cow rewards, or to redeploy one's resources in an alternative market in which one's relative strengths are greater. Growth with the industry may require considerable financial, managerial or other resources; and may also imply a commitment to a rapidly changing technology. To pass such growth opportunities by, however, and continue to operate on an increasingly small scale relative to the market leaders may involve experiencing a considerable cost disadvantage. This position is likely to become progressively untenable as in time the market growth rate itself diminishes. We have noted, however, that firms may combine low market share with superior profit and growth performance providing appropriate strategies are adopted. The firm in a market leader position as the market growth rate falls must recognise the need for a Cash Cow strategy. New investment in the market should be restricted to that necessary to maintain a leadership position. Cash flow in this situation will be strongly positive; and management, in order to ensure the long-term development of the firm, must garner these resources and finance product-market interests that will replace the present ones following the application to these in due course of a harvesting strategy.

For single-product firms in low-growth markets which are not leaders – and this category must include a large number of businesses today – the response to this situation must be to find a niche within the market in which there are reasonable growth prospects, where competition with the market leader or leaders is avoided, but within which the firm can ensure a reasonable return based upon the cost levels that obtain in respect of a smaller level of operations and prices which can be achieved in the chosen market niche. The basic problem of British Leyland, by contrast, may well be its strategy of attempting to operate across the whole range of motor vehicles in a low-growth market in which it is in world terms a small-scale producer.

The BCG and Shell matrices can be more obviously applied to multi-product businesses. For such firms the value of the matrices is to emphasise the contribution that products at each stage in their development have to make to the success of the company, and the need constantly to renew the product base of the business. Evidence at the time of its near acquisition by Robert Maxwell's British Printing & Communications Corporation suggests that John Waddington, the games and packaging group, had not fully developed its product portfolio. At that time games accounted for 22 per cent of group sales, plastics for 25 per cent and packaging 25 per cent.[13] The company's games division – including of course Monopoly – which should have been a Cash Cow for the firm, had been allowed to drift into losses, thus possibly holding back growth in the expanding plastics subsidiary. The group has a paper packaging subsidiary which is in the low-growth, narrow profit margin category, but equally requires funds to expand from a presently very small market share in the developing security printing business, including stamps and secure forms. The continued survival and development of such firms depends upon the profitable operation of Cash Cow products (Waddington's games division), a continued monitoring of low-growth, low-share market sectors in order to ensure that they do not become cash traps (paper packaging in the case of Waddington), an ability and willingness to invest in potential Star products (plastics), and a search for new ventures that are capable of being funded into Star and eventually Cash Cow positions (security printing). By contrast, and to take an example in the news at the same time as Waddington, the American firm Motorola, which is the world's second largest manufacturer of semiconductors, has fuelled its success in the growth field of integrated circuits by remaining in the mature discrete semiconductor sector manufacturing transistors and diodes and using this product area as a Cash Cow. Continued operation in this latter sector, in which Motorola remains highly profitable, has helped the firm to remain in a Star position in integrated circuits; while Motorola's dominance in land communications (it has just under 75 per cent of the mobile radio market in the United States) is the base for its investment in the growth field of cellular telephones.[14]

In addition to its use as an operational tool, the portfolio approach to strategic planning should serve to increase the general level of business analysis. As one British consultant has put it, 'it will encourage thinking. There seems to me a tremendous value in using the technique firstly to help managers to think as a group about their markets, the competition and the relative strategic value of their portfolio to the company. Secondly, the portfolio approach provides a useful way of communicating strategic guidelines to different business units'.[15] One result of portfolio planning, for example, may well be an administrative reorganisation of the firm. Strategic business units may have to be defined separately from operating units, and a more careful examination made of the purpose of strategic units, their goals and performance targets. This identification of strategic business units should be correspondingly linked to the capital investment programme and other significant inputs such as research and development, marketing expenditures and personnel for each unit. In his survey Haspeslagh found that 70 per cent of all firms covered started off their introduction of portfolio planning by comprehensively re-examining the definition of each of their businesses, and that in 75 per cent of these cases this re-examination resulted in strategic business units being redefined and distinguished from operating units.[16] This question of the alignment of operating and strategic units highlights but one of the administrative difficulties of introducing the portfolio planning approach to business strategy. Where manufacturing costs are a high proportion of the total, there will always be a tendency to want to define business units in cost rather than market terms. Other difficulties in the adoption of portfolio planning include matching the business unit's administrative and managerial reward systems to the chosen strategy (for example, expansion or harvesting), and the fact that the implementation of portfolio planning must nearly always result in some managers being worse off in terms of capital allocations or scale of operations than before, even if this results from the inevitable elimination of previously marginal activities. In particular some divisional managers may find it difficult to accept that they are not expected to maximise short-term profits (in the case of Star products) or that they are not allowed to reinvest surplus cash funds in profitable Cash Cow ventures. Correspondingly, top management must find a way of motivating divisional heads to behave according to the dictates of the portfolio planning approach in respect of their divisions and not, for example, reward all divisional heads on the basis of return on investment.

This chapter has been concerned with the means by which one can combine the analysis of market environments and business resources with the strategies available to firms in such a way as to match the strategy and the individual firm's environment/resources situation. The issue can be seen most easily in diagrammatic form in terms of a simple matrix whose axes measure market attractiveness and business competence, and within whose boxes one can prescribe individual strategies. Of course, neither of the approaches considered here – the BCG and Shell matrices – is perfect. In the case of the former the assessment of market attractiveness in terms only of growth and the measurement of competitive advantage solely by reference to relative market share represent a very summary or even simplistic approach.[17] On the other hand, the greater detail of the assessment built into the Shell matrix inevitably makes the positioning of the products within the 3×3 matrix more subjective and the choice of strategy apparently less precise. Used sensibly, however, these approaches can help firms to recognise explicitly the major strategic variables affecting their products and markets as a prelude to the actual making of the strategic business decision. It is to this final process of decision-making that we now turn in Chapter 6.

References

1. A good concise exposition of this by a director of the Boston Consulting Group is contained in B. Hedley, 'Strategy and the "Business Portfolio"', *Long Range Planning*, February 1977, pp. 9–15.
2. Ibid., p. 11.
3. The product-market life-cycle concept implies that the volume of sales of any product follows a particular pattern over its life of tentative beginnings, a period of rapid growth followed by a plateau period during which sales are pretty well constant, and a final phase of decline as sales fall off markedly.
4. See J. Harvey, *Business Policy and Strategic Management* (Columbus, Ohio: Merrill Publishing, 1982) pp. 187–90.

5. See K. R. Harrigan and M. E. Porter, 'End-game Strategies for Declining Businesses', *Harvard Business Review*, July–August 1983, pp. 111–20.

6. See S. St. P. Slatter, 'Common Pitfalls in Using the BCG Product Portfolio Matrix', *London Business School Journal*, Winter 1980, pp. 18–22.

7. See R. D. Buzzell and F. D. Wiersema, 'Successful Share-Building Strategies', *Harvard Business Review*, January–February 1981, pp. 135–7; but see also research which indicates that factors in addition to market dominance will influence the profitability of market leaders. These factors include the nature of the market environment, product characteristics, the basis of competition in the market, and the degree of autonomy of market leader business units within their total organisation. See C. Y. Koo, 'Market-Share Leadership – Not Always So Good", *Harvard Business Review*, January–February 1984, pp. 50–4.

8. See W. S. Howe, *Industrial Economics* (London: Macmillan, 1978) pp. 86–8.

9. See R. G. Hamermesh *et al.*, 'Strategies for Low Market Share Businesses', *Harvard Business Review*, May–June 1978, pp. 95–102.

10. J. Thackray, 'The Five-Star Management of Ball', *Management Today*, March 1984, pp. 66–71.

11. T. Lester, 'The Giant Planning Problem', *Management Today*, June 1982, p. 76.

12. See S. J. Q. Robinson *et al.*, 'The Directional Policy Matrix – Tool for Strategic Planning', *Long Range Planning*, June 1978, pp. 8–15.

13. See 'Tactics of a Reluctant Takeover Target', *Financial Times*, 7 September 1983.

14. J. Thackray, 'Motorola's Leading Edge', *Management Today*, November 1983, pp. 76–83.

15. D. E. Hussey, 'Portfolio Analysis: Practical Experience with the Directional Policy Matrix', *Long Range Planning*, August 1978, p. 7.

16. P. Haspeslagh, 'Portfolio Planning: Uses and Limits', *Harvard Business Review*, January–February 1982, p. 65.

17. See R. Wensley, 'PIMS and BCG: New Horizons or False Dawn?' *Strategic Management Journal*, 1982, Vol. III, pp. 147–58.

Strategic Decision-Making and Implementation

6

A strategic decision is the choice by the decision maker of a course of action from among the alternatives available. Strategic management involves making the decisions which will ultimately determine the organization's survival. — D. F. Harvey, *Business Policy and Strategic Management* (Columbus, Ohio: Merrill Publishing, 1982) p. 206.

6.1 Introduction

Chapters 2–5 in this text have taken us through a logical sequence by which business strategists arrive at those decisions which in Harvey's words above determine the survival of the organisation. We started by looking at the essence of business objectives, and then examined the way in which the firm should analyse its external environment and internal resources in order to clarify these objectives and choose those product-market areas in which it wishes to operate. Chapter 4 dealt with a number of possible strategic directions in which a business could move, together with the goals and limitations attaching to these. Finally, in the last chapter two particular techniques were presented by the use of which management could determine specific strategies to be applied to individual product-market areas or strategic business units.

In this attempt to present the material in a coherent and logical manner a number of issues have up to this point been consciously glossed over, while at the same time the spreading of the material over a number of chapters has dispersed the picture of strategic decision-making. The purpose of this chapter is to use the analysis of the making of strategic decisions to pull together a number of strands of thought developed in the earlier chapters, to present a more compact picture of this process, and also to consider some of the organisational features of the implementation of strategic decisions.

Strategic decisions are those which take a business from the determination of its goals to the achievement of these via choices about how the organisation's resources shall be deployed. As such, strategic decisions have a number of significant characteristics which heighten the importance of the process of arriving at them:

1. They involve the allocation of resources across the firm as a whole and thus have an impact upon the total organisation.
2. They normally involve disposing of sums of money which for the organisation concerned are large.
3. Strategic decisions involve choosing from among a number of possible courses of action, and by deciding upon one particular strategy a firm is denying itself the opportunity of taking up other possibilities, at least in the medium term.
4. Such decisions will therefore commit the business to a particular strategic direction for some time into the future and are normally reversible only at considerable cost.
5. Strategic decisions involving a specific commitment of the firm's resources are usually made relatively infrequently, and each decision must be regarded as unique. It is therefore not easy to learn form one's previous experience in this area.
6. Strategic decisions have to be made under conditions of partial ignorance of some important variables, and the outcomes are correspondingly uncertain.
7. These decisions in Ansoff's terminology are non-self-generative. That is, management itself must recognise that a particular strategic decision requires to be made and must decide when to make it.

All of these features combine to make strategic decision-making one of the most difficult as well as the most important areas of management activity.

6.2 The Decision-Making Process

Table 6.1 indicates Witte's five-stage model of strategic decision-making, together with implementation. Below we discuss each of the stages in turn.

**Table 6.1
Decision-Making Steps or Phases**

---

1. Identification of the problem
2. Obtaining necessary information
3. Production of possible solutions
4. Evaluation of solutions
5. Selection of strategy
   Implementation

Source: E. Witte, 'Field Research on Complex Decision-Making Processes – The Phase Theorem', *International Studies of Management and Organisation*, 1972, p. 164.

Even within this chapter it will be necessary for us to simplify our exposition of the decision-making process in comparison with the results of empirical studies. Witte, for example, in his analysis of the decision by businesses to install EDP systems, found that the five steps leading up to implementation indicated in Table 6.1 were not necessarily undertaken discretely or in sequence, and that information gathering, the development of possibilities and evaluation of these were carried out simultaneously rather than sequentially. With regard to the findings of his empirical study on the phasing of decisions, Witte concluded that the 'test presents a dismal picture of the validity of phase hypotheses', and suggested as an explanation: 'We believe that human beings cannot gather information without in some way simultaneously developing alternatives. They cannot avoid evaluating these alternatives immediately, and in doing this they are forced to a decision. This is a package of operations, and the succession of these packages over time constitutes the total decision-making process'.[1] Interestingly, too, Witte found no evidence to suggest that decisions made as a result of adhering to the phase process were any more efficient than others in terms of speed, thoroughness or reduced friction. For purposes of exposition, however, we now outline the process of strategic decision-making in terms of the sequence of activities in Table 6.1.

1.   Problem identification

Given the non-self-generative characteristic of strategic decisions, the first and most important stage in the process is the recognition of the need to make a strategic decision. This involves the recognition of the need for a decision and an acceptance that it is a strategic rather than an administrative or operating decision that is required. The crucial trigger mechanism here is assumed to be an actual or potential gap or deviation between the planned performance of the organisation and its achievements. This is likely to be most apparent when a negative gap arises concerning the firm's profitability or growth. However, in this event – if the present return on investment is 10 per cent against a planned target of 15 per cent – there is a range of possible explanations. First, the strategy currently being implemented may be the most appropriate one for the circumstances of the business, in which case the firm must accept that these circumstances necessitate a downward revision of its original profitability goal. Second, the shortfall in performance may arise from the incorrect implementation of the chosen strategy. In this case the strategy may be assumed to be correct, and what is required of the business is a revised set of administrative or operational decisions. The third possibility is that circumstances relating to the environment or resources of the firm have changed in such a way as to invalidate the original strategy, in which case, of course, a reassessment of these variables is required in order to arrive at a new strategy.[2]

One of the most important types of management decisions is to distinguish between the second and third possibilities above: that is, to distinguish between the requirement for administrative or operational adjustments and the need for a strategic reassessment.

In choosing between these two alternatives management is all too likely to adopt an 'operational' approach to remedying its failure to achieve performance goals: that is, to reduce prices or increase advertising expenditures in response to a sales shortfall rather than to ask more fundamental questions regarding the product-market strategy of the firm. This temptation may be further enhanced by the late recognition of the trigger and a necessary resort to a quick reactive solution, 'because you don't form a committee when the house is on fire'.

Triggers for identifying strategic problems thus have to be timeous: sufficiently so to allow management to appraise the nature of the problem and, if necessary, arrive at a considered strategic decision. Ideally, of course, the trigger is not the performance gap itself but some event occurring ahead of this such as a warning report from the sales force which will allow the firm to take the necessary action even before a performance gap emerges. One further difficulty in this area is that strategic decisions may also be required when performance is ahead of target but when this favourable variance is due to fortuitous changes in the business environment. In these circumstances an upward revision of certain performance goals is necessary, with action being taken to ensure that these revised targets can be met.

The implication for management of this part of the strategic decision-making process is that the organisation should be constantly sensitive to triggers, particularly those such as the loss of long-standing customers or generally declining order books which give early notice of threats. As emphasised in Chapter 3, one purpose of ongoing environmental analysis – both general and task – is to forewarn the business of the need to react strategically to changes in such variables; and this applies equally to environmental scanning for opportunities such as unsatisfied demands or possible extensions of one's existing markets.

2. Analysis of information

It follows naturally from what we have said above that before a business commits itself to a particular strategy, and having accepted the need to make a strategic decision, that a complete analysis of the business's environment and resources must be undertaken. The form of this analysis was set out in Chapter 3 above under the headings of environmental analysis for opportunities and threats, and resource analysis for strengths and weaknesses. Each time a new strategy decision is required, a fresh analysis must be carried out, as the need for such a new decision implies that the earlier strategy is no longer valid: either environmental or resource variables have changed or the previous analysis of these was incorrect. A minor deviation or performance gap may justify a fairly rapid review of these variables. A more significant shortfall will require the firm to reappraise its whole approach to its current business and question whether it should continue to operate in its present product-market area(s). Such appraisals may lead to a total change of strategic direction for the company. This is what happened to one of the firms in the traditional jute industry, researched by the author, which moved from being the market leader in this sector to making a major investment in North Sea oil-related activities. These now account for the largest proportion of the firm's turnover.

3. Development of possibilities

The most innovative part of the strategic decision-making process is the generation of possible strategies for the achievement of the organisation's goals. These strategic possibilities must comply with three conditions: (a) they must be capable of leading to the achievement of the goals of the organisation in terms of profitability, growth, etc.; (b) they must be consistent with the present or likely future resources of the business; and (c) they must not transgress any of the external constraints or internally generated responsibilities faced by the firm. While complying with these criteria the firm should try to develop as large an initial list of strategic possibilities as it can. This requirement gives added impetus to the need on the part of the organisation to react sufficiently far in advance of the necessary implementation of a strategy to be able to undertake a wide-ranging review. The strategic possibilities initially identified will normally be related to the firm's existing activities. These will be the possibilities most familiar to the firm's present management, and they may also be regarded as those most conducive to enhancing profitability or to achieving growth, unless the market is in significant decline. Thus

Thomas lists the way in which a business following an expansion strategy may start from considering increasing output of its existing product range and explore alternative strategies outwards to those involving diversification away from its existing markets. These possibilities are set out in Table 6.2.

Table 6.2
Possible Strategies for Business Expansion

(a) Further development of existing markets and types of customer by one or more of marketing, distribution, or product improvements;

(b) Exploration of new markets and customers within the same countries and product groups as hitherto;

(c) Export operations either as a new outlet or through extension to new national markets;

(d) Widening of product range within the same industry and product group with some product innovation;

(e) Widening of product range to include related groups using common technological base;

(f) Divergent product search and development involving deliberate move into unrelated fields.

Source: R. E. Thomas, *Business Policy* (Oxford: Philip Allan, 2nd edn., 1983) p. 114.

The strategic possibilities identified at this stage set out routes which the business may follow in achieving its objectives. It is essential at this stage, therefore, that any major inconsistencies such as attempted growth within a market which itself is relatively stagnant and competitive, or expansion by acquisition without the necessary financial resources, should have been eliminated. The essence of stages 2 and 3 of the strategic decision-making process outlined in this chapter is to use the results of the SWOT analysis to create a range of viable strategies from among which senior management can make a final choice on a more judgemental basis.

4. *Evaluation*

Each of the possible strategies developed in terms of the preceding subsection satisfied the requirements of being capable of leading to the achievement of the firm's objectives, being consistent with the resources of the business, and being able to be implemented within the constraints and responsibilities to which the business is subject. The evaluation process that follows is likely to be the decision-making phase containing the greatest element of judgement. Although the strategic possibilities developed in the preceding subsection will each have compiled with certain basic criteria, assuming that the firm has only a limited amount of financial and other resources available, only one project can be undertaken – one which, as we noted earlier, precludes the possibility of undertaking other projects and which commits the business to a significant and largely irreversible expenditure for a number of years. In making this judgement a range of intangible variables is likely to have to be considered, for it is extremely unlikely that the single project could be chosen simply by rank ordering the possibilities by their discounted cash flow net present values or internal rates of return, even assuming that profitability was a key variable. Variables such as risk (or more properly uncertainty), compatibility with existing management values and styles, synergy and acceptability within management's 'responsibilities' are extremely difficult to evaluate. Nor should one forget that the final decision relating to a new strategy in an organisation of any size but the smallest is likely to be a group one. A group decision in particular is likely to evolve as a result of a process of political bargaining. As Thomas puts it, 'once a firm becomes multi-unit, even more once it acquires different activities, competition for resources is inescapable. Business policy [therefore] has to do with power and politics ... [it] is inseparable from the question of power, not only over the firm as such but over a somewhat wider "immediate environment"'.[3]

Ansoff refers to the adaptive search process in the area of business strategy as a 'cascade', and describes this in the following way:

> [At] the outset possible decision rules are formulated in gross terms and are then successively refined through several stages as

the solution proceeds. This gives the appearance of solving the problem several times over, but with successively more precise results. The first step is to decide between the two major alternatives: to diversify or not to diversify the firm. The second step is to choose a broad product-market scope for the firm from a list of broad industrial categories. The third is to refine the scope in terms of characteristics or product-markets within it.[4]

Using this technique, the firm successively narrows down the range of possibilities, starting at the broadest level and concluding with a final specific decision. In addition to the fact that we shall consider an illuminating example of this approach below in the case of the Imperial Group's acquisition of the US Howard Johnson hotel chain, the cascade technique accords closely with the findings of Witte's research (see note 1). That is, although the decision-making process starts with the recognition of the need for a decision and concludes with its implementation, the intermediate processes of information gathering, generation of possible solutions and their evaluation do not take place in an orderly sequence. Rather, as Ansoff emphasises, '[An] important characteristic of this [cascade] process is feedback. Since the cascade is a process of search for the best solution, information may develop at later stages which casts doubts upon previous decisions'.[5]

5. Selecting the strategy

The final step in making a decision in this field is the selection of a single strategy from the list of possible courses of action generated as described in the subsection on 'development of possibilities' above and evaluated according to the processes outlined in the last subsection. A number of factors influence how, and how well, the final strategy is chosen. The first is the amount of time that is available for carrying out the selection process. Too often, as we have emphasised before, senior management is in a situation in which it is necessary to do *something now*. Not only is such a situation likely to generate an operational or administrative reaction to changed business circumstances rather than a thought-out strategic decision, but the quality of any strategic decision-making is likely to suffer under these conditions. This emphasises again the point that where possible managemnet ought to put itself in a position in which it can make an anticipative or proactive strategic response to an issue rather than a kneejerk reaction.

Just as the issue of risk or uncertainty entered into the evaluation process above as a variable associated with strategic proposals, so management's attitude to risk (however imperfectly assessed) will have a major impact upon the selection process. Every strategic decision involves some trade-off between the expected value or reward associated with a policy and the risk attaching to it. The question is how much greater an anticipated reward a manager or management group demands in return for a given increase in the degree of risk. A high risk-taker is prepared to adopt a strategy which, if it turns out well, will provide considerable rewards even though there is some likelihood of failure. The more risk-averse strategist chooses a route along which, even if the likely returns are more modest, they are virtually guaranteed. One variable that may influence the ultimate choice in this direction is the nature of the returns and the group to whom they accrue. The wealthy owner/manager may be prepared to gamble over a marginal addition to his fortune. The professional manager, who is not necessarily going to be rewarded proportionately to the financial success of the strategy but who may lose face in the event of failure, is more likely to support a low-risk strategy.

In the preceding subsection we noted that part of the complexity of strategic evaluation arose from the fact that such decisions were inevitably group ones, and that each participant might evaluate each variable differently. In the same way there is a strong tendency for the strategy finally adopted to be a consensus one – one which has the effect of bringing managers together. Not only is this likely to lead to earlier rather than later agreement on the decision, but it is also likely to produce greater commitment to the implementation of the decision.

As in the case of evaluation, so with the final selection of a strategy there is likely to be a mixture of the rational and the less rational. The personal values of managers (including attitudes towards risk-taking), the group dynamics of the decision-making situation, and the influence of past strategy are each likely to play a part. As Harvey puts it, 'Managers often approach decisions in intuitive, erratic ways, rather than as a mechanical procedure'.[6]

Accepting this and having traced the steps involved in arriving at the strategic decision, the next stage is to analyse the processes involved in strategic implementation.

6.3 Strategic Implementation

Implementation of the chosen strategy follows on from Witte's five-stage strategic decision-making sequence, and is by any measure one of the most vital phases in the decision-making process. Indeed, most of the texts in this area aphorise the worthlessness of a good strategy for whose implementation no provision has been made: 'Better a first-class implementation procedure for a second-class strategy than *vice versa*', wrote one Arthur D. Little senior consultant.'[7]

Strategic implementation as an activity embraces all of those actions that are necessary to put a strategy into practice. In detail this implementation involves identification of the key tasks to be performed, allocation of these tasks to individuals (i.e. delegation), providing for co-ordination of separated tasks, the design and installation of an appropriate management information system, the drawing up of a specific programme of action including a time schedule down to the level of operating budgets or standards, setting up a system for comparing actual performance with those standards, and the design of a system of incentives, controls and penalties appropriate to the individuals concerned and the tasks to be performed.[8] More broadly, Glueck divides such actions into three categories: leadership implementation, organisational implementation and functional implementation, and we shall use these headings to highlight the actions necessary to ensure effective strategic implementation.[9]

The first step is to put the right people in the right places to ensure that the strategy has the best chance of success, following which it is desirable to ensure that adequate incentives are available to motivate senior managers to achieve the chosen strategic goals. Although it may not be possible for top management to choose an entirely new team to implement a new strategy, in allocating responsibilities one should try to match the requirements of the strategy and the characteristics of the individual managers. Research has shown how different manager characteristics or management styles such as entrepreneurial, scientific management, conservative or democratic may be more or less appropriate to a particular strategic environment when the latter is assessed in terms of such variables as turbulence, hostility, diversity and technological complexity.[10] One practising businessman has summed up the implications of these considerations: 'If you have a business you want a lot of cash out of instead of growth, you don't put a high-powered marketing man in charge, and if you want growth, you don't put a conservative accountant in charge'.[11] What these comments recognise is both the significant role in strategic choice and implementation of the senior executives in any organisation, and the influence of their values in strategic choice and implementation. Research in this latter area indicates that executives of different backgrounds and values will even interpret the same environmental variables in accordance with their own cultural views; and such may be the influence upon them of these values that the executive's effectiveness in a strategic situation which clashes with his basic motivation will be severely reduced.[12]

Following the choice of the right person for the job, it is necessary to ensure the correct motivation. The most obvious form of this is to relate management salaries to the achievement of strategic goals. This is fairly straightforward when the corporate objective is short-term profitability or growth. It will, however, become difficult to design incentives that are closely related to longer term or more complex strategies, in which case qualitative monitoring may be all that can be achieved – for example, when a manager is in charge of a divestment situation.

In addition to choosing the right people to implement a strategy, implementation involves the business in adopting the right organisation structure for the strategy. Stressing this dimension of implementation reflects the view that organisation structure can be related to strategy, and that to neglect this is to jeopardise the likelihood of achieving the firm's goals. Thus, 'If organizational structure is not adapted to its context, then opportunities are lost, costs rise, and the maintenance of the organization is threatened'.[13] Research in the late 1950s and early 1960s first began to draw attention to the relationship between certain important variables in a firm's environment and its internal organisation structure. Burns and Stalker, for example, aligned turbulent environments in terms of competition and changes in technology with 'organic' organisation structures that were less formal and hierarchical, and contrasted these with businesses whose stable environments led them to adopt 'mechanistic' structures with an emphasis upon formally established roles and relationships within a strict hierarchy.[14] With regard to the impact of different types of technology, and the strategic considerations associated with these, Woodward found that job, batch, mass and flow production technologies confronted firms with different environments, and that these influenced the strategic emphasis and organisation structure of individual firms.[15] Undoubtedly the most influential writer in the area of strategy and organisation structure is Chandler.[16] The Chandler hypothesis is that structure is determined by strategy, and correspondingly that the successful implementation of a strategy can be aided by the adoption of an appropriate organisation structure. Chandler's hypothesis derived from his observations as a business historian of the way in which the adoption by American firms of more complex strategies – developing from single-product, single-stage, single-country businesses to multi-product, multi-stage (vertically integrated), multinational corporations – was accompanied by a change in organisation structure from the unitary business to the multidivisional form of enterprise. The unitary or functional business structure, where devolution of responsibility within the organisation is by functions such as production, sales, finance, etc., and where it was both necessary and possible for the manager to be fairly closely associated with the day-to-day operations of the business, was appropriate when both the size and product and geographical scope of the firm were limited. With an expansion of the operations of the business to embrace a range of products and geography it was both less possible and less appropriate for senior management to be involved in the detailed operations of the firm. A clear distinction then arose between strategic and operational management decisions, and this was reflected in the multidivisonal organisational form. Under this, illustrated in Figure 6.1, responsibility for operations is devolved to product or geographical areas, and senior management is concerned solely with strategic issues. The data in Table 6.3 illustrate the way in which by the late 1960s those large American manufacturing firms that had adopted strategies which took them away from their original product-market interests ('related' and 'unrelated' product businesses) had also overwhelmingly adopted the multidivisional organisation structure. By contrast 'single' and 'dominant' product businesses had moved much less in this direction. A comparable study of the evolution of organisation structures in UK manufacturing industry has borne out this hypothesis that as strategies became more complex in terms of the scale and product or geographical range involved, so the multidivisional organisational structure was more commonly adopted.[17]

Figure 6.1
Multidivisional Organisation Structure

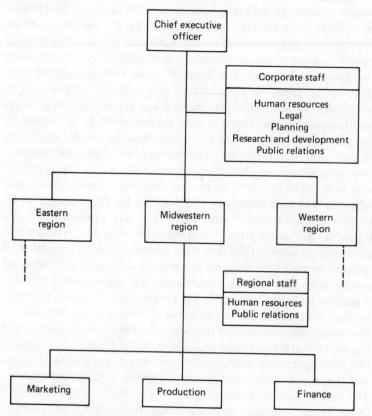

Source: L. L. Byars, *Strategic Management* (New York: Harper & Row, 1984) p. 168.

Table 6.3
Strategy and Organisational Structure in US Manufacturing Industry (based upon a 20 per cent sample from the *Fortune* 500 firms, late 1960s)

Strategy	No. of firms	Organisational structure	
		functional	divisional
Single Product Business	6	6	0
Dominant Product Business	14	5 (36%)	9 (64%)
Related Product Business	60	3 (5%)	57 (95%)
Unrelated Product Business	20	0	20
	100		

Source: B. R. Scott, 'The Industrial State', *Harvard Business Review,* March–April 1973, p. 138.

Moreover, although Child appeared to doubt that one could demonstrate that the choice of the most appropriate organisation structure significantly affected the performance of the organisation, there is evidence relating to both the United States and this country that the choice of the multidivisional organisation structure by diversified firms does have a significant impact upon profitability. In the case of the UK study, for example, it was concluded that 'the internal organization structure of the firms in our sample exerted a statistically significant and large influence on their profitability. Evidently organizational form matters'.[18]

Obviously the broad distinction between functional and multidivisional organisation structure is not necessarily sufficient to guide an indidivual business in choosing a structure appropriate to its strategy. The recognition of the strategy-structure link should, however, lead strategists to consider how best to structure the organisation to ensure the implementation of strategly. Is the business to be organised functionally or multidivisionally? Is multidivisionalisation to be on the basis of product or geography?

What is the appropriate size for each strategic business unit? What is to be the balance between centralisation and decentralisation? The answers to these questions will depend upon some of the features mentioned above as characterising the strategic environment: turbulence, competitiveness, complexity, etc. The point is that these more detailed aspects of business administration must also be related to the strategy of the organisation. Recently reported research in this field indicates that business unit growth and return on investment can be improved by taking account not only of strategic variables such as the environment and business competitiveness, but also of the administrative relationship between corporate headquarters and the business unit in terms of the degree of autonomy enjoyed by business unit managers and the independence they enjoy in functional areas such as marketing, production, etc. In dynamic business environments, for example, growth was significantly greater in business units enjoying a high degree of autonomy from headquarters, whereas business units in the same environment whose policies were closely controlled from the centre performed significantly better in terms of return on investment. Clearly, combining the goal of the business unit with the balance of autonomy/independence improves performance. In the words of the authors, Hamermesh and White, 'we found that corporate managers can have as much impact on a business unit's performance by attending to its administrative ties to headquarters as they can by managing according to detailed strategic portfolio analyses. Moreover, executives can affect the organizational context more easily than they can the competitive and environmental conditions confronting that unit'.[19]

In the previous chapter we noted that one of the problems of applying individually appropriate strategies to strategic business units was that it was sometimes difficult to structure SBUs separately from operating units. This problem is repeated again at the level of strategic implementation. Existing organisation structures and hence centres of authority and responsibility may be dictated by considerations of manufacturing plant organisation, the organisation structures existing prior to an acquisition, or legal and tax considerations. While accepting the validity of determining the organisation of the firm on such bases for certain purposes, it is essential for strategic management to identify SBUs, develop an appropriate strategy for each one, and establish objectives for these. Only if this is achieved will it be possible to ensure that correct strategies for the individual components of the organisation are generated and in turn effectively implemented.[20]

The last of Glueck's implementation areas is functional policy implementation. By this is meant the allocation of resources so as to allow chosen policies to be implemented, and the relating of individual unit or functional policies to those of the organisation as a whole. At a very simple level this means allocating capital within the organisation in accordance with the strategy adopted and not according to some existing rule of thumb such as restricting new investment to funds generated by that activity or division.

The relating of individual business unit or functional policies to the corporate strategy involves communicating the corporate strategy to divisional or functional managers, ensuring their commitment to the strategy, and backing this up with a formal set of objectives at the division/function level to which management salaries may in part be tied. If, for example, the corporate objective is growth and a broad strategy of expansion of sales in existing markets has been chosen, then this strategy must be communicated to production and sales managers and those concerned with finance so as to ensure both a common commitment to this goal and co-ordinated action. A growth approach must then be adopted in the marketing strategy, production must be geared to this, and the necessary finance sought. The task of senior management in this context is to uncouple unit or function policies from previous strategy, which may for example have emphasised short-run profitability, and couple the approaches adopted further down the organisation to the new corporate strategy.

This linking or coupling of the views of strategists and more specialist managers – often between those who predominantly look outwards from the organisation and those whose tendency is to look inwards – can only be accomplished as a result of continual communication between all of the persons involved.[21] This is an important part of strategic decision-making and one that has to be positively implemented by senior management. Businesses would presumably wish to avoid the situation pictured by the *Financial Times* in respect of the committee responsible for co-ordinating group strategy at The Distillers Company whose workings 'are deliberately kept a mystery to most people outside the group – and to not a few within it'.[22] Obviously, any major potential incompatibility between a proposed strategy and, say, financial resources should be highlighted at stage 3 of the strategic implementation process. Even without major incompatibilities, however, a lack of coupling as outlined above may seriously delay or dilute the implementation of a strategy. Once a strategy and its implementation have been agreed upon, clear targets or objectives must be set, monitoring devices established, and managers rewarded for the achievement of these goals.

Problems in the area of strategic implementation are merely illustrations of there being many a potential slip between the cup of strategic planning and the lip of practical implementation. An aggravating factor is that implementation comes at the end of the whole strategy process. One author summed up an understandable reaction on the part of those involved in the implementation of acquisition strategy as 'a natural tendency to relax once the merger is legally consummated and the usual premerger hassles have faded into memories',[23] while Hobbs and Heany explained part of the generally poor record of strategic implementation in terms of the executives involved being 'exhausted before they translate their strategic concept into specific functional support programs'.[24] Compounding this difficulty is the fact that strategic implementation is more largely an operational and administrative task. In contrast to most of the work of strategists, implementation involves the internal workings of the organisation as much as its relationship with the external environment. Harvey, for example, lists task notification, clarification, job assignment and routine stabilisation as among the important components of strategic implementation.[25] The manager whose talent is for for the designing of broad strategy may be much less effective in the field of implementation. Again, implementation of a new strategy will involve not only the coupling issues which we spoke of above, but also in some cases a complete change of attitudes on the part of staff in the organisation. Roy Ash, in turning round the ailing American office equipment firm Addressograph-Multigraph, spoke of the need to 'develop a much greater attachment of everybody to the bottom line – more agony and ecstasy'. 'As he sees it', a commentator wrote, 'the really important change in a company is a process of psychological transformation'.[26] This dimension of strategic implementation demands considerable organisation development talents on the part of senior management concerned. Again, these abilities may not be possessed in sufficiently large measure by the manager whose real talent is for strategic design.

6.4 An Example

In order to illustrate the sequence of strategic decision-making dealt with in this chapter, consider the material in the Appendix relating to a single strategic decision made by a large diversified UK manufacturing firm. The Imperial Group (formerly Imperial Tobacco), with its dominant share of the highly competitive and slow growing UK cigarette and tobacco market, had followed a path of diversification during the 1960s and 1970s in the process of which it had acquired Courage Breweries, HP Sauce, Smedley's, the Ross Group in frozen foods, Allied Farm Foods, J.B. East-wood in poultry, egg and international meat trading, together with Golden Wonder Crisps. The material in the article from the *Financial Times* set out in the Appendix illustrates the way in which Imperial went about making a further strategic decision, involving an expenditure of £280 million, within the context of three broad goals which it had set itself and which derived quite logically from the group's situation at that time of being very largely a UK firm still dependent in 1979 for 52 per cent of its sales and 50 per cent of its profits upon cigarettes and tobacco. Imperial's three goals, expressed in the company's own words, were, first, 'to aquire direct trading assets which will enhance our growth prospects' and hence 'the need to concentrate more of our assets in businesses with higher growth potential'; second, 'to lessen our dependence upon the single market which we domin-ate', and third, 'to lessen our dependence on UK earnings'.[27] As stated above, these goals may be reduced to a desire for growth, and at the same time to the perceived need to achieve this on a broader product and geographical front than previously, thus contributing to a greater stability of earnings and growth.

We now turn to the strategic decision-making process as exem-plified by the Imperial Group–Howard Johnson case. The immedi-ate *trigger* here appears to have been twofold: a threat by the EEC competition policy authorities to take action to improve competi-tion in the tobacco industry (hence the sale of the Imperial Group shareholding in BAT), along with the continuing desire by the company to move in the direction of its goals of growth combined with product and geographical spread. The sale of the BAT shares provided Imperial with a £250 million opportunity with which to make 'a major splash'.

The *information-gathering* process in this case appears to have been extremely thorough: 'Imperial spent over two years of intensive market analysis, embracing some 18 countries ... and going on to study over 1,000 different market sectors in depth'. Consideration of the general environment created a strong bias towards the USA or continental Europe because of the legislative complications likely to apply in respect of UK acquisitions and the possible cultural problems associated with Far East ventures. The healthy and stable general business environment encouraged the firm to choose the USA rather than Europe. 'In the long run the US must have the strongest economy ... It is the last bastion of capitalism and also the most exhilarating nation on earth', said the company chairman in an interesting mixture of economic analysis, political ideology and personal predeliction. The *production of possible solutions* phase here appears to have proceeded in a cascade manner of selecting initially 1,024 sectors of the US economy and narrowing these down to 42 and subsequently 16, from which 60 companies were initially selected.

In this and later parts of the decision-making process, certain criteria for *evaluation* emerged. Desired characteristics were long-term growth prospects, possession of a high level of existing management competence by the acquired business, a history of good quality earnings, a minimum size to provide a springboard for growth, and compatibility with Imperial's philosophy of corporate and individual integrity (hence avoiding gambling). Sectors which Imperial wanted to avoid in the light of its own background and experience (i.e. its perception of its own strengths and weaknesses), together with its goals, were basic research-intensive or capital-intensive industries, those which had low profit margins or which were highly cyclical, markets which were fragmented or characterised by low growth, or those classed as highly competitive. These criteria were narrowed down even further when it came to the evaluation of individual companies: strongly branded goods, high added value, coast-to-coast coverage, etc. The final *selection* process, which 'now increasingly involved a set of value judgements', comprised weighing up all of the factors above in the light of the goals of the organisation, its background strengths and weaknesses, the results of the environmental analysis and the evaluation criteria developed.

The issue of *implementation* is not specifically dealt with in the case as recounted in the Appendix, although it is interesting to note that even in the circular to shareholders seeking their approval prior to the acquisition, two Imperial Group directors have been specifically allocated responsibility for Howard Johnson in the event of the acquisition going ahead. It is relevant, too, to note that the Howard Johnson acquisition could all the more easily be fitted into the Imperial Group portfolio because of the new multidivisional structure which the group had adopted as a reflection of its policy of diversification. Thus in the Imperial Group's 1978 annual report the following development was highlighted:

Just as the fundamental nature of our business has evolved from that of a tobacco company in search of appropriate openings for diversification to that of the multidivisional (i.e. multiproduct) business we have now become, *so it has been necessary to adapt our organisation [structure] so that it reflects the changed nature of Imperial* and assists all levels of the Group to plan for the future. Accordingly, we have taken further steps over the past year to develop our systems for assessing risks and opportunities in every field, for formulating business plans and for resource allocation. (*emphasis added*)

These actions and comments reflect clearly the leadership and organisational aspects of implementation highlighted by Glueck (see note 9).

This case indicates that even if the 'stages of decision-making' model is not necessarily followed step by step, it does provide a framework within which to examine strategic decisions and decision-making. The example certainly illustrates the fact that all of the decision-making steps are necessary, but gives more support to the cascade approach to arriving at the final decision as opposed to an ordered mechanical sequence. In particular, although this case may be a little unusual in this respect, the role of information-gathering and analysis together with the time required for these activities are especially emphasised.

6.5 Conclusions

The purpose of this chapter has been to draw together the material covered in Chapters 2–5 within a 'phases of decision-making' context in order to consider the strategic decision-making and implementation processes as a whole. The importance of doing this stems from the fact that the previous stages in the strategic decision-making process are only a prelude to making strategic decisions, and that implementation is an often neglected component of strategy.

Thus although we have commented frequently in this chapter on the discrepancy between the model of decision-making behaviour as a series of ordered activities and the process as found in practice, strategists ought, whatever the precise sequence of events followed, to engage in each of the activities dealt with in this chapter and summarised in Table 6.1 above. Strategic implementation is a difficult and relatively neglected area. The tide appears, however, to be turning. 'The point is that today, not strategic planning, but instead *implementation* of strategies is all the rage among consultants', wrote one commentator on the American scene, and quoted the president of Arthur D. Little: 'One trend today is the recognition of the importance of the inter-relationships between strategy and operations'.[28] Thus we have brought our consideration of the strategic decision-making process not to an end in itself but to the point where it is translated into practical relations with administration and operations. Equally, however, with the ongoing monitoring and evaluation of strategy the system has come full circle. Any business which finds as a result of such monitoring that it has not achieved its goals must recommence the strategic planning process of considering its objectives, analysing its environment and resources, choosing again among new strategic possibilities and implementing improved strategies. Thus business strategy is in these two senses an ongoing process, through implementation and re-evaluation. Part II of this text looks at these activities in a number of specific strategy areas.

Appendix: The Long Search That Led To Howard Johnson's Door

(reprinted with permission from the *Financial Times*, 17 December 1979)

The Imperial Group's controversial $630m. bid for the Howard Johnson restaurant and motel chain in America will be decided by today's extraordinary general meeting of Imperial's shareholders.

Whatever its outcome, it will remain significant for the process that preceded it; an unusually thorough acquisition 'search'.

Imperial spent over two years of intensive market analysis, embracing some 18 countries, before confirming its instinctive preference for the US, and going on to study over 1,000 different market sectors in depth.

Imperial thus decided to join the growing bank of UK food and drinks companies which are turning their backs on Europe and looking instead to the US as the prime growth market to be in over the next decade.

Some of the British moves into the US over the past year have been substantial – such as Cadbury Schweppes' move for Peter Paul, a confectionery maker – but most so far have been small in scale. But Imperial's bid for Howard Johnson shows that large-scale acquisitions are still very much on the cards. Imperial's bid is the largest ever made by a UK company of any sort for a US organisation.

Seemingly open mind

Unlike most expansive companies which have a good idea of at least the country and sector (if not the company) in which they want to invest, Imperial started the overseas takeover trail with a seemingly open mind – as well as up to £250m. to spend.

Even though Imperial professed an 'open mind' at this stage, it soon became clear that it really wanted to make a major splash by acquiring a single large and well-known company.

Imperial was in its fortunate financial position mainly as a result of the sales – in two stages, completed earlier this year – of its long-held shareholding in BAT (formerly British American Tobacco). This holding dated back to 1902, when BAT was founded by Imperial and a US company, to trade in the world tobacco markets; its position kept Imperial itself out of them. This was one of the reasons why the EEC was beginning to threaten action to improve competition between the two tobacco giants, a factor which spurred the sale.

But Imperial had been planning a major overseas move since the early 1970s, having spent several years lessening its dependence on tobacco by diversification at home, first into foods, and then into brewing with the acquisition of the Courage brewery group.

After this, Imperial felt the possibility of further substantial UK growth by acquisition was likely to be limited by Government competition policy. But its overseas expansion ambitions were put into abeyance by the problems facing its food, drink, and tobacco divisions in the mid–1970s as a result of the oil crisis, steep commodity price rises, and the economic recession.

Finally, just over two and a half years ago, Imperial's group board gave the go-ahead to serious consideration of overseas acquisition targets. The task of finding the right overseas venture was given to Imperial's group strategy centre, a revamped version of its existing corporate planning department.

The centre's task was to compile an extensive dossier on about 18 countries which were large enough, and had sufficient growth prospects, to be worth an investment of the order Imperial was considering. The review split the countries into four groups: Europe, the Commonwealth, developing countries, and the US.

On the basis of published information, the strategy centre considered the likely future trends in each country's economy and the probable trend in political stability. The centre was also concerned to choose countries which were compatible with Imperial's somewhat insular way of thinking: it seemed unlikely that the Far East, for example, would be suitable.

Inevitably, Imperial was heavily biased in favour of the US as the prime area for overseas expansion. In some respects, it would be fair to say that the object of the world survey was simply to ensure that no other growth economy was overlooked as a result of Imperial's prejudices.

For Imperial – and other UK companies for that matter – the attraction of the US is obvious: that, despite its own economic problems, it is still the biggest and most politically stable, most potentially lucrative market in the world; because of the size of the investment Imperial was planning, it was particularly keen to ensure that it was secure. 'In the long run the US must have the strongest economy', says Sir John Pile, Imperial's chairman. 'It is the last bastion of capitalism and also the most exhilarating nation on earth.'

Having firmly settled on the US, Imperial was faced with the mammoth task of deciding on the right sector for expansion, and then on which company to acquire.

Imperial says it started out with no preconceived ideas of the type of business it wanted to be in. Initially, it sought a panoramic over-view of the entire US economy before getting down to specific acquisition targets. It enlisted the aid of a major US consultancy firm, Booz, Allen & Hamilton to help with data collection and advice.

Imperial told Booz Allen that its basic acquisition criteria were fourfold: first, and most important, a market sector had to be identified which showed long-term growth prospects. Second, Imperial made clear that the company eventually chosen for acquisition should have a high level of management competence, and especially that the key management should be willing to stay with the company after the takeover. Third, it wanted evidence of a good and consistent earnings track record, emphasising that it was not seeking a turn-around opportunity but a long-term market investment. Fourth, the company had to be significant enough to be used as a springboard for further growth. And, finally, Booz Allen was told that the company had to be compatible with Imperial's basic philosophy – a philosophy which basically expects a high level of corporate and individual integrity. (In other words, it was looking for a good, solid company run by good, solid people.)

The result of this first panoramic survey was to specify 1,024 sectors or sub-sectors of the US economy. Imperial's strategy team in London and Booz Allen in the US then began the long process of discarding sectors. Imperial decided against those, for example, where costly basic research was a primary factor, such as aerospace or computers. Heavy industries, such as oil, mining and construction were also excluded because they were so capital-intensive.

Imperial wanted to avoid commodity sectors in the US which offered low margins and a highly cyclical business (factors it was well aware of from its UK activities). Small, fragmented sectors were excluded and non-growth markets obviously also went.

This selection process necessarily required a great deal of data collection and analysis. It left Imperial with 42 possible sectors for investment. Although the acquisition trail so far had been largely a mechanical one – simply gathering information and classifying it – Imperial's task now increasingly involved a set of value judgements which had to be traded off against each other.

It therefore took the 42 sectors and applied a new set of criteria. As before, size of the market and its growth prospects represented a major factor, but Imperial also considered the competitive environment, such as whether the industry was too fragmented and too highly competitive. (Grocery retailing would probably fall into this category.)

A complex distribution process was also an unfavourable factor. Imperial looked at consumer trends, profitability, capital investment, research and development, and the possibility of government intervention. Highly unionised industries were also considered a negative factor – as were industries with a 'non-Imperial' image, such as gambling.

Obviously, some of these criteria were contradictory and extremely subjective, and forced Imperial to make continual decisions of judgement. It also made it well aware of potential problems at an early stage. (The crucial problem of transferring ownership of liquor licences from Howard Johnson to Imperial was foreseen at this point, says the company.)

As a result of this analysis, Imperial put the 42 sectors into three groups, in order of priority. The first division, which Imperial now concentrated on, comprised 16 sectors.

It was at this stage that it decided to switch from sector examinations to identifying possible company takeover targets. With Booz Allen's help, some 60 different companies within the chosen sectors were identified and studied in detail over a three-month period.

Again, a new set of criteria was formulated by which to select the base candidates irrespective of whether they were available. The first test was that the company should have strongly branded goods or services, in line with Imperial's general belief in a strong trade brand. (In the UK, for example, it has John Player and Embassy cigarettes, Ross Foods and Courage beer.)

Then Imperial looked for a company's strength in adding value, since this was where it believed the key profits growth lay. A single large company with coast-to-coast coverage was favoured, although a smaller company would reluctantly be considered if the opportunity existed for adding on further ones.

The analysis also covered whether the company was dependent on cyclical markets or raw material supplies. And each company's management structure and problems were reviewed, as well as its business reputation. (The help of the consultants here was invaluable, since Booz Allen's wide US business experience meant that it was able to provide some of the 'off the record' background to a company's management problems.)

And, of course, the financial track record of each company was considered in some detail.

This systematic collection of existing data and background information enabled the 60 companies to be pared down to a final 12 by the autumn of 1978. These were then subjected to an even more intensive scrutiny, using the same criteria as before, but also looking in greater detail at its potential compatability.

Imperial's path along the acquistion trail was troubled at this time by the energy and economic problems emerging in the US. It enlisted the further aid of another set of consultants to look at the energy and economic prospects and decided as a result to re-affirm its basic decision: that it believed in the long-term prospects for the US economy.

The result of its long search finally emerged early this year when the Howard Johnson company came top of the list. Not surprisingly, Imperial refuses to reveal who was number two on the list.

Liquor licence problems

Imperial's methodical approach was then taken a stage further: Howard Johnson was even more extensively researched. The problem of liquor licences led to Imperial using the same lawyers who had successfully dealt with a similar situation when Pepsico had acquired the Pizza Hut chain.

Imperial went ahead with its bid in September this year – and then ran into sharp criticism from the financial press and some shareholders that it was paying too much. Imperial argues that it had to pay a premium on the shares to persuade the Howard Johnson family to sell. It also stresses its belief that it is paying for the long-term investment potential of the company.

Sir John Pile believes the takeover will be given the go-ahead at today's shareholders' meeting. But he points out that the studies undertaken by Imperial have 'had two by-products which make the exercise worthwhile in itself.

'First, in order to look for new opportunities it was necessary for us to look harder at ourselves. The motivation which made us seek new opportunities elsewhere has also made us take a long cold look at our existing interests, and we are a tougher company in consequence.

'Second, we now know more clearly our real role as a company as part of British industry, and in the economy, and understand where we can develop in the future and where we can not. We are better equipped, therefore, to succeed in the uncertainties of the future.'

References

1. E. Witte, 'Field Research on Complex Decision-Making Processes – The Phase Theorem', *International Studies of Management and Organisation*, 1972, pp. 173 and 180.
2. There is, of course, a fourth and less palatable possibility, namely that the shortfall in performance is due not to imperfect implementation of an original strategy, nor to changes in the business environment, but simply to the fact that the original strategic decision was wrong!
3. R. E. Thomas, *Business Policy* (Oxford: Philip Allan, 2nd edn, 1983) pp. 3, 51 and 136.
4. H. I. Ansoff, *Corporate Strategy* (Harmondsworth: Penguin, 1968) p. 32.
5. *Ibid.*, p. 33.
6. D. F. Harvey, *Business Policy and Strategic Management* (Columbus, Ohio: Merrill Publishing, 1982) p. 228.
7. A. A. Owen, 'How to Implement Strategy', *Management Today*, July 1982, p. 51.

8. K. R. Andrews, *The Concept of Corporate Strategy* (Homewood, Ill.: R. D. Irwin, revised edn. 1980) pp. 110–12.
9. See W. F. Glueck, *Business Policy and Strategic Management* (New York: McGraw-Hill, 3rd edn, 1980) p. 305.
10. See P. N. Khandwalla, 'Some Top Management Styles, Their Context and Performance', *Organization and Administrative Sciences*, Winter 1976–77, pp. 21–51.
11. W. W. Wommack of Mead Corporation, quoted in *Business Week*, 27 March 1978, p. 105.
12. See W. Lamb, 'Motivating by Strategy', *Management Today*, March 1984, pp. 81.
13. J. Child, 'Organizational Structure, Environment and Performance: The Role of Strategic Choice', *Sociology*, 1972, Vol. VI, p. 8.
14. See T. Burns and G. Stalker, *The Management of Innovation* (London: Tavistock Publications, 1959).
15. See J. Woodward, *Industrial Organisation: Theory and Practice* (Oxford: Oxford University Press, 1965).
16. See A. D Chandler, *Strategy and Structure* (Cambridge, Mass.: MIT Press, 1962).
17. See D. F. Channon, *The Strategy and Structure of British Enterprise* (London: Macmillan, 1973).
18. See Child, 'Organizational Structure', pp. 1–22; and the evidence in D. J. Teece, 'Internal Organization and Economic Performance: An Empirical Analysis of the Profitability of Principal Firms', *Journal of Industrial Economics*, December 1981, Vol. XXX, pp. 173–91; and P. Steer and J. Cable, 'Internal Organization and Profit: An Empirical Analysis of Large UK Companies', *Journal of Industrial Economics*, September 1978, Vol. XXVII, pp. 13–30.
19. R. G. Hamermesh and R. E. White, 'Manage Beyond Portfolio Analysis', *Harvard Business Review*, January–February 1984, p. 105.
20. See Owen, 'How to Implement Strategy', pp. 51–2.
21. See J. M. Hobbs and D. F. Heany, 'Coupling Strategy to Operating Plans', *Harvard Business Review*, May–June 1977, pp 119–26.
22. *Financial Times*, 28 January 1984.
23. F. W. Searby, 'Control Postmerger Change', *Harvard Business Review*, September–October 1969, p. 5.
24. Hobbs and Heany, 'Coupling Strategy', p. 125.
25. Harvey, *Business Policy*, pp. 238–9.
26. 'Roy Ash is Having Fun at Addressogrief-Multigrief', *Fortune*, 27 February 1978, p. 47.
27. These statements are taken from the letter from the Imperial Group chairman to shareholders concerning the Howard Johnson acquisition, and from the Group's 1978 and 1979 Annual Reports.
28. J. Thackray, 'The Consulting Cornucopia', *Management Today*, December 1983, p. 73.

Analysis of Strategies

II

Business Growth 7

Nothing is so compelling as the need to survive. However, there is little doubt as to how, overwhelmingly, this choice is exercised: it is to achieve the greatest possible rate of corporate growth as measured in sales. — J. K. Galbraith, *The New Industrial State* (London: Hamish Hamilton, 1967) p. 171.

7.1 Introduction

In Part I of this text we examined the sequence in which firms make strategic decisions. In Part II we shall examine a range of individual business strategies that are used to achieve corporate objectives. The first of these individual strategies to be examined is growth. This has been chosen because growth embraces most of the major directions of strategic decision-making. Indeed, only divestment as a business strategy falls out with the ambit of growth, and even in that case individual divestments by a firm may simply be a prelude to a new phase of growth.

The plan of this chapter, after a preliminary consideration of the appeal of corporate growth to businesses, is to consider the major barriers to growth, the directions in which firms may choose to expand, and finally, as a prelude to Chapter 10 on acquisitions, to consider the choice which expansionist businesses have to make between internal and external growth.

117

7.2 Incentives to Growth

Few business people today need to be persuaded that firms should be growth-oriented. The firm that does not attempt to grow, it is argued, is likely not merely to stand still but to stagnate and die. This attitude is likely to be particularly common among professional managers. They receive little direct financial benefit from increased profitability on the part of the firm, but would appear to enjoy both pecuniary and broader benefits from business growth.[1] In Marris's view, 'Well-planned and well-executed expansion . . . is both stimulating and self-sustaining, and may thus represent to the executive a challenge similar to the challenge of difficult climbs in mountaineering'.[2] Johnson and Scholes report in their research reference by managers to the benefits arising from growth in the form of personal challenge and satisfaction, the opening up of further business opportunities, and keeping ahead of the competition. Growth for some of these managers was seen as a 'natural, normal, "instinctive" state of affairs'.[3] In addition to the managerial stimulus to business growth, expansion is likely to confer tangible financial benefits to the firm. Providing growth is not disproportionately expensive, and particularly if it is horizontal in direction, the productivity of the organisation may rise as the rate of output increases ahead of costs. At least in the short term this is likely to be the case as an expansion of output merely results in an elimination of spare or underutilised capacity. The firm may benefit at this stage, too, from moving down the learning curve as it accumulates experience of operating in its markets. Furthermore, as growth increases the size of the firm, the business may also reap the benefits of economies of scale. If expansion takes place within a single market, such economies may be reaped at both the production and managerial levels. Even if the firm grows by diversifying into a range of product-market areas, the increased size of its total operations may allow it to enjoy advantages of economies of scale in such areas as marketing or finance, or in the use of certain management functions. Thus at certain rates of growth (and as we shall see below, this is an important caveat) the very activity of expansion on the part of the firm may lead to increased productivity and profits.

Horizontal expansion by a firm may also provide benefits arising from market dominance. Indeed, in terms of the structure of the business environment in a product-market area it may be essential for a firm to grow in order to maintain its size and market position *vis-à-vis* its suppliers, competitors or customers.

Thus both in respect of business costs and revenues growth within certain limits is likely to confer not only professional satisfaction but also tangible economic benefits to the firm. Most organisations therefore place a considerable emphasis upon growth. There is, however, a range of difficulties or constraints that are likely to confront firms following expansionist strategies, and these are considered in the section below.

7.3   Constraints upon Growth

Expanding businesses face five major constraints: finance, other non-managerial inputs, management, the impact of growth upon profitability, and markets.

Finance

Business growth implies not just an increased level of sales by the firm but an expansion of its whole scale of productive activity. For this expansion access to additional finance is necessary. In seeking to expand, firms may be confronted by institutional barriers to raising additional finance, or there may be some limit to the *rate* at which additional capital may be raised. Institutions such as the clearing banks or other financial intermediaries may not be willing to extend their services to firms beyond a particular size or for particular forms of investment such as research and development. The firms affected are thus faced with a 'gap' in the financial institutions which acts as a barrier to expansion and which at least for a time creates an effective ceiling to their size or rate of expansion. The Wilson Committee concluded in 1979 that capital for small businesses was more difficult and more expensive to obtain than was the case for larger companies. Venture capital was reported to be especially hard for small firms to obtain. Although it is accepted that these difficulties often simply reflect correspondingly higher costs and risks on the part of financial institutions in lending to small organisations rather than any systematic bias against them, such circumstances undoubtedly place financial restrictions upon the growth of smaller firms.[4]

Given the importance of retained earnings or undistributed profits for business expansion, a more immediate growth barrier for firms is the existing level of return on capital employed and the rate at which savings can be accumulated from this. The maximum rate at which a firm which is dependent entirely upon additional internal finance for expansion may grow is the product of its current return on investment and the savings or retention ratio. That is,

$$g = \frac{\text{profits}}{\text{capital}} \times \frac{\text{savings}}{\text{profits}}$$

where g is the maximum internally financed growth rate, profits are measured net of all business expenses including interest and taxes, and savings comprise profits less equity dividends. Thus for a firm presently earning 15 per cent as defined above, and distributing 40 per cent of the profits as dividends, the maximum possible growth rate is 9 per cent. To achieve a growth rate in excess of this would require the firm to increase its present return on investment or be prepared to save a greater proportion of its profits. The situation in practice is more complicated if we allow for the possibility of the firm financing its expansion through a mixture of internal and external funds. Then further matters such as the gearing ratio (that is, the proportion of debt to equity finance) and dividend policy have to be taken into consideration. In particular, given the desire by a firm to grow at a rate beyond that which can be financed internally (9 per cent in our example above), the optimal financial strategy may be for the firm not merely to fill the gap between that rate and the desired expansion rate by raising additional external funds, but to *reduce* its savings rate in order to increase its share price and so lower the cost of new equity capital. In this way although more new capital will require to be raised, the earnings per share may be increased. From these points it will be seen that finance may act as a significant brake upon the rate of business growth, and that whatever the other attractions of such growth a price may have to be paid in terms of increased financial costs.

Non-managerial factors

A shorter-term barrier to business expansion may be the lack of material or personnel resources. Raw materials may be in inelastic supply as a result of lead times which suppliers face. The expansion of world demand for computers and other electronic equipment has currently (early 1984) resulted in a significant shortage of microchips with semiconductor manufacturers having to ration customers.[5] Supplies of primary commodities such as phosphate for fertiliser manufacture may be inelastic arising from the time taken to obtain access to new supplies and also to acquire the expensive, specialist mining equipment. At the peak of the boom in fertiliser demand in the mid-1970s, for example, it was reported that in the United States there was a five-year waiting list for the massive drag lines necessary for phosphate mining; and at the same time it was estimated that the lead time for bringing a new ammonia fertiliser plant on stream was three years.[6] Certainly, access to reserves of clay for cement or brick making, or to quarry materials for roadstone or land for housebuilding must enter into the expansion plans of businesses in those sectors; and the presence or absence of these may dictate the speed, direction or form of expansion undertaken.[7] Shortages of personnel may also restrict business growth. Even in a period of generally high unemployment, skilled and specialist labour may be in short supply. The cost of rapid expansion in the east of Scotland offshore oil industry has at times been increased by shortages of certain types of skilled labour, thus reducing the attractiveness of such expansion.

Management

The emphasis put upon the significance of management in the growth process, and the analysis of the limitations placed upon the rate of business growth imposed by the rate of expansion of the management team by Edith Penrose has led to such restrictions becoming known as Penrose effects.[8] In her analysis of growth, while accepting that the size of the firm was not determinate, Penrose emphasised that its rate of growth was particularly circumscribed through being dependent upon the existing management team and the rate at which this team could be expanded effectively. Business growth implies a plan for its achievement, and therewith a management team to plan and implement growth. Not only is there a present limit to the amount of such planning and implementation that a firm's existing management team can undertake, but there is also a limit to the rate at which such a management team itself may be expanded. This limit arises not simply from the need to hire additional members to supplement the existing team (although in keeping with what has been said about other personnel shortages, skilled managers too may be difficult to recruit), but from the fact that there must be a limit to the rate at which additional new managers can be effectively integrated into the present team. In Penrose's own words,

> **if a firm deliberately or inadvertently expands its organization more rapidly than the individuals in the expanding organization can obtain the experience with each other and with the firm that is necessary for the effective operation of the group, the efficiency of the firm will suffer ... in extreme cases this may lead to such disorganization that the firm will be unable to compete efficiently in the market with other firms.**[9]

Management itself, therefore – the making and implementation of strategic and administrative decisions – may act as a major brake on the rate of business growth. Such growth is likely to be particularly costly if it is being attempted in a complex and turbulent environment where there is a wide range of variables to be considered in making strategic decisions, and where the environment is subject to rapid change and uncertainty.

Growth and profitability

Although in discussing the incentives to business growth we instanced a number of efficiency advantages which certain growth rates might confer upon a firm, one of the ultimate restrictions upon business growth is the depressing effect that higher rates of growth may have upon profitability. The statistical analysis of business growth normally involves treating growth as the dependent variable, and independent variables such as firm size, profitability or diversification are used to explain variations in observed growth rates among a cross-section of firms. Growth in this case is normally strongly associated with profitability (indicating its dependence upon this variable), but not with firm size.[10] On the other hand Marris has tested for the dependence of profitability upon growth,[11] and the existence of a negative relationship between these two variables beyond certain rates of growth is a crucial assumption in Marris's theory of 'managerial' capitalism.[12] The negative relationship between growth and profitability as the former rises beyond a particular level obviously has the effect of curtailing growth in so far as it is dependent directly or indirectly upon profitability. The damaging impact that growth then has upon profitability will reduce the level of internally generated finance available for growth; and the fall in share prices consequent upon reduced profits will increase the cost of external funds. This negative relationship between the rate of growth and profitability arises as the firm begins to experience increased operating costs at high growth rates and also encounters severe Penrose effects. Increased competitive costs, or reduced earnings, accompanying high rates of growth will also result from the difficulties inevitably encountered in attempting to expand one's markets. This problem is dealt with below as the final major barrier to growth. The conclusion here is that for any firm, according to its strategic circumstances – the environment in which it operates and its blend of strengths and weaknesses – there will be a maximum rate at which it can expand without encountering a negative relationship between growth and profits. Any growth strategy must therefore have particular regard to the resources of the business and the match between these and the identified opportunities for market expansion.

Markets

This leads us to the final constraint upon business growth: markets or customers. The barriers to growth we have discussed so far relate to the increasing costs of expansion. Difficulties in generating additional sales represent the demand constraint upon growth. The firm pursuing a strategy of horizontal growth is constrained in its environment by the rate of growth of the market, and also by its competitiveness *vis-à-vis* other sellers in the field. Organic growth – that is, without resort to acquiring other independent sellers – is limited to the rate of expansion of the market itself unless the firm can envisage increasing its market share. Such an increase in market share will involve the firm in using additional resources to reduce the proportion of the market held by competitors. This will be attempted by adopting a strategy that recognises the key factors for success or key dimensions of competition in the product-market area, and which exploits the strengths of the firm relative to its competitors' weaknesses. The intensity of competitiveness in the market will depend upon the growth rate the firm wishes to achieve relative to that at which the market is expanding, the attitude of the remaining sellers to the firm's growth plans, and the balance of competitive advantage among all sellers in the market. When the expansion plans of one business imply a significant reduction in market shares for others, and when these remaining sellers have a strong desire to remain in the market and are well matched against each other in terms of resources, an industry may well experience a prolonged price war or severe competition along some other dimension. By contrast, expansion by a firm within its existing market through acquisiton, since it involves no addition of capacity or supply in the market *vis-à-vis* the current level of demand, is at first sight an attractive proposition where the market growth rate is low and where the firm's strengths are financial rather than technical or marketing. As we shall see in Chapter 10, however, an acquisition strategy does not in general appear to offer an easy or immediate route to profits. There are significant managerial problems likely to be encountered in any acquisition strategy; and if a number of firms in the same market are attempting to expand externally, the cost of appropriate acquisitions may well rise to a level which threatens the prospect of acceptable returns on this form of investment.

The market difficulties associated with horizontal expansion often encourage firms to seek growth by undertaking a wider range of functions within a given product-market area – vertical integration – or by expanding into other markets altogether, that is by diversification. Vertical integration, as we shall see in Chapter 8, may be undertaken for a variety of reasons other than growth. As a growth strategy alone vertical integration may, however, combine the disadvantage of offering no real escape from a static or declining market while at the same time confronting firms with potential technical, marketing or management problems in moving backwards or forwards along the vertical market chain. For this reason firms may consider the real alternative growth strategy to horizontal expansion to be diversification.

The attraction of diversification as a growth strategy – despite evidence of the poor profit returns and high risks attaching to it[13] – is that by releasing itself from the confines of its original market, or indeed any market which does not offer sufficient growth prospects, the firm escapes all demand constraints upon expansion. These demand constraints may well, however, by replaced by management difficulties, by no means all of which can necessarily be overcome by entering new markets by acquisition. Thus diversified expansion, while apparently surmounting one set of restrictions on business growth, highlights the management constraint upon growth very much along the lines emphasised by Penrose.[14]

A firm's success in expansion depends upon its ability to cope with the constraints we have outlined in this section. While the broad financial constraint for smaller firms may have been somewhat reduced with the development of the Unlisted Securities Market (USM) since its establishment late in 1980,[15] product markets have remained a serious constraint for firms of all sizes. Success at this general level of expansion strategy involves a recognition of the major growth constraint, and an assessment of the firm's strengths and weaknesses in this area. It implies, too, an understanding of the key factors for success in the market(s) involved. In the process of considering the nature of demand constraints above, possible directions of business growth were outlined. These are now considered in more detail below, together with the strategies associated with them.

7.4 Directions of Expansion

Horizontal growth

The most obvious direction in which a firm may expand is by increasing output of its existing product(s). The principal factors for the firm to consider in pursuing this strategy are the aggregate market growth rate, the key factors for success in the market, the match between these and the firm's resources, and the balance of competitiveness between the firm and its competitors. The potential restrictive impact of the market growth rate upon individual business expansion has already been commented upon. If this factor is likely to impinge upon the firm's growth ambitions, then it is vital for the firm to analyse the key factors for success in the market and to compare these with its own strengths and weaknesses. Market success in this respect will depend upon a recognition of what it is that consumers want from a product and what influences them in buying it. In some markets success depends upon attaining a low cost position, while in others technological virtuosity is essential. In some sectors marketing skills are all-important, whereas in others considerable financial resources are needed when customers do not make progress payments during an extended construction period or expect to be granted generous credit. By identifying these and matching or developing one's resources to market needs, growth may be obtained even in comparatively static markets. The final dimension of analysis involves assessing one's own capabilities relative to those of other sellers. The result of this assessment, combined with the previous elements discussed above, will indicate the likelihood of the firm achieving its planned rate of growth in the face of market competition.

Research in this area indicates that even in markets having low overall growth rates, firms can succeed on the basis of well-chosen strategies.[16] These strategies may be divided into three categories: segmentation, innovation, and low-cost leadership. Each involves identifying the key characteristics of a market and exploiting these on the basis of existing or developed resources. Segmentation involves exploiting growth sectors in otherwise sluggish markets. Speciality chemicals, quality cigars and recreational bicycles are examples of market areas in which success has been possible in a growth segment within markets characterised by low aggregate growth and severe competition. The point at issue here is that most markets, and even those whose aggregate rate of growth is modest, have growth sectors. Expansion for a firm under these circumstances is most dependent upon marketing skills in recognising and exploiting these segments rather than technology.

This latter strength dimension is, however, the basis for growth through innovation, although it should also be accompanied by an accurate recognition of market needs. Consumption of food, for example, is expanding very slowly in this country. Between 1969 and 1979 total consumer expenditure on food grew at only 0.5 per cent per annum in real terms. Over the same period, however, convenience food expenditure increased markedly. In the case of quick frozen foods it rose from 4p per person per week to 21p in current terms, and similar increases occurred in respect of canned and other convenience foods.[17] Firms that have benefited from this trend have done so not only by recognising the growth in demand for convenience foods stemming from the increased proportion of working women in the economy and the trend towards snack meals, but also through new product innovation, as in the cases of instant mashed potato, oven-ready chips, etc. As a particular example in another field one firm has even managed to expand rapidly in the sewing machine market, where sales halved during the 1970s, by using the latest electronic technology to add a range of special features to its machine.[18] Competition in technology and new products not only provides for expansion in low-growth markets but also avoids potentially mutually destructive price competition among sellers. It may therefore be the preferred dimension of competition in concentrated, low-growth markets, particularly where the level of aggregate demand is not sensitive to price reductions. Competition by advances in product technology rather than price has, for example, been the predominant competitive weapon between the oligopoly competitors in the wet-shave market.

The final possible growth strategy involves achieving a low-cost position in the market and using this to establish a leadership position. This approach is most appropriate where price is the major competitive dimension, and where a seller can set a low price without appearing to compromise on product quality. This strategy may be adopted where the seller is prepared to grow slowly and where, as output expands, access is gained to economies of scale.[19]

The point emphasised in this section is that by identifying the key factors for success in a market or market segment – price, technology, etc. – and by concentrating business resources upon particular markets or market features, even firms having modest resources may compete and succeed in low-growth markets. Our conclusion, therefore, is that although horizontal growth – the most obvious direction of business expansion – is undoubtedly limited by market and competitive conditions, careful strategic analysis of the market and its segments, of the key factors which determine success in the market, and of one's own competence relative to competitors, followed by the pursuit of a clearly identified strategy, can provide opportunities for horizontal growth in a range of market areas.

Vertical integration and diversification

Horizontal growth has been dealt with at greater length than wider directions of expansion in order to indicate the ways in which strategic analysis can be used to achieve expansion under competitive conditions. By contrast, because separate chapters are devoted to them below, vertical integration and diversification are referred to only briefly here in a growth context.

Vertical integration provides firms with an opportunity to expand within a market by increasing the number of successive stages within the product-market chain that are undertaken rather than by increasing output of existing products. It should be noted that in the case of backward vertical integration it is the value added measure of output that will rise and not sales revenue. By means of vertical integration the firm may avoid having to increase its range of customers. It may be able to expand its scale of operations without adding significantly to capacity; and many fewer problems are likely to be encountered in adapting its management to a previous or subsequent stage of manufacturing as distinct from moving into entirely new markets. The advantages of a strategy of vertical integration additional to growth are analysed in the following chapter. However, there we shall also find not only that vertical integration may involve strategic risks, but also that the management skills required at successive stages in the product-market chain may differ significantly in ways that must limit the scale or speed of growth that may be achieved by this strategy.

Diversification as a growth strategy most obviously releases the firm from the market or customer constraint on expansion.

Indeed, in being able to move from one growth market to another in a series of diversification moves the firm may appear to have eliminated this ultimate barrier to growth. As we shall see in Chapter 9, however, there may be significant managerial growth problems involved in expanding by diversification. Firms that have expanded by diversification into totally unrelated markets seem to have a particularly poor record of profitability or survival.[20] Chapter 9 below analyses the major difficulties involved in managing diversified businesses, and also considers in some detail the way in which diversification opportunities may be assessed.

7.5 Forms of Growth

So far we have only mentioned in passing the possibility of firms achieving growth by acquisition as an alternative to internal or organic expansion. In particular it has been suggested that the acquisition route to growth allows firms to bypass some of the restrictions upon the rate of expansion considered above. Growth by acquisition offers three advantages over organic expansion: speed, immediate access to factors (including management) and customers, and the purchase of a corporate vehicle which has, so to speak, been run in. Each of these advantages, although capable of being analysed separately, is related to the others. Acquisition offers a faster rate of growth in so far as another company may be bought for shares in the acquiring business rather than with the cash resources slowly accumulated out of profits with which suppliers of plant, etc. have to be paid. Moreover, in gaining access to customers and management by acquisition the slow, competitive increase in sales and the Penrose managerial limits to growth are avoided or relaxed. Finally, in buying a presently working business model the painful piecing together of assorted human and material factors which must accompany internal expansion is avoided altogether. In particular, where material factors are scarce or in inelastic supply, where necessary management expertise is at a premium, and where powerful competitors are strongly entrenched behind market entry barriers, there may be no alternative to growth by acquisition. In many instances a major barrier encountered in expanding internally is the creation of a working enterprise. Difficulties are likely to be encountered from market, technical and Penrose problems, all of which may be alleviated by purchase of the required business.

As we shall emphasise in Chapter 10, however, the acquisition process is not without its difficulties and drawbacks, and these apply to growth as much as to other strategies. Appropriate candidates for acquisition may simply not be available to an expanding firm. The working package of resources purchased may not be as compatible as one would like in terms of size, product interests or other required strengths, and may be even less attractive upon acquisition than it appeared in prospect. In particular there is no guarantee that the acquired management will stay and work effectively with the acquiring firm; and the whole process of planning, implementing and consumating a corporate marriage may be as difficult and time-consuming for management as any internal expansion. These and other problems associated with acquisitions are dealt with in more detail in Chapter 10 below.

Before leaving the issue of mergers and growth it is worth mentioning that one means of expanding is for a firm to allow itself to be acquired. In this case the victim firm is relying upon its new parent to provide it with a means of growth which would otherwise not be open to it. It must also be assumed that under its new parent the victim firm retains considerable management autonomy, or the expansion achieved is very much that of the acquiring firm rather than the victim. An example of this phenomenon is Wilkinson Sword, the 'razor blades to garden shears' manufacturer. In 1974 Wilkinson joined forces with the British Match Corporation: their respective annual sales at that time were £25.3 million and £66.2 million. Wilkinson was acquired by BMC but gained access to significant additional financial resources from BMC's matches cash cow with which to compete with Gillette, then as now the dominant firm in the wet-shave market. It was, moreover, Wilkinson's management that dominated the combined organisation Wilkinson Match. In 1980 Wilkinson repeated earlier history when the combined firm was acquired by the American Allegheny International. Again, at the time of the acquisition Wilkinson's sales were less than half those of its new parent. The UK management now plays a subordinate role in the total operations, although it appears to enjoy autonomy within Wilkinson itself. Being taken over has again, however, increased the competitive scale of Wilkinson Sword, as it is now called, and in

particular has given the firm increased capital investment resources with which to compete against Gillette and Bic.[21]

7.6 Conclusions

This chapter commences our analysis of individual business
strategies. As mentioned in the first section above, growth
embraces almost all of the strategies which firms may adopt. Our
discussion of the incentives, constraints, directions and forms of
growth, together with the use made in these contexts of the
concepts of strategic analysis developed in Part I of this text,
should serve as a prelude to the further analysis in Part II. As in
the case of growth, any corporate strategy must be considered in
terms of the goals it is intended to achieve, the constraints and
limits in using the strategy to achieve corporate goals, and the
form in which the strategy may be achieved. In particular the
strategy should have regard to the goals of the organisation, the
market environment, and the resources of the business.

Part II of this text now proceeds by considering two expansion
strategies: vertical integration and diversification. This is followed
by an analysis of merger or acquisition as a particular route to
business goals. Two rather newer areas of strategy – divestment
and business turnaround – are examined in Chapters 11 and 12
respectively, and Part II closes with some general conclusions on
the topic of business strategy.

References

1. See, for example, G. Meeks and G. Whittington, 'Directors' Pay,
   Growth and Profitability', *Journal of Industrial Economics*, September 1975, Vol. XXIV, pp. 1–14.
2. R. Marris, *The Economic Theory of 'Managerial' Capitalism* (London: Macmillan, 1964) p. 58.
3. See G. Johnson and K. Scholes, *Exploring Corporate Strategy* (New
   Jersey: Prentice-Hall International, 1984) p. 151.
4. See Interim Report of the (Wilson) *Committee to Review the Func-
   tioning of Financial Institutions* (London: HMSO, 1979, Cmnd 7503)
   Ch. 9.
5. See *Financial Times*, 9 February 1984.

6. See J. Thackray, 'The Year of W. R. Grace', *Management Today*, January 1975, p. 72.
7. See, for example, London Brick Company's approach to valuing its reserves of Oxford clay in *Financial Times*, 10 February 1984.
8. See E. T. Penrose, *The Theory of the Growth of the Firm* (Oxford: Blackwell, 1980 edn) Ch. 4.
9. *Ibid.*, p. 47.
10. See the evidence on this quoted in W. S. Howe, *Industrial Economics* (London: Macmillan, 1978) pp. 87–8.
11. R. L. Marris, 'Incomes Policy and the Rate of Profit in Industry', *Manchester Statistical Society*, December 1964, pp. 23–8.
12. See Marris, *The Economic Theory of 'Managerial' Capitalism*, pp. 250–3.
13. See T. J. Peters and R. H. Waterman, *In Search of Excellence* (New York: Harper & Row, 1982) pp. 296–7.
14. See Penrose, *The Theory of the Growth of the Firm*, Ch. 7.
15. See S. Caulkin, 'The Unlimited Explosion', *Management Today*, February 1984, pp. 42–4.
16. See R. G. Hamermesh and S. B. Silk, 'How to Compete in Stagnant Industries', *Harvard Business Review*, September–October 1979, pp. 161–8.
17. See W. S. Howe, 'Competition and Performance in Food Manufacturing', in J. Burns *et al.* (eds), *The Food Industry* (London: Heinemann, 1983) pp. 101–26.
18. See *Sunday Times*, 19 February 1984.
19. See W. K. Hall, 'Survival Strategies in a Hostile Environment', *Harvard Business Review*, September–October 1980, pp. 75–85.
20. See R. Biggadike, 'The Risky Business of Diversification', *Harvard Business Review*, May–June 1979, pp. 103–11; and for some rather more optimistic UK evidence C. W. L. Hill, 'Conglomerate Performance Over the Economic Cycle', *Journal of Industrial Economics*, December 1983, Vol. XXXII, pp. 197–211.
21. See Monopolies Commission, *British Match Corporation Ltd and Wilkinson Sword Ltd* (London: HMSO, 1973, Cmnd 5442); and S. Caulkin, 'Wilkinson's Second Safety Match', *Management Today*, September 1983, pp. 50ff.

Vertical Integration 8

Vertical integration . . . competing with suppliers and supplying competitors. — Robert Heller, *The Times*, 20 June 1971.

8.1 Introduction

Vertical integration as a business strategy involves a firm in undertaking two or more successive stages in the process of converting raw materials into finished goods in the hands of the ultimate consumer. By this means two or more successive technologically distinct production or distribution processes are carried out by a single enterprise. We noted in Chapter 4 (see Table 4.1, p. 55) and in Chapter 7 that vertical integration constituted a significant potential growth path for the firm. In addition to the prospect of growth that vertical integration offers, there is a range of further advantages that may be gained from the adoption of this strategy. In this chapter we shall analyse the nature of these possible advantages, consider the potential strategic drawbacks of such a policy, and examine how management can arrive at an optimal strategy in this area.

8.2 Strategic Gains from Vertical Integration

Porter discusses the potential gains from vertical integration under the headings shown in Table 8.1.[1]

Table 8.1
Potential Gains from Vertical Integration

1. Economies of integration
   economies of combined operations
   economies of internal control and co-ordination
   economies of information
   economies of avoiding the market
   economies of stable relationships
2. Tap into technology
3. Assurance of supply and/or demand
4. Offsetting bargaining power and input cost distortions
5. Enhanced ability to differentiate
6. Elevation of entry and mobility barriers.

The economies of vertical integration as Porter describes them are the most significant in the list of advantages. Not only are these effects likely to be more quantifiable than the other considerations, but if there are no such economies – if indeed there is a sacrifice of efficiency involved in vertical integration – then this must constitute a cost of attaining the other benefits.

The economies of integration argument in favour of this policy rests essentially upon the assumption that a single organisation can better achieve by management co-ordination what might otherwise be undertaken as a result of arm's length market transactions. Thus there are instances where the administrative linking of successive stages in the provision of goods or services is cheaper or more reliable or convenient than the invisible hand of the market. This will occur as successive operations are combined under one roof, eliminating transport costs, cooling, preservation and reheating of metals, and in some cases utilising otherwise 'spare' capacity. Such arrangements may also provide for a more efficient managerial co-ordination of supply and demand for components, and there may be consequent reductions in the necessary levels of stockholding. It may also be argued that a whole range of functions including selling, purchasing, pricing, negotiating and other transaction costs are eliminated or significantly reduced when goods move between divisions of a single enterprise rather than between two independent commercial organisations.

Finally Porter argues that once a selling and buying relationship has been established between an upstream and downstream unit within a single organisation, each may be able to reduce costs further by investing in specialist equipment on the basis of a guaranteed throughput. Given a stable flow of demand, the upstream unit may be willing to provide a specific product for its internal customer. Where both the seller and the buyer in a market-based situation have to recognise that this relationship may be terminated by either in favour of a competitor, there is no incentive to employ specific cost reducing techniques or provide products for which there is no general demand.

The remainder of the advantages of vertical integration – that is, in addition to the straightforward potential economies outlined above – stem from broader strategic advantages which the adoption of such a policy may confer. Backward integration by manufacturers into a previous stage of production or into raw material supplies gives them an insight into the supply process. This insight may provide a means of monitoring price and cost conditions at the earlier stage of production, or of increasing familiarity with the technology. Furthermore, although such integration may initially be partial (that is, the firm may still obtain most of its supplies from the market) such a policy will provide a basis for deciding upon the complete adoption of vertical integration. Correspondingly a manufacturer may integrate partially forward in order to increase its familiarity with the market for its product and with its customers' requirements.

One of the most obvious advantages sought through backward or forward vertical integration is control over raw materials or customers respectively. Forward integration in this context may, however, be a short-sighted policy. Acquisition of customers in a market that is in long-term decline merely extends the firm's commitment to more than one stage of the market. Such a policy should only be adopted in order to protect the upstream unit from a rapid rate of decline in the market from which the firm should divest in the longer term. A more rational advantage of vertical integration in this context is the positive defence of one's sources of supply or distribution. Thus if there is any risk of raw material shortages, and particularly if there is any danger of the supply of these being controlled by competitors, backward integration will become the norm in the industry, as in the case of petroleum refining. In the same industry forward integration into petrol retailing is explained by the planning restrictions relating to such outlets and the need felt by petroleum refiners to control distribution of the product. The decision by a firm to integrate backwards or forwards may also be stimulated by apparently excessive profits being earned by either suppliers or customers. The aim of vertical integration in this case for the expanding firm is to arrogate to itself these profits. In some cases the mere threat of integration may lead suppliers to reduce their prices for components, or customers to offer more attractive terms. Alternatively the symbolic act of partial integration may be all that is required to alter the bargaining power in the trade. However, it should not be forgotton that even if one's suppliers appear to be earning excessive profits there is no guarantee that a firm integrating backwards will be able to achieve such returns. A supplier's profits are a function of the prices charged and its cost levels. If a supplier's profits are largely the outcome of the low level of costs arising from scale economies or certain absolute cost advantages over other existing and potential suppliers, then entrants to the market will not necessarily enjoy such handsome returns. Partial vertical entry by customers may, however, lead a supplier as a matter of prudence to reduce its prices generally in order to discourage further entry into the market.

Without necessarily intending this to be the case, vertical integration by firms in a sector raises the entry barriers to potential new entrants into that market. Integration by existing suppliers will increase the capital requirement of entry into a market, will put potential entrants at a cost disadvantage, and may also lead to a situation where a new entrant producer has to rely upon its integrated competitors for the distribution of its product. Any firm wishing to enter the UK brewing industry on a national scale would face precisely such a combination of disadvantage arising from the existing vertically integrated structure of the market.

8.3 Costs of Vertical Integration

So far we have emphasised the strategic advantages of vertical integration arising from potentially reduced costs or increased prices, or a more advantageous strategic position in the market. There may, however, be situations in which vertical integration involves the firm in increased costs. Equally, under certain circumstances there are strategic drawbacks arising from vertical integration. Frequently, therefore, a firm contemplating integration will face both potential costs and benefits, and will have to weigh the former carefully against the latter. One of the most obvious costs of vertical integration, the existence of which explains why in many markets firms do not operate on an integrated basis, is the requirement for large specific capital investment and the existence of economies of scale. In respect of a policy of backward vertical integration the existence of these explains why, for example, motor car assembly firms rely upon specialist suppliers of electrical equipment, tyres and certain mechanical components such as clutches rather than provide their own supplies. In these cases it is recognised that any economies of integration for motor car assembly firms in combining assembly operations with the production of a range of components would be offset by a loss of economies of scale in the manufacture of the latter in comparison with the cost of purchasing these from specialist producers.[2]

As an extension of this argument against vertical integration, a firm which lays down manufacturing capacity for its own material or component supplies inevitably commits itself to this source of supply regardless of the present and future cost of obtaining such requirements through the market. Unilever's early experience of purchasing sources of several of its primary commodity inputs in Africa illustrates the outcome of this inflexibility. In this instance lack of familiarity with the management of these, and a fall in the world market price of the commodities meant that backward vertical integration, 'instead of bringing independence, security and profit . . . could bring bondage, insecurity and loss'.[3] Where forward vertical integration has taken a group into retailing, and where it is essential to keep pace with rapid changes in customers' demands, it has to be accepted both that the retail operation must be free to buy where it can hope to meet its customers' requirements and that correspondingly the manufacturing unit must not regard the retailing division as a captive market. One of the major changes of recent years at Tootal, the third largest integrated textile group in the UK, has been the move away from a situation in which salesmen were employed to sell what the mills were producing or where products were marketed in order to help increase fabric sales. Tootal stores such as Van Allan, or garments such as Rael-Brook shirts cannot therefore guarantee a demand for the output of Tootal's mills.[4] Manufacturing units in this situation are thus required to serve a range of customers beyond their integrated partners.

In a number of manufacturing industries one requirement in cases where two successive operations are brought together by a single firm is for some degree of matching of the capacities of the processes. The milling firm that integrates forward into baking must ensure that it experiences neither a significant excess of demand for flour relative to its own ability to supply, nor an excess of flour output in relation to the needs of its bakery division. Failure to achieve a reasonable balance here will mean, as one financial journalist has put it, that the firm ends up competing with its suppliers or supplying its competitors.[5] In our example the integrated miller-baker either ends up selling surplus flour to competing bakeries, or has to buy additional flour for its bakeries from competing millers. Not only is such a situation likely to emerge as the integrated firm cannot easily adjust capacities in its adjacent operations to match requirements, but in neither case is the integrated firm likely to enjoy a good relationship with suppliers or customers who will regard it as an unstable source of custom or supply.

One of the strategic problems arising from operating a vertically integrated business is that once integration has been adopted, it may be difficult to sever the relationship, or even to appraise each integrated division separately. One of the divisions may come to dominate the other to the benefit of neither. In theory separate profit-and-loss assessment of integrated units is possible. Transfer pricing techniques can be used to place a value on goods as they move between divisions: providing an output value for the upstream division and a cost figure for the downstream division.[6]

As another possibility divisional managers may be permitted to buy or sell in the market as an alternative to in-house suppliers or customers. Unfortunately both in theory and practice transfer pricing techniques may be a far from satisfactory solution to this issue. Although permitted to do so, managers may in practice be unwilling to buy or sell outwith the organisation in competition with their company colleagues unless there are significant price discrepancies involved. The outcome of this is that once an in-house facility has been established it may well continue to be used regardless of its efficiency. This may be a particular problem where retailers possess manufacturing facilities. The latter division may regard the retailing arm of the business as a convenient means of distributing what the manufacturing division chooses to produce. Recovery in the American supermarket group A & P (formerly the Great Atlantic & Pacific Tea Co.) in the late 1970s was hampered by retail merchandising decisions being based upon the needs and abilities of its integrated manufacturing units which provided the A & P private label goods.[7] A similar example of this failure in the case of the tailoring group Montague Burton in the UK is analysed in more detail in Chapter 12 below.

The dominance of an integrated manufacturer-distributor organisation by the former function may generally lead to a more exclusive concern with production considerations regardless of ultimate market demand. Accusations along these lines have been made of Courtaulds, the leading integrated UK textile firm. Here 'the vertically integrated structure . . . caused managers to look inward, within the group, where they often found their largest and most profitable customers'. Increased competition in textile markets meant a rethink of Courtauld's philosophy of integrated operations, including a realisation by manufacturing management 'that they could not try to operate by forcing oceans of pink acrylic down the (integrated) textile pipeline when the consumer actually wanted something different'.[8]

More generally, one of the inefficiencies associated with vertical integration is the loss of specialisation, and a failure to realise that operations at different stages in the production and distribution of goods require special management characteristics for success. Distribution in particular may call for a very different management approach from manufacture. Thus in addition to retailers' needs for flexibility in sources of supply it may be unwise for manufacturers to integrate forward into distribution without a full consideration of the managerial implications. Failures of such strategies have been ascribed in part at least to the management of retail operations being handicapped by a 'manufacturing mentality'.[9]

From our analysis immediately above it will be apparent that the strategy of vertical integration carries with it potential penalties as well as rewards. At the very least considerable financial investment may be necessary to establish the required manufacturing base at the previous or subsequent stage of operations. If there are economies of scale in production at a previous stage, then unless a manufacturer's needs are considerable, or unless output at minimum efficient scale surplus to requirements can be sold on the market, the unit costs incurred in providing in-house supplies may well be higher than prices obtaining in the market. Such an in-house provision, particularly if it has required considerable capital investment, also denies the downstream operation the opportunity to purchase flexibly in the market over a period of time. It was noted above that this may be a considerable drawback when the downstream operation is involved in retail distribution. In manufacturing operations in particular it will normally be desirable for there to be a fairly close matching of the output and requirements of successive integrated operations. At the same time production conditions may make this difficult to achieve as output levels change; and the market may not easily provide or accept shortages or surpluses arising from a mismatch of output and requirements. Finally, integration of successive operations may result in one unit being dominated and made subservient to the needs of the other. The risk here is greater for downstream units. These, despite requiring for their own success a sensitivity and responsiveness to changing market demands, may be treated as convenient and captive depositories for what an upstream unit produces in a lopsided view of the firm's affairs which we referred to above as a manufacturing mentality.[10]

8.4   Policy on Vertical Integration

The optimal integration strategy for an organisation is one which confers the maximum benefits of integration while minimising the costs. The firm should seek to obtain as many of the immediate economic benefits from combining adjacent operations, internalising control and co-ordination, together with the broader advantages of an assurance of supply and/or demand, without incurring the inflexibilities of integration involved in committing oneself entirely to a single source of supply or custom.

Vertical integration is a particularly complex area of business strategy. The range of variables that must be taken into account in arriving at the most appropriate integration strategy is emphasised in a recent detailed analysis. Harrigan points out that an integration strategy itself on the part of the firm has four dimensions. These are: the *breadth* of integration, which is concerned with the range of functions previous to or following the firm's existing activities; the number of market *stages* or the extent to which a firm has integrated in any area of breadth; the *degree* or coverage of integration as measured by the proportion of components manufactured or output distributed; and the *form* of the vertical integration relationship in terms of the legal or financial link between the integrated production or distribution functions. Harrigan also emphasises that the strategic choices regarding breadth, stages, degree and form of integration will be determined by the firm's objectives and a range of market or environmental variables unique to the business, and that such a policy may correspondingly have to alter with changes in the exogenous variables.[11] The conditions determining the appropriate vertical integration strategy, in addition to the firm's objectives, include the stage of development of the industry, the volatility of the industry structure, and the firm's bargaining power *vis-à-vis* both preceding and succeeding manufacturers/distributors and also rival sellers in its current market. Harrigan's analysis includes a total of thirty-three variables. The point about this is not only the complexity of the initial vertical integration decision which the need to take account of such a range of variables creates in respect of the breadth, stages, degree and form of integration, but also the potential requirement for change in policy as these conditions alter. For as Harrigan stresses, 'The combination of corporate needs and competitive conditions which make one vertical strategy better than another at a particular time may change; as a result, strategies which were once effective become disadvantageous'.[12]

Full integration strategies, as we shall see, are not only in many cases disproportionately expensive in terms of capital investment but also commit a firm inflexibly over a period of time to one source of supply or distribution. Subsequent changes in market conditions can, for example, leave the firm at a distinct cost disadvantage. A case at the present time is that of Ford in the UK, which currently estimates that it costs the firm 60 per cent more to make its own castings for cylinder blocks and gaskets than to buy them from outside suppliers.[13] A similar situation applies in respect of variations in output levels. Purchase of a component from a supplier results in all of such costs being variable and thus correspondingly reduced as output falls. Vertical integration, by contrast, introduces an element of fixed costs which will penalise the firm in unit-cost terms as requirements fall. All of this emphasises the fixed commitment of a vertical integration strategy, and while for some firms part of this may be avoided by partial integration, which is discussed below, the strategy nonetheless remains a difficult one for firms to optimise.

Two possible alternatives to a policy of complete integration are partial or tapered integration and vertical quasi-integration. Partial integration involves a firm in supplying a proportion of its component requirements in-house or acquiring a captive source of custom for part of its output. The essence of this policy is that the extent of a firm's integrated activities should be sufficient to confer upon it the economic and other advantages of integration. At the same time the firm will not have committed itself to a single source of supply or custom, while its extent of integration may be sufficient to provide enough market power over supplies to obtain favoured terms. Thus partial vertical integration is designed to achieve some of the direct economic benefits, increased security of supply and improved co-ordination, while avoiding the need for high levels of investment or an inflexible commitment associated with full or complete integration.

Despite the fact that partial vertical integration opens up the prospect of competing with one's suppliers or supplying competitors, it clearly offers an alternative either to complete dependence upon market transactions or total integration. In the case of wire rope-making, although most of the rope makers have their own wire drawing plants, these manufacturers also purchase roping wire from other suppliers, including competitors. The market leader, Bridon, not only buys steel wire from integrated competitors but also sells roping wire to other producers.[14] Clearly there may be markets in which the relationship between competing firms is such that it is not necessary for firms to adopt a strategy of full integration, nor to ensure a complete matching of capacities of adjacent functions.

In contrast to partial integration, vertical quasi-integration involves no investment in productive resources upstream or downstream from one's existing activities. Rather the quasi-integrating firm puts itself in the position of a 'large customer' relative to its suppliers.[15] By this is meant that the buying firm purchases a significant proportion of the supplier's output, such that a withdrawal of this custom would mean losses for the supplier, at least in the short term. The power of the buying firm in this situation rests upon the buyer being able to satisfy its requirements flexibly from a number of potential sources, while the seller has no corresponding reserve of alternative customers in the short term should the existing large buyer adopt another source of supply. Were the relationship symbiotic in the sense that the two independent businesses in a seller-buyer link are mutually dependent upon one another, then the downstream buyer would not enjoy the advantages of vertical quasi-integration. Where a 'large buyer' position has been established, however, the buyer may obtain many of the advantages of vertical integration in terms of cost savings (arising from market power), continuity of supply, fulfilment of special requirements, etc. without any of the capital expenditure, inflexibilities or other costs associated with complete or even partial vertical integration. The key to success in this respect for the purchasing firm is to be in a position where it accounts for a significant proportion of the sales of its suppliers, but where at the same time the purchasing firm can obtain access to other independent sources of supply (either at home or through imports) at fairly short notice, or where in the longer term the purchaser can integrate into the market either by establishing its own capacity or through acquiring an independent supplier.

Vertical quasi-integration does appear to operate in a number of markets in which large-scale manufacturers or retailers exert significant buying power over some of their suppliers. Blois, for example, quotes one managing director of a motor vehicle component supplying firm as saying that in the industry, 'the customer and the supplier virtually function as a single unit, and we are, in effect, merely an extension of their production facilities'.[16] In this same industry the significantly lower levels of profit that electrical component suppliers obtain on their original equipment sales to motor vehicle assembly firms compared with those earned on replacement sales to garages testify to the superior bargaining power of the former group of customers.[17] Retailers may similarly exert considerable buying power over their manufacturing suppliers. The rapidly growing discount furniture chain Harris Queensway, for example, is able to obtain many of the advantages of being a large buyer relative to some household furniture manufacturers. Christie-Tyler has committed 20 per cent of its total output to Harris, with some items being manufactured exclusively for that chain. On the basis of this relationship, according to *Management Today*, 'Harris will not only get bespoke sofas, but also power to control output in the Lebus [Christie-Tyler] factory, switching production lines as necessary to meet the stores' changing stock requirements'.[18] A further example of vertical quasi-integration by a retailer is, of course, Marks & Spencer, which has no equity investment in the manufacturing facilities upon which it draws but undoubtedly enjoys the advantage of being a large customer in respect of many of them. A number of Marks & Spencer suppliers have been with the firm for over forty years in a relationship variously described as 'not a bed of roses', and on the part of Marks & Spencer, as 'one of benevolent dictatorship rather than ownership'.[19]

In addition to the adoption of a policy of full vertical integration, firms may therefore resort to partial integration or to that particular relationship with suppliers which we have called vertical quasi-integration. In all cases the objective must be to maximise the strategic advantage for the firm through balancing the benefits and the costs involved.

8.5 Conclusions

Business historians have suggested that as an economy develops, the increased scale of markets permits greater specialisation by firms and thus a trend to 'disintegration'. Along with economic growth, specialist businesses develop to undertake functions which previously had to be carried out 'in-house'. Evidence suggests that in the United States there was a trend away from vertical integration between the inter-war period and the mid-1960s, but that by the early 1970s the situation had stabilised.[20] Casual observation in the UK over recent decades indicates, however, that integration has increased as, for example, motor vehicle assembly firms have taken over the manufacture of some of the components, such as body parts, which were previously bought in, the large flour millers have integrated forward into bread baking and even into retailing, and specialist tool manufacturers have invested in steel-making and forging facilities.[21]

The statistical evidence on vertical integration is sparse, but those data that do exist suggest that the strategy of integration should be undertaken with a certain amount of caution. Buzzell, for example, found that as the degree of integration increased, so the return on investment fell until the degree of integration as measured by the ratio of value added to sales rose above 70 per cent, at which level return on investment recovered. That is, there was found to be a distinct V-shaped relationship between the degree of integration and the dependent variable return on investment.[22] Further analysis of the same data suggested that the cause of this relationship was that as vertical integration increased, so did the ratio of investment to sales. Increased integration reduced investment productivity as measured by capital turnover. Firms following a strategy of integration thus have to undertake a disproportionate increase in investment such that even though sales margins increase, these are more than offset by the reduction in capital turnover, resulting in a fall in return on investment.[23]

This finding suggests that although vertical integration may reduce certain ongoing costs such as production, transport and marketing, and provide firms with other opportunities for increasing the sales margin, capital is used overall much less productively by integrated businesses. Buzzell shows that achieving the combination of high capital turnover and high vertical integration is not easy. The scale of business also appears to have some impact upon the profitability of vertical integration. Although the evidence is not robust, there is some to suggest that firms operating on a larger scale profit more from adopting a strategy of integration. This supports the view that the benefits of integration come through more strongly when a firm is operating its integrated divisions at output levels which enable it to enjoy scale economies at each of the linked stages in the production-distribution sequence. A statistical analysis of vertical integration thus indicates that the strategy yields few automatic gains, and that other policy variables combined with integration may significantly affect profitability. Vesey, for example, suggests that the rapid introduction of new products under conditions of vertical integration depresses returns, indicating that integration reduces flexibility, or increases the costs of achieving this, by committing the firm to more than one stage of production or distribution.[24]

In Sections 8.2 and 8.3 of this chapter we outlined a range of possible benefits and costs associated with the strategy of vertical integration, and in Section 8.4 a range of approaches within this strategy was dealt with. Given the finely balanced nature of these benefits and costs and the adverse impact that vertical integration may have upon profitability, it is essential that firms have a very clear idea of the objectives they are seeking to achieve by this strategy, together with an accurate and realistic view of the industry environment and the firm's own strengths and weaknesses. If the firm believes that there are significant economies to be gained by integrating backwards or forwards in the market, that it has the quantity and quality of resources to achieve this, that the strategy is appropriate to the market environment, and that there are no significant inflexibility costs attached to the strategy, then it would clearly seem to be an appropriate path to follow. As we have noted, however, vertical integration may be a disproportionately costly strategy in terms of capital investment. Operating at previous or subsequent stages of the market to one's existing activities may require significantly different technical, marketing or managerial skills. Even if a market is expanding it may be quite inappropriate for a manufacturer to integrate forwards if there is, for example, an efficient established wholesaler network. Such a forward integration strategy could merely antagonise one's range of distributors. Finally, unless carried out as part of a considered long-term strategy, one would not advocate integration in declining markets as this merely accentuates the firm's dependence upon a falling market, although forward integration here would increase sales in the short term.

The existence of the problems discussed above perhaps explains why it is that firms that wish to expand and at the same time reduce their exposure to the business risks of one particular market follow a strategy of diversification. This is the topic of the following chapter.

References

1. See M. E. Porter, *Competitive Strategy* (New York: Free Press, 1980) pp. 303–9.
2. In the case of clutch mechanisms motor car manufacturers fairly early abandoned production of their own requirements, relying on specialist suppliers such as Automotive Products, which now dominates the UK market. Economies of scale in clutch production and assembly appear to be such that there are considerable cost savings for a large specialist supplier operating at a scale of output far beyond that required to meet the needs of a single motor car assembly firm. See Monopolies Commission, *Clutch Mechanisms for Road Vehicles* (London: HMSO, 1968, HCP 32).
3. See C. Wilson, *The History of Unilever* (London: Cassell, 1954) Vol. I, p. 265.
4. See T. Lester, 'Tootal's Vertical Theme', *Management Today*, June 1975, p. 49.
5. R. Heller, 'Vertical Disintegration', *The Times*, 20 June 1971.
6. See W. S. Howe, *Industrial Economics* (London: Macmillan, 1978) pp. 199–203.
7. See P. W. Bernstein, 'Jonathan Scott's Surprising Failure at A & P', *Fortune*, November 1978, pp. 34–44.
8. See *Financial Times*, 3 December 1983.
9. R. D. Buzzell, 'Is Vertical Integration Profitable?', *Harvard Business Review*, January–February 1983, p. 94.
10. Hayes and Abernathy suggest that backward integration, too, leads to an inflexible commitment to in-house sources of supply and hence also to a manufacturing as opposed to a marketing orientation on the part of the firm. These problems of integration must again be greater when markets or technologies are changing rapidly, and when it will pay the firm to 'stay loose'. See R. H. Hayes and W. J. Abernathy, 'Managing Our Way to Economic Decline', *Harvard Business Review*, July–August 1980, pp. 72–3.
11. See K. R. Harrigan, *Strategies for Vertical Integration* (Massachusetts: D. C. Heath, 1983) Ch. 1.
12. *Ibid., p. 8.*
13. *Sunday Times*, 26 February 1984.
14. See Monopolies Commission, *Wire and Fibre Ropes* (London: HMSO, 1973, HCP 2) paras 11, 76, 119–20.
15. See K. J. Blois, 'Vertical Quasi-Integration', *Journal of Industrial Economics*, July 1972, Vol. XX, pp. 253–72.

16. Quoted in Blois, *ibid.*, p. 269.
17. See Monopolies Commission, *Supply of Electrical Equipment for Mechanically Propelled Land Vehicles* (London: HMSO, 1963, HCP 21) para. 705.
18. See D. Isaac, 'Harris Queensway's Flying Carpet', *Management Today*, January 1984, p. 56.
19. See *Financial Times*, 31 October 1974; and *Sunday Times*, 5 February 1984.
20. See G. J. Stigler, 'The Division of Labour is Limited by the Extent of the Market', *Journal of Political Economy*, June 1951, Vol. LIX, pp. 185–93; A. B. Laffer, 'Vertical Integration by Corporations, 1929–1965', *Review of Economics and Statistics*, February 1969, Vol. LI, pp. 91–3; and I. B. Tucker and R. P. Wilder, 'Trends in Vertical Integration in the US Manufacturing Sector', *Journal of Industrial Economics*, September 1977, Vol. XXVI, pp. 81–94.
21. See Monopolies Commission, *British Motor Corporation Ltd and Pressed Steel Company Ltd* (London: HMSO, 1966, HCP 46) paras 19, 24 and 44; National Board for Prices and Incomes, *Bread and Flour* (London: HMSO, 1965, Cmnd 2760) paras 12 and 46; and C. Caulkin, 'The Drill at Sheffield Twist', *Management Today*, April 1975, p. 43.
22. See Buzzell, 'Is Vertical Integration Profitable?', pp. 96–7.
23. Return on investment is the product of the sales margin and the capital turnover ratio. That is, (profit/sales) × (sales/capital) = profit/capital.
24. J. T. Vesey, 'Vertical Integration: Its Effect on Business Performance', *Managerial Planning*, May–June 1978, p. 12.

Diversification

9

> The primary principle that must be grasped is that diversification is fundamentally a negative strategy. Diversifiers are always running away from something. — M. L. Kastens, 'How Much is an Acquisition Worth?' *Long Range Planning*, June 1973, p. 53.

9.1 Introduction

Despite the above observation by an American management consultant, coming at a time of great popularity of diversified acquisitions, diversification over the past twenty or thirty years in this country has been a common strategy on the part of business organisations. Studies by economists relating to diversification have encountred a number of statistical problems in measuring the extent of this phenomenon and its trend over time. For example, Standard Industrial Classification data upon which such studies are usually based do not necessarily reveal accurately the extent of market diversification that is at the heart of business strategy in this area. Nor is it even possible on the basis of such data to distinguish clearly between the strategies of diversification and vertical integration. There appears, nonetheless, to be some evidence to suggest that since the late 1950s in this country diversification in some form has become an increasingly common business strategy.[1] However, the most up-to-date study of the UK

149

published data did caution that some recent economic analyses may have overstressed the extent of corporate diversification in this country, and in terms of 1972 data emphasised that in diversifying most firms do not tend to move far from their existing technological base, and that this (1972) data ran 'counter to the popular view of a small number of very large conglomerates with tentacles stretching into every corner of industry'.[2] In market terms, however, many of the largest manufacturing businesses in the UK are significantly diversified, as the following summary of AEI's activities by the chief executive of the firm (now, of course, part of GEC) indicates:

> **At the beginning of 1960 AEI was a complex international industrial concern, with annual sales of over £200m. and deliveries to most countries of the world. Its products ranged from the largest turbines to electric kettles; from large radar equipment for tracking and control and early warning to the smallest domestic lamps; from electron microscopes and linear accelerators to washing machines; and from equipment for geothermal power generation in New Zealand to floodlighting for British castles and football grounds.[3]**

From a management point of view one of the most illuminating sets of data is that provided by Channon in his study of strategy and structure in the UK economy, and reproduced in Table 9.1. Channon's study, following the pattern of similar analyses in the USA, distinguishes between single product firms (with at least 95 per cent of sales in a single product area), dominant product firms (where secondary product lines account for 30 per cent or less of total sales), related product businesses (with secondary market interests related by technology or markets to their principal products accounting for more than 30 per cent of total sales), and unrelated product businesses, which have expanded into a wide range of markets and technologies to such an extent that again these secondary interests account for more than 30 per cent of sales. The Channon data indicate that the evolution of these 100 largest manufacturing businesses, which in 1970 accounted for about 60 per cent of UK manufacturing assets and sales, has taken them from a situation in 1950 where having subsidiary or secondary interests accounting for more than 30 per cent of total sales was

Table 9.1
UK Manufacturing Industry, 100 Largest Firms (1970) by Turnover

Category	1950*	1960*	1970*	1980**	US Manufacturing industry†
Single product	34	20	6	3	6
Dominant product	41	35	34	34	14
Related product	23	41	54	54	60
Unrelated product	2	4	6	9	20
	100	100	100	100	100

Sources:
* D. F. Channon, *The Strategy and Structure of British Enterprise* (London: Macmillan, 1973) p. 67.
** This column of data has been produced by the author in an attempt to update Channon's 1950–70 data. It has been derived from company annual reports alone, and thus in respect of the detailed research and strict comparability of approach the data here should be compared with those of Channon with some caution. This having been said, there appear to have been relatively few changes involved. Of the 100 companies in 1970, eleven had ceased independent existence by 1980: two through acquisition by one firm outwith Channon's largest 100, the remainder through acquisition by others in the population (most significantly the merger of the Reed Group and IPC in 1971 and the acquisition of EMI by Thorn in 1980), while Slater Walker Securities had removed itself from the manufacturing sector by becoming a purely financial organisation. 'Upward mobility' in the product classification between 1970 and 1980 was surprisingly limited. In the cigarette and tobacco market BAT moved from 'single product' to 'unrelated', and the Imperial Group from 'dominant product' to 'related'. The Reed Group/IPC merger changed these two 'related product' businesses into a single 'unrelated' one.
† See B. R. Scott, 'The Industrial State', *Harvard Business Review*, March–April 1973, p. 138. These data are based upon a 20 per cent sample from the Fortune 500 in the late 1960s.

characteristic of only 25 per cent of the group, to one in 1970 where 60 per cent of the group was in this situation. It is also interesting to note that while in 1970 only 6 per cent of the firms fell into the 'single product' category, correspondingly only 6 per cent of the businesses could be described as conglomerate. The more tentative analysis by the author relating to 1980 indicates a slowing down in the rate of diversification by this group of firms since 1970. As indicated in the second footnote to Table 9.1, the changes were the result of two or three significant moves by the companies involved; and interestingly, the overall proportion of firms in the dominant product and related product categories remained unchanged over the decade to 1980.

These UK data thus add weight to Utton's conclusions quoted above (note 2). As revealed in the final column in Table 9.1, they also provide a rather different picture of the extent of conglomeration compared with the situation in the USA at the end of the 1960s. The explanation for the US position is complex, and almost certainly includes the impact of different antitrust legislation in America from that in this country. There appears to be no doubt, however, that the trend towards conglomeration among big business has proceeded much further on the other side of the Atlantic.

This chapter continues by examining the reasons for businesses pursuing a policy of diversification, a consideration of why diversification strategies do not always prove to be successful, an analysis of some of the factors that ought to be taken into account in pursuing such a policy, and some conclusions relating to the future of diversification strategies.

9.2   Diversification

At a general strategic level Ansoff suggests three reasons why firms diversify. First, their objectives cannot be achieved by continuing to operate in their existing markets. Thus since continued operation in these markets is not able to satisfy the profit, risk or growth objectives of the business, achievement of these must be sought in new market areas. Second, where a business has excess financial resources beyond those necessary to satisfy its expansion plans in its existing markets, then rather than retain these resources in liquid form the business may invest them in new market areas. Third, if greater opportunities are presented to the firm in new market areas than accrue from its existing activities then a diversification programme may be undertaken to benefit from these.[4]

The major reason for a business adopting a strategy of diversification is therefore to allow it to reduce its dependence upon a single market area. Obviously firms can reduce some of the risks involved in operating in a single market by diversifying their sources of raw materials or avoiding undue dependence upon a small number of customers, as well as maintaining an adequate supply of liquid financial resources. Beyond this, however, any single-product firm is to some extent a prisoner of the market to which it has restricted itself. At the general level, as one contributor to the *Harvard Business Review* puts it, 'The world changes. Evolution takes its toll. The businesses most vulnerable to the march of events are those concentrated in single, non-evolving (or only slowly evolving) technolgies, in single product categories, and in industries characterised by large aggregates of fixed and inflexible plants and equipment.'[5] Such industries as traditional textiles, cement, paper and certain metal-working sectors would appear to fall into this category; and for firms in these sectors diversification is an important strategy to be considered.

Thus even businesses which have by all accounts been a success in their single chosen market must recognise in time to take appropriate action that sooner or later their continued expansion and perhaps profitability will be dependent upon moving into new market areas. A case in point is Marks & Spencer, with, according to *Management Today*, a store in almost every desirable High Street in Britain, 14 million shoppers per week representing almost 25 per cent of the population, accounting for £1 out of every £7 spent nationally on apparel, and with more than half the market in some garments. Here, however, as *Management Today* put it in the light of this approaching saturation of the market, 'Its awesome statistics on market penetration are thus equally signs of its limited prospects for growth'.[6] Hence the significant drive by that organisation for overseas expansion to maintain its past momentum in its chosen market.

The most frequent reasons for diversification on the part of individual businesses are the achievement of growth and risk reduction. With regard to growth, any firm that attempts to expand within a single industry immediately faces two limitations: the rate of growth of the market itself, and the ambitions and reactions of its market competitors. Thus, not surprisingly, mature, low-growth industries such as food and tobacco have seen considerable diversification on the part of their largest constituent firms in particular – for example, Cadbury-Schweppes's movement into a wider range of convenience foods, beverages and groceries; BAT and the Imperial Group into cosmetics, retailing, paper and packaging, and convenience foods, brewing and packaging respectively. Any business seeking to achieve a growth rate above the aggregate rate of expansion of the market to which it is currently confined is implicitly or explicitly envisaging an increase in its market share. Not only is such a move likely to be resisted by market competitors under most circumstances, but in markets themselves characterised by low growth and populated by a small number of large firms, such a policy of expanding market share is likely to be achieved only at considerable cost in terms of price competition or, more likely, significant additions to promotional or product costs. Although, as we shall see below, diversification is not a policy which easily yields short-term benefits in terms of profitability, it may be considered relatively safer for an expanding firm to try to build up product interests elsewhere rather than embark upon the more obviously costly strategy of growing at the expense of its immediate market competitors.

The other major reason given by businesses for pursuing a strategy of diversification is the reduction in certain types of business risk which such a policy is thought to confer. Firms are thus distributing their corporate eggs among a number of market baskets. If in its present market a firm's profits are subject to variability over time as a result of being particularly affected by changes in interest rates, cyclical demand or the weather (as in the case of sales of beer or ice cream), then by combining such activities with those that are less affected by these factors, or are ideally affected inversely by them – as in the case of convenience foods and ice cream, whose fortunes are inversely related so far as the impact of extremes of summer weather on their sales are concerned – the overall riskiness or time variability of profits can be reduced. Tunnel Holdings, Britain's third largest cement manufacturer is a company that possesses many of the characteristics listed above (note 5) as suggesting the need for a diversification strategy. In the light of the likely medium-term situation in the cement market, its position in that market, and the cyclical nature of demand in the industry, Tunnel has moved to a wider geographical base, deliberately scaled down its commitment to the cement industry by about one third, and diversified into the fields of speciality chemicals and toxic waste disposal.[7] Christian Salvesen, until recently one of the largest private companies in the UK, is another example of a business that has sought risk reduction through diversification, in this case moving away from its earlier dependence upon fishing and fish processing through expanding its cold storage services, increasing its activity in housebuilding, and also participation in North Sea oil servicing. A case study of this firm highlighted the benefits of diversification by showing not only a rise in average annual gross trading profits from £3.84 million to £10.25 million comparing the two periods 1967–72 and 1973–78, but also a decline in the variance of these from 2.59 in the former period to 0.82 in the latter.[8]

These two cases illustrate the way in which a strategy of diversification has been adopted by organisations that occupy difficult or risky markets. The case of Salvesen in particular emphasises the fact that it is essentially the combination of market interests that reduces business risk, and not the nature of the added market (in this case construction) itself.

9.3 Management Issues

In spite of the sometimes persuasive rhetoric surrounding the adoption of diversification strategies by businesses, there appears to be little clear evidence that such policies benefit company profits in anything other than the long term, or that profit variability can be thereby automatically reduced. At the individual firm level it would appear that for some time after diversification moves are undertaken, businesses remain highly dependent upon their principal product interests for profitability.[9] There are probably many firms that have shared BAT's experience of diversification ventures, 'some of which have combined a formidable hunger for cash with, at best, an indifferent performance', even if they have not gone so far as the experience of the Automobile Association, which built up a loss of £5.8 million over a three-year period in the mid 1970s during its initial phase of diversification.[10] Certainly, aggregated studies in the UK – although these are disappointingly few and far between – confirm that diversification does not confer immediate benefits upon businesses in the anticipated directions;[11] and the more recent and detailed study by Biggadike of diversification experience on the part of a sample of US businesses suggests that firms have to wait on average twelve years (if their new ventures survive that long) before diversifying businesses contribute a return on capital employed similar to that of established, mature activities.[12]

Problems of diversification

There are a number of reasons for poor diversification performance. First, there does not appear to be clear evidence of businesses having a diversification strategy as such. Because diversification by nature offers a wide remit to strategists, there is perhaps a reluctance to establish diversification guidelines. Diversification ventures, particularly those arising from acquisitions, may tend to be made on an *ad hoc* opportunistic basis rather than as part of a long-term diversification strategy based upon the goals of the organisation and following a thorough investigation of the markets and the individual ventures concerned. Indeed, there is every risk under certain conditions that diversification becomes an end in itself. In the case of BAT mentioned above (note 10), during the 1960s and 1970s the firm invested and divested itself of ice cream and electronics in the UK, printing machine manufacture in France, and fish processing in the US as part of its attempts to reduce dependence upon tobacco and cigarettes.[13]

Second, management often appears to be somewhat over-optimisitc in respect of its ability to manage varied interests, or insufficiently well prepared for differences between the new venture that it undertakes and conditions in its principal market.

Some firms have clearly recognised the existence of problems of the transferability of managerial talent from one market to another. For example, in contrast to the policy of Tunnel Cement, Rugby Portland Cement, the second largest UK cement manufacturer, has consciously avoided diversification as a strategy for dealing with precisely the same market conditions as the remainder of the firms in that market, recognising its limited management resources and expertise available to pursue such a strategy.[14] This reticence may be contrasted again with BAT's experience in moving into the cosmetics field, where 'Top management was surprised to find that the scope for economies of scale was so small: that losses couldn't necessarily be converted into profits by combining the companies, and making and selling their products as though they were cigarettes'.[15]

Third, management in diversifying companies may again be over-optimistic regarding the rate at which diversified interests will generate profits. This situation may itself be a product of insufficent care on the part of management in examining diversification markets and individual ventures before entering into them, combined with over-optimisim regarding its ability to cope with the managerial and technical problems arising. Whatever the sources of such difficulties, this last issue is a particular problem for firms that are looking to diversified ventures rapidly to replace profits or growth in a company's principal market, and which may have limited reserves of cash on the basis of which to nurture new business interests. This was a diversification issue that the author encountered in the context of firms adopting this strategy in order to reduce dependence upon a rapidly declining textile market. In failing to react sufficiently early to this market decline, and in underestimating the period of time required to build up alternative business interests, such firms encountered situations where, according to company chairmen, 'profits from the expansion of other activities and entry into new activities have to bear not only development charges but also finance charges until new installations become commissioned and profitable', and problems of 'the time lag between building up profitable diversifications, which utilise much capital, whilst at the same time maintaining the capital employed in our jute manufacturing activity, which is declining in profitability'.[16]

Fourth, there appears to be evidence to suggest that diversified businesses adopt an uncritical, passive attitude to the management of their varied interests. Corporate management of a diversified company must involve the careful assembly of a rational group of businesses in the light of the company's objectives, the creation of an appropriate administrative structure for managing these, and positive management of the portfolio of interests rather than simply an 'investment trust' approach to holding a bundle of assets. While there is evidence in the USA and the UK that an increasing proportion of diversified companies are organised on a multi-divisional basis in order to reflect this corporate strategy, positive management of diversified interests – what one author refers to as 'process portfolio planning' – does not appear to be highly developed. This approach involves dividing the firm's business interests into strategic business units possessing similar strategic characteristics (and these strategic business units may not be coterminous with operating units), analysing the strategic position of these units on the basis of market characteristics and business strengths, and setting strategic objectives and correspondingly allocating resources for individual units on the basis of unique strategic analysis. Until or unless such an approach to the management of diversified firms is adopted, it is argued, then the full benefits of a strategy of diversification are unlikely to be realised.[17]

These experiences suggest that companies undertaking diversification should do so only in the context of an explicit policy regarding what the objectives of such a strategy are and how diversification is going to achieve these objectives; that not only should individual ventures and their markets be examined in detail prior to any specific strategy being implemented, but that management should adopt a harshly realistic view of the problems likely to be encountered and its available resources for overcoming these; and that particular regard should be had to the time horizons adopted for such a strategy so that management reacts to the need for diversification sufficiently early to make full allowance for the frequently protracted time period over which diversified ventures become profitable. Finally, as emphasised in Chapter 6 on strategic implementation, the organisation structure of a diversified firm should be carefully chosen to reflect and accommodate this strategy.

9.4 Strategy variables

Biggadike, in his detailed study of diversification experience by American businesses, provides in effect a checklist of items that ought to be considered by any firm undertaking diversification.[18] This is combined below for our purposes in Table 9.2 with a reference to the relative merits of internal and external diversification. Internal diversification occurs when a business enters a market unrelated to its existing product interests by purchasing the necessary plant, premises, etc., hiring the required workforce (including management), and creating a business out of these. External diversification, or diversification by acquisition, occurs when a business purchases as a going concern another firm in an unrelated market. The broad case for a business following the external diversification route is that the acquisition of a diversified interest provides the diversifier with a 'working package', particularly with regard to the management skills required in the new market area; and that since external diversification does not immediately add capacity to the entered market, then expensive market entry and competitive costs are thereby avoided. On the other hand internal diversification increases the flexibility of the diversifier so far as the timing and size of the new venture is concerned, and also allows the firm to assemble a unique package of diversified assets rather than accept those accruing from an acquisition. It may also be argued that internal diversification is likely to result in a greater compatibility and integration between the various interests of the business, and also a greater commitment on the part of management to the new ventures. Thus the checklist in Table 9.2 comprises those factors which management should take account of in choosing diversified interests, and which should also influence the choice between internal and external diversification.

As a first consideration management should examine the relatedness or otherwise of a potential new venture to its current operations. How similar are these in terms of technology, markets served or management skills to the firm's existing operations? Is the firm seeking to apply its existing technology to a new market area, or will entry into the new market require knowledge of an

Table 9.2
Checklist for Diversifying Businesses

Variables		Mode of diversification	
		Internal	*External*
1. Relatedness:			
technology	common to existing products	high	low
economies of scale	shared production or other facilities	some	none
marketing	same group of consumers	similar	different
management	assumed management familiarity	familiar	unfamiliar
2. Entered market characteristics:			
sellers/buyers	number of sellers	many	few
	number of buyers	many	few
products	differentiated/ undifferentiated	undifferentiated	differentiated
entry barriers	height of various entry barriers	low	high
market	product life-cycle situation/growth rate	new/high growth	mature/ low growth
3. Entry strategy:			
role of price, promotion, etc.	likely impact of price and promotion entry strategies	less significant	important
role of innovation	how profitable is such strategy likely to be	unimportant	significant
likely reaction of existing sellers	reaction in terms of output, price, promotion, etc.	accepting	aggressive

Table 9.2 (continued)
Checklist for Diversifying Businesses

Variables	Mode of diversification	
	Internal	*External*

4. Performance and resources:

existing ROI	comparison with market to be entered
finance	relative to demands to be made
production,	assessed relative to existing sellers in the market
marketing,	to be entered, and in relation to key areas of
technology,	competition in that market
management,	
etc.	
competence	
market share	potential market share assessed on basis of
	reaction of competitors and significance of
	market share for ROI.

entirely different technology? The first heading Table 9.2 provides the diversifying firm with a focus for comparing the potential problems and benefits from the relatedness of its existing activities and the product-market area into which it is planning to diversify. The greater the extent of relatedness involved in diversifying, the more easily will the benefits of synergy be realised from the combined operations, and the fewer are likely to be the problems of managing the enlarged business. Thus in respect of technology, while one may imagine a brewing firm transferring its knowledge of microbiology into certain pharmaceutical markets (as Guinness did at one time), it may be more difficult for a traditional metal container manufacturer to diversify into the market for plastic or other synthetic containers. Similarly, the diversifying firm has to assess whether diverse market interests can share any facilities such as production, research and development, or other overheads. Firms diversifying into new product areas may be approaching their existing customers with new products, or they may require to identify themselves with a new group of buyers. In the latter case in particular there is a strong incentive to diversify by acquisition. Finally in respect of relatedness, there is the issue we have touched upon already of how familiar or otherwise management is likely to be with the new products and markets from a general management point of view.

The issue of the relatedness of a firm's existing product-market position to its new interests forms the basis of the distinction between concentric and conglomerate diversification. Concentric diversification involves a firm entering new market areas where there is a degree of overlap with existing products in terms of customers or technology or distribution channels. Here there is more obvious scope for synergy between the product interests. In the case of conglomerate diversification there is no such overlap, and the potential for synergy is likely to be restricted to the areas of finance or management. Although there may be instances where conglomerate diversification is necessary for a firm widening its market base – because the firm's existing base or technology is very narrow or specialist and therefore limits any prospect of concentric diversification – it would appear from the studies by Utton and Channon that in this country concentric diversification embracing the 'related product' category in Table 9.1 above is by far the more common diversification strategy. Thus managements appear to prefer to stay fairly close to their product-market base when diversifying, even where some of the difficulties in going beyond this boundary may be overcome by diversified acquisitions.

In considering these variables the firm has to balance the synergy, adaptation or control advantages of a related diversification policy against the greater degree of risk reduction or other market attractions of entering a product area further removed from its existing activities. In balancing these considerations the firm has a choice between internal and external diversification. Where the degree of technology, production, marketing and management relatedness is high, there should be no barrier to internal diversification. Indeed, given the managerial difficulties involved in the acquisition process itself, unless the speed with which diversification must be achieved is of the essence, internal diversification should be preferred, other market conditions being equal. However, where management may expect to encounter difficulties in adapting by itself to new technologies, production methods, customers or the management environment in entering a different market then external diversification or diversification by acquisition may be more attractive.

The second of the headings in Table 9.2 above, the entered market characteristics, defines the environment into which the firm may move, and thus helps to identify the opportunities and threats likely to be encountered. Although each of these factors may be separately identified, diversifying management has to arrive at a judgement as to the balance of the attractiveness of the market. This judgment must be made in the light of the resources of the firm relative to those of its new market competitors – involving an analysis of comparative strengths and weaknesses – and the forecast reaction of these existing sellers to new entry into their market. Thus headings 2, 3 and 4 of Table 9.2 should be considered together. The dimensions within heading 2 focus on the attractiveness of the market in terms of its size, growth and stage of development, upon those structural characteristics which make markets more or less competitive, and upon the likely dimensions of competition in the market. Sectors where the rate of growth of demand is low, where a small number of existing sellers compete among themselves by product differentiation, and where entry barriers are high are obviously more difficult to diversify into unless the diversifying firm possesses particular skills *vis-à-vis* these rivals. As in the case of the issue of relatedness, a firm moving into a new market may avoid some of the threats in the entered market environment by adopting the acquisition route. This strategy is likely to be particularly appealing in the market conditions outlined above: where demand is growing only slowly, and where an oligopolistic group of existing sellers enjoys the protection of market entry barriers such as economies of scale or absolute cost advantages over potential entrants. For the externally diversifying firm, however, the problem to be overcome is that of securing an appropriate acquisition at a price that will allow it to earn a satisfactory return on its investment in the market conditions following entry.

Headings 3 and 4 in Table 9.2 contain the dimensions which, taken together with the entered market characteristics, will determine the likely performance of the diversifying firm in its new market. These headings comprise an identification of the basis of competition in the market – determining the key factors for success – and the anticipated reaction of existing market sellers. The outcome for the diversifying firm in so far as the key factors for success are concerned depends upon the relative strength of the firm in these areas. In some markets price competition will be all important, in which case comparative cost levels will be crucial to success. In other sectors success depends more upon marketing or technological skills. If the diversifying firm is not confident of its relative superiority in the key competitive dimensions, then an acquisition entry into the new market must be considered, although success with such a policy is again dependent upon securing an appropriate acquisition at a realistic price, and overcoming the management problems of the acquisition process itself. The reaction of existing sellers in the entered market may be a crucial determinant of success or failure for the diversifying firm. If the particular market is important to existing sellers, and if they consider themselves to be competitively placed *vis-à-vis* a potential entrant, their reaction to such entry will be aggressive. Output levels may be maintained, price reductions implemented or promotional expenditures increased, all in an effort to deter the entrant from remaining in the market. It may even be worthwhile for existing sellers as a group to accept losses in the market for a period if they estimate that the competitiveness and 'staying power' of the new entrant is limited. Anticipating such reactions any potential entrant may avoid moving into such an aggressively defended market except through acquisition of an existing seller.

This analysis suggests that any diversification strategy should be based upon an assessment of the benefits arising from the degree of overlap between the firm's existing and potential new operations, the opportunities and threats presented by the new market (including reference to the key factors for success in that market and the likely reaction to entry on the part of existing sellers), and the strengths and weaknesses of the organisation assessed in the context of the entered market environment. As a result of this form of analysis, the diversifying firm should be in a position to estimate the post-entry return on investment in the market and to decide upon the basis on which it is going to compete in the market. In particular, the more appropriate form of entry into the market – internal or external – can be chosen.

9.5 Conclusions

Over the past thirty years the UK manufacturing sector has become steadily more diversified in its structure, and while this trend appears to have slowed down over the last decade, diversification strategies and the management of diversification (which may include selected divestment of some diversified interests and the acquisition of others) are an important part of corporate strategy.

Strategic decision-making in diversified companies not only confronts senior management with more complex issues but opens up greater opportunities than exist in the context of single-product organisations. The diversified firm has the potential to be more than the sum of its divisional parts. However, top management in diversified companies has the additional burden of combining divisional strategies into a coherent whole, ensuring that divisions play a role within the *corporate* strategy of the organisation. Strategic planning and implementation in diversified firms is therefore of necessity more formal and protracted than in smaller, single-product firms. Vancil and Lorange, for example, indicate the need for diversified firms to go through a series of strategic planning cycles – involving corporate consideration of divisional goals, calling for business-unit environmental analysis, co-ordinating all divisional strategies at a corporate level, and considering divisional budgets – as the firm moves from corporate objectives to an agreed allocation of funds to individual divisions.[19]

Portfolio analysis is a particularly useful tool for diversified business strategies. This should be combined with an M-form organisation structure to provide for personal detachment from divisional considerations on the part of those responsible for formulating corporate strategy and who require to take a 'big view' of the organisation, which divisional managers cannot be expected to. Advantage can also be taken of the M-form structure to measure divisional performance in terms of profitability or growth in a way that is not open to single-product firms organised on a functional basis. Furthermore, the M-form structure of business units in a diversified portfolio should facilitate easier entry into and exit from market areas as the product market environments of individual units change or the business modifies its overall or corporate goals. Thus in contrast to strategic management in single-product organisations, where the emphasis is upon reacting to a limited range of strategic variables associated with a single-product market and supervising co-ordination of functions within the organisation, strategic planning in a diversified firm extends to the choice of overall objectives, the achievement of portfolio balance, the allocation of funds among divisions, and the designing of appropriate and possibly differentiated reward systems for divisional managers.[20]

Corporate diversification as a strategy has not lived up to expectations. Although the UK data in this respect are not as good as those in the USA (nor as good as they should be) there is evidence to suggest that, in terms of profitability at least, diversification strategies have not proved uniformly successful.[21] The reasons for this poor performance are many, but the material in Section 9.3 above concerning management attitudes and approaches to diversification suggests not only room for improvement in this area of strategy but also some inevitable management limitations to success. Peters and Waterman, for example, noting the almost total absence of any financial evidence to support the case for highly diversified businesses, appear to argue that given the importance for business success of strong management identification with the values of a particular market, it is only to be expected that diversification – and in particular widespread diversification by acquisition – is a problematic strategy. These two authors point out, as we have done above, that the transition from one market area to another is often much more difficult to achieve than many managers anticipate.[22]

All of this may well explain some apparent lessening of diversification activity since the early 1970s. Department of Industry data, for example, show that diversified mergers as a proportion of the total have fallen off since a peak in the early 1970s.[23] Furthermore a recent survey, albeit covering a more limited period during the late 1970s, indicated in an analysis of divestment activity an apparent trend against diversification. The survey data showed that while 22.9 per cent of horizontal divestments and 23.8 per cent of vertical divestments were in turn conglomerate acquisitions, thus implying an increase in the extent of diversification, 47.2 per cent of conglomerate divestments constituted horizontal acquisitions for the acquiring business, and a further 10.3 per cent of such divestments were vertical acquisitions.[24] Such data strongly imply that over this period there was a dominant tendency for divestment activity to result in a reduced degree of product diversity in the UK manufacturing sector. There is also evidence from the United States that many previous diversification strategies are being put into reverse, at least to the extent of producing more concentric rather than conglomerate diversified businesses.[25]

The emphasis in this chapter is not, however, designed to argue that diversification is an undesirable business strategy. It is true that the past financial record of diversifying firms provides little comfort. Some part of this may be explained by the fact that managers have not always given as much thought as they should have done to the design and implementation of diversification strategies. Moreover it is inevitable that some businesses will be forced by market circumstances to diversify in order to maintain reasonable growth and profit rates. For such firms there is no escape from diversification. It is clear also that diversification should contribute to a reduction in the level of business risk or uncertainty for a firm.[26] The key to success in diversification is to develop a balanced portfolio of product market interests as analysed in Chapter 5, to have regard to the issues of strategic implementation relating to multi-product businesses as discussed in Chapter 6, and to identify clearly the issues relating to any individual diversification programme as set out in Table 9.2 above. In particular, success in diversification is likely to be significantly influenced by the quality of management of the acquired business interests, the synergy that can be created between the different fields of operation, and the manner in which diversified expansion is implemented.

One of the means used by diversified companies to implement significant as opposed to incremental change in the balance of their portfolios is acquisition and divestment. Since the logic of diversified firms is often strategic and financial rather than industrial, it would seem natural that these external means of adjustment to environmental and resource circumstances should often be preferred to internal or organic changes. The next two chapters examine acquisition and divestment strategies as they relate not only to diversified businesses but also to a range of other strategic circumstances.

References

1. For an overview of the data see W. S. Howe, *Industrial Economics* (London: Macmillan, 1978) pp. 120–21.
2. See M. A. Utton, *Diversification and Competition* (Cambridge: Cambridge University Press, 1979) p. 19.
3. J. Latham, *Takeover: The Facts and The Myths of the GEC–AEI Battle* (London: Iliffe, 1969) p. 21.
4. H. I. Ansoff, *Corporate Strategy* (Harmondworth: Penguin, 1968) pp. 113–14.
5. T. Levitt, 'Dinosaurs Among the Bears and Bulls', *Harvard Business Review*, January–February 1975, p. 42.
6. See S. Salmans, 'Mixed Fortunes at Marks & Spencer', *Management Today*, November 1980, p. 67.
7. See N. Newman, 'How Tunnel Saw the Light', *Management Today*, June 1981, p. 74ff.
8. See K. Wilson, 'Growth and Planning in Christian Salvesen', *Case Clearing House of Great Britain and Ireland*, Cranfield Institute of Technology, 1979, p. 11.
9. For an earlier example relating to the British Match Corporation's diversification at the end of the 1960s out of matches and into associated activities, see the data quoted in W. S. Howe, *Industrial Economics*, p. 127. Here, although by 1973 matches accounted for only 53 per cent of turnover, they provided the firm with 75 per cent of its profits.
10. See G. Foster, 'BAT Buys Bigger', *Management Today*, February 1983, p. 45; and B. Bell, 'The Big AA Speed Trap', *Management Today*, March 1981, p.148.
11. See M. A. Utton, 'Diversification, Mergers and Profit Stability', *Business Ratios*, Spring 1969, pp. 24–7; and N. Hood and S. Young, 'Growth, Performance and Strategy in 400 UK Holding Companies', unpublished paper, Paisley College of Technology (1975).
12. For a shortened report of his findings see E. R. Biggadike, 'The Risky Business of Diversification', *Harvard Business Review*, May–June 1979, pp. 103–111.
13. See Foster, 'BAT Buys Bigger'.
14. See G. Foster, 'Rugby after Reddish', *Management Today*, February 1981, p. 47.
15. See Foster, 'BAT Buys Bigger', pp. 45–6.
16. See company annual reports quoted in W. S. Howe, *The Dundee Textiles Industry* (Aberdeen: Aberdeen University Press, 1982) pp. 79 and 98.
17. See P. Haspeslagh, 'Portfolio Planning: Uses and Limits', *Harvard Business Review*, January–February 1982, pp. 58–73.
18. E. R. Biggadike, *Corporate Diversification: Entry, Strategy and Performance* (Cambridge, Mass.: Harvard University Press, 1979). The deriving of this checklist from Biggadike's book does not of course do full justice to this very insightful and readable study.

19. See R. F. Vancil and P. Lorange, 'Strategic Planning in Diversified Companies', *Harvard Business Review*, January–February 1975, pp. 81–90.
20. See J. H. Grant and W. R. King, *The Logic of Strategic Planning* (Boston: Little, Brown & Co., 1982) Ch. 2.
21. See note 11 above and the US data in R. P. Rumelt, *Strategy, Structure and Economic Performance* (Cambridge, Mass.: Harvard University Press, 1974).
22. See T. J. Peters and R. H. Waterman Jr, *In Search of Excellence* (New York: Harper & Row, 1982) pp. 296–7.
23. See Office of Fair Trading data in Chapter 10, Appendix Table 10.3.
24. See B. Chiplin and M. Wright, 'Divestment and Structural Change in UK Industry', *National Westminster Bank Quarterly Review*, February 1980, pp. 42–51.
25. See J. Thackray, 'The Disinvestment Boom', *Management Today*, January 1982, pp. 46ff.
26. The evidence for this is unimpressive. At least one pair of authors has suggested that shareholders would do as well by investing in their own portfolio of shares as by investing in a comparably diversified firm. See M. S. Salter and W. A. Weinhold, 'Diversification via Acquisition: Creating Value', *Harvard Business Review*, July–August 1978, pp. 166–76.

Acquisitions and Mergers 10

In the takeover battle between Bendix and Martin Marietta, the fate of two important American companies has now been decided after a lurid soap opera, complete with cliff-hangers, boardroom dramas, court scenes, and even a spot of romantic interest. Business considerations appear to have taken second place amid the mighty clash of management egos, and the spectacle of two large companies trying to swallow each other up has pulled in audiences from well beyond the confines of Wall Street. — *Financial Times*, 27 September 1982.

10.1 Definitions and Statistics

As the statistics in Appendix Table 10A.1 indicate, mergers and acquisitions are a significant part of corporate strategy activity both with regard to the economy as a whole and for individual businesses. The first two data columns of Appendix Table 10A.1 show that in each year recently some 400 companies on average acquire a total of around 550 other businesses, with some 15 per cent of these acquired businesses constituting overseas acquisitions. Appendix Table 10A.2 emphasises that expenditure on acquiring other businesses constitutes a significant proportion of applications of company funds. Over various periods recently it is estimated that acquisitions and mergers have accounted for between one-quarter and one-half of business growth; and, of importance to economists and those concerned with government policy in this area, it is variously estimated that external growth has accounted for between 40 per cent and over 100 per cent of the increase in market concentration in the UK economy.[1]

Our concern in this chapter is with merger or acquisition as a means of achieving corporate goals, and a point to which we shall return several times in this chapter is the need clearly to see acquisitions or mergers as a means to various possible ends rather than as ends in themselves, and thus the necessity for comparing the acquisition route to achieving strategic goals with the internal route. Although it may be considered that there is some merit in distinguishing clearly between acquisitions and mergers on the basis of the degree of acquiescence of the parties to a new corporate ownership arrangement, the survival or loss of identity of one or both of the parties involved, and the relative size of the two constituents, we shall nevertheless in this chapter use the two terms more or less synonymously, except when an individual issue or problem is being discussed which is the likely outcome particularly of one of these two events.

The sequence of the remainder of this chapter is first to analyse the general goals of merger activity and to examine the case for achieving these goals by acquisition. After this the performance record of mergers in the UK over recent decades is looked at as an introduction to a more extended discussion of the findings in the management literature of why mergers are not generally successful. This leads naturally to a further main section on guidelines for success in merger activity, and this is followed by some general conclusions in this area of corporate strategy.

10.2 Acquisition and Merger Goals

It is feasible to use acquisitions as a means of achieving several possible business objectives. Those considered here are growth, market entry, diversification, improved operating efficiency, and profitability.

Growth

Acquisition is a particularly attractive means of growth because of the rapidity with which this can be achieved through the external route of acquiring an existing business as opposed to the internal route of building up capacity by purchasing the necessary assets such as premises, plant, etc. Providing appropriate 'victim' businesses are available, acquisitions not only secure for the expanding firm the necessary working plant and equipment but may also avoid for the firm the growth problems of access to scarce raw materials and distribution networks. With regard to the question of access to markets and customers, one would expect the external or acquisition route to growth to be particularly characteristic of low-growth markets, where profit margins are already fairly low, and where the alternative to such a policy is severe price or product competition. By contrast, businesses operating in new, fast-growing and profitable markets may have neither the need, nor indeed the opportunity, to grow by acquisition. If an expanding business considers that it lacks the management resources either to implement the actual growth process or to manage the expanded volume of business, then such 'Penrose' management restrictions on growth can be overcome by acquiring an existing business possessing the necessary management competence.[2] Thus, given the numerous attractions of increased size or market share for businesses and their managers, it is not surprising that 'the security provided by bigness' or 'desires to move towards increased control of the market and the necessity to take defensive action to preserve existing market and industrial positions' have been seen as major explanations of merger activity.[3]

Growth by acquisition would thus seem to be an attractive strategy. However, certain restrictions and disadvantages apply. Even asusming that a suitable, as opposed to merely available, corporate partner can be found, and that there is no legislative barrier to acquisition arising from the operation of the Monopolies and Mergers Commission, external growth imposes its own constraints. It is essential for an expanding business to find an acquisition which clearly fulfils its strategic needs in terms of the desired size of the planned increase in output, the range of products being sought, the technology to be used, the functional strengths needed, or correspondence of organisational characteristics, including management style.[4] These conditions are far from easy to satisfy, whereas the success of a merger is likely to be crucially dependent upon a high proportion of these criteria being met. Thus in this as in other areas of business strategy there is a need to consider carefully the appropriateness of acquisition as a means of achieving the business goals in the light of a range of factors relating to the firm and its markets.

Market entry

As a means of achieving market entry acquisition would seem to be a particularly appropriate strategy. This is especially true where a market is growing only slowly, if at all, where demand is inelastic with respect to price reductions by individual firms, where existing market shares are strongly entrenched behind patronage entry barriers sustained by product differentiation and advertising expenditure, or where competitors are characterised by a high level of operating efficiency and are thus capable of responding to any price competitoin, or have significant financial resources and are consequently able to sustain short-term losses associated with a pricing policy designed to make entry into the market extremely costly for new firms. Thus unless a potential entrant to a market is particularly advantageously placed relative to existing sellers in respect of cost levels, management capability and capacity to attract existing or new customers to its product, there is a natural tendency to consider acquisition as the more appropriate means of entering a market. Finally, if institutional restrictions apply in respect of the distribution of a product – as in the case of brewing, where a considerable proportion of sales is through public houses controlled by brewers – then if one does not envisage being able to establish such distribution facilities oneself, acquisition of an existing brewer is the only realistic growth medium.

Diversification

Businesses adopting a policy of diversification face additional problems beyond those of simply expanding or increasing their share of an existing market. Factor inputs, technologies, products and customers may all present management with new problems additional to those of expanding the scale of existing operations; and the extent of the difficulties will depend upon the relatedness of the firm's existing and potential new activities, together with management's view of the transferability of its own competence from one product-market area to another. Under these circumstances a firm is especially likely to choose the external route to diversification, placing particular emphasis upon the quality of the management of the acquired business. Even in this case, however, there are likely to be costs as well as benefits arising from choosing the acquisition route. As in the case of all acquisitions, there is the question of the business finding an appropriate partner. In the particular case of diversified expansion it might be thought that the choice of the appropriate product-market sector to be entered, the complementarity of existing and new ventures, and the question of management styles would be just as important as in the case of horizontal growth. But while there may be considerable advantages for a firm in diversifying through acquisition, taking account of the fact that it is acquiring a company in what for the expanding business is a new market area, the acquiring firm's appraisal of it is likely to be even less accurate than in the case of horizontal mergers. This may be one particular case where acquisitions can provide not only ready-made solutions but also a set of ready-made problems for the unwary purchaser.[5]

Operating efficiency

One of the most publicised advantages of a large number of proposed mergers or acquisitions is the projected increase in operating efficiency of the combined business. This may be based upon an intended increase in the efficiency of the acquired business or, more frequently, the result of access to economies of scale in production, joint operation of marketing or research and development activities, or benefits at a broader financial or managerial level all arising from rationalisation and the release of synergy to the combined business. These are, of course, perfectly reasonable and laudable justifications for merger or acquisition. Several factors have nonetheless to be borne in mind in considering how realisable such gains are likely to be.

First, in some of the areas of anticipated benefit it may be unrealistic to expect major improvements in the performance of the business either because there is little scope for these or because the area in which the advantages are anticipated is insufficiently clearly specified. For example, in the case of production economies of scale there is evidence to suggest not only that existing levels of firm size are well beyond those that could be justified by reference to the need to have plants of minimum efficient scale (m.e.s.), but also that the unit cost penalty attaching to operating plants of, say, 50 per cent of the m.e.s. is often quite small. Thus while in the cases of electric motors and refrigerators or washing machines an incentive to horizontal mergers in the quest for scale economies is suggested by the fact that m.e.s. plants would account for 60 per cent and 50 per cent of UK output with 50 per cent m.e.s. unit cost penalties of 15 per cent and 8 per cent respectively, in the case of cement manufacture, brewing, bread baking and machine tools the proportions of the UK market accounted for by m.e.s. plants are 10, 3, 1 and 0.5 per cent respectively, suggesting that given the existing levels of market concentration in these areas the scope for economies of scale from further mergers is negligible.[6] This is not to say that access to economies of scale cannot be the foundation of a merger; and examples exist of considerable achievements in this direction at the operational level in the case of television set production, and at a more general level in the field of computers.[7] Unfortunately, however, there are too many instances of the experiences reported by Kitching and Newbould below for one to place too much emphasis upon this factor as an area of likely major gains from mergers. On the other hand, anticipated economies arising from combined operation of complementary interests resulting from increased 'substance' in the markets involved sound rather generalised to be a strong basis for a merger.[8]

The second point about many sources of operating economies in merger situations is that they appear to require much more effort to achieve them than management is prepared to devote to the task. In the case of operations such as retail stores or commercial banks involving branch networks, horizontal mergers may fairly easily give rise to considerable operating economies. In other cases such rationalisation of activities may be much less easy to achieve. Indeed, in his classic study of the outcomes of mergers in the

United States, Kitching pointed out that in the view of the executives involved, in comparison with other sources of economies anticipated from mergers, rationalisation or combination of manufacturing facilities was the most difficult area in which to achieve economies.[9] In Newbould's study of UK merger activity in the late 1960s (which, it should be noted, was restricted to horizontal mergers) in more than two-thirds of the cases there was 'negligible' activity following the merger in the direction of closure of plants or administrative units (including head offices). An even greater proportion of the mergers considered by Newbould (71 per cent) was characterised by negligible subsequent disposal of assets, although in 29 per cent of the mergers there were significant shopfloor redundancies following the amalgamation.[10] Thus it would appear from these and other detailed studies that although bidders in merger situations may genuinely believe that such amalgamations will lead to an improvement in operating efficiency for the combined business, not only is the scope for significant tangible benefits in this area likely to be limited in many cases, but such economies are by no means easy to achieve, and there is evidence to suggest that in the event management does not even devote much effort to trying to achieve such merger gains.

Profitability

Finally, and despite the evidence we shall examine below relating to post-merger profitability, it is worthwhile looking at the potential profitability gains from mergers. Given our reservations expressed above regarding the operating efficiency gains from mergers, it is likely that the major profit gains, other than the short-term benefits pejoratively referred to as arising from asset stripping, are likely to stem from changes in market structure to which mergers lead. Thus increased company size *vis-à-vis* suppliers, competitors and customers is likely to lead to a reduction in some costs and increased sales margins. However, whether the reductions in costs are the result of genuine economies for suppliers or simply a reflection of the bargaining power of buyers is a moot point. Whatever the rationale, this is a recognised source of gains from amalgamations, as Sir Adrian Cadbury pointed out in the aftermath of the Cadbury-Schweppes merger. According to Sir Adrian, one of the advantages of increased size following a merger is 'the ability to obtain better terms from suppliers and to resist similar demands from customers. Some [trade] discounts . . . can be improved by making use of the leverage that comes with size'.[11] Horizontal mergers leading to market dominance may be especially motivated by the desire to enjoy increased profits. One analysis of the amalgamation of the two largest UK metal window manufacturers spoke of 'Hope's [belief] that a merger with Crittall's would enable them, by virtue of their dominance of the market with more than sixty per cent of standard window sales, to raise prices'.[12] A more general study of the phenomenon of mergers and market concentration suggested that the elimination of competition between suppliers was a major motive in a range of industries.[13] One particular study has suggested that this motive for mergers may have been especially strong in the period following government legislation designed to eliminate common trade pricing agreements.[14] With respect to the Crittall-Hope case mentioned above, the former chairman of the firm subsequently wrote that, 'A financial merger between Hope's and Crittall, even if they traded as separate companies, would allow the two companies to agree common selling prices between themselves without breaking the law'.[15]

This section has considered a range of corporate strategies for which mergers or acquisitions may be appropriate. In the areas of growth and market entry acquisition obviously offers a speedy route to these goals, avoiding in particular the competition associated with internal expansion, and enabling firms to surmount the patronage and scale economy entry barriers. In respect of diversification and growth, managerial barriers to the speed of adjustment and to the absorption of new product-market situations are also avoided. In the cases of growth and diversification, however, it was noted that external expansion by a firm might well impose its own problems on the adjustment process, and this should be a reminder to business people that acquisitions should be undertaken only after considering the alternative approach and in the light of all of the circumstances in the market.

10.3 Merger Performance

Having examined under a number of headings some of the corporate strategies that might be best achieved by merger or acquisition, it is logical to consider the track record of mergers. Most of the analysis of this issue has been based upon examination of the profitability of businesses following a merger, comparing the profitability of the combined firm with that of the previously independent constituents. Utton, for example, considering a sample of UK manufacturing firms over the period 1961–70, found that firms which were merger-intensive had significantly lower levels of profitability both during and after the period of intense merger activity than a random sample of firms that had expanded internally.[16] Meeks's study of the results of takeover activity for the period 1964–72, involving a comparison of the performance of acquiring and victim firms in the three years previous to the acquisition with the performance of the combined businesses over a subsequent period during which no further merger activity took place, revealed that in the years following the merger there were significant declines in profitability compared with the profit performance prior to the merger.[17]

Firth's research covering individual acquisition bids in the years 1972, 1973 and 1974 considered movements in share prices (that is, in the wealth of shareholders) following merger. Firth's interesting finding is that while over this period there were no significant changes in the combined market capitalisation of the two merging firms compared with their previous separate capitalised values, the small net reduction in the capitalisation – which remained in existence for twenty-four months after the merger – was made up of a combination of a very significant reduction in the share value of the acquiring firm together with corresponding increases in the wealth of the acquired company shareholders. The reduction in the wealth of the acquiring firm shareholders appears to be influenced by the payment of 'excessive' premiums for victim firms.[18]

There seems to be no doubt from the evidence above that mergers have resulted in significant reductions in the business efficiency of firms undertaking them as measured by profitability, and also in the wealth of acquiring firm shareholders. The persistence of such corporate behaviour is thus more likely to be explained by managerial motives. Given the divorce between business ownership and effective control, and also the pecuniary and other attractions to senior management of firm size, growth and increased market share,[19] it would not be surprising to find management, within certain limits, pursuing acquisition activity for the benefits of corporate growth, etc., always provided that there was not an excessive clash between the pursuit of such goals and the interests of shareholders. Support for such a thesis is found in a study of the experience of American merging firms. S. R. Reid's analysis of the performance of 478 large US industrial firms over the period 1951–61 considered the performance of four groups of firms ranked by merger intensity according to management interest variables (three measures of company growth) and shareholder interest variables (increases in share prices and profits). Reid's finding was that there was a significant positive association between merger intensiveness and the management interest variables on the one hand, and a significant negative relationship between merger intensiveness and the shareholder interest variables. This result applied both to the sample as a whole and to the firms analysed by industry, although in the latter case the effect was somewhat reduced.[20]

At a general level, therefore, mergers have not been successful from the point of view of shareholders. The explanations for this 'poor' performance of mergers are likely to be many. Our purpose in the next section of this chapter is to suggest reasons for this situation at the strategic or management level, and to follow this with suggestions on how merger or acquisition performance could be improved.

10.4 Reasons for Merger Failure

Given the evidence relating to the poor performance of mergers – at least from the point of view of shareholders if not of management itself – it is worthwhile considering some of the reasons for this failure. This analysis provides a basis for Section 10.5 on guidelines for mergers or acquisition activity. The major reasons for merger failure may be listed as follows:

1. Failure to establish objectives for an acquisition which fit into the overall corporate strategy.
2. Failure to compare acquisitions with alternative means of achieving corporate objectives.
3. Ignoring the financial dimension of mergers.

4. Insufficient familiarity on the part of the acquiring company management with the business of victim firms.
5. Insufficient attention to post-merger planning and to the need for such planning to realise the potential gains from merger.

An acquisition or merger, as we have stressed before, is one means of achieving certain strategic goals. Mergers should therefore stem from corporate strategy, but Kitching, following his classic study of the outcome of mergers in the USA, concluded that a major reason for the low success rate was that 'acquisitions are largely accidental, and do not fit into a pattern of planned strategic growth: and that, even if acquisitions do form part of a thought-through management programme (as opposed to pure reactions to opportunity), the business thinking that lay behind the acquisition is often dangerously shallow'.[21] Combining this point with a reference to the speed with which mergers are undertaken, another author spoke of 'Too many acquisitions [being] based on an attractive-looking balance sheet and earnings statement plus a quick trip to the plant'.[22]

As a particular example of this failure to distinguish the means (acquisition) from possible corporate ends (strategic goals), consider the evidence on the comparison by senior managers of the relative merits of the internal and external routes to their objectives. Despite the fact that most senior managers would agree with those in Kitching's American sample that merger is a much higher risk activity than internal expansion, Newbould in his study of 38 horizontal mergers in the UK found that in 35 cases (92 per cent) internal growth was neither formally nor informally considered as an alternative before any of the mergers in question was undertaken. This strongly suggests that merging *per se* was a major goal of the firm rather than a means.[23] It was pointed out in Section 10.2 above that the balance of advantage between internal and external growth was often finely balanced and dependent upon individual business circumstances. Unless these considerations are carefully analysed, the scales of success or failure may be strongly tipped against mergers or acquisitions from the beginning of the process.

Not only is there little evidence to suggest that management seriously considers the relative merits of internal and external means of achieving corporate goals, but there apears to be at times an almost reckless attitude towards prices paid for acquisitions.

One corporate merger broker's comment relating to the pricing of acquisitions, that 'if there is community of interest, the price is almost a formality', does not suggest a rigorous approach to this aspect of acquisitions. The 'premiums' that acquiring businesses pay for their victims demonstrate on occasions considerable over-pricing of acquisitions.[24] In one of his studies of mergers that had actually taken place, Newbould showed that in order to achieve a 10 per cent net of tax return on their investment in new sub-sidiaries (which at the time seemed a reasonable figure) acquiring businesses would have had to achieve quite dramatic increases in the victims' earnings over a five-year period following the acquisi-tion. In the case of 49 per cent of the sample, the required *annual compound* growth of earnings over the five-year period exceeded 15 per cent, and in 9 per cent the rate exceeded 50 per cent.[25] Whatever the reason for such excessive assumptions, they hardly suggest circumspection in acquisition pricing, but rather a desire to buy other businesses almost regardless of the costs or consequ-ences.

Mergers and acquisitions typically involve very large sums of money. The Business Statistics Office data in Appendix Table 10A.1 value the average merger in 1984 at £10.3 million. C. S. Jones, in his excellent book on the management of acquisitions, devotes considerable space to a consideration of the planning of mergers: to the internal organisation of merger planning, the search pro-cess and acquisition valuation techniques.[26] Newbould's empirical study of merger behaviour, however, reveals that the gap between the first discussion of a merger possibility and public announce-ment was typically very short. Indeed, if we omit the firms which took a year or more, then 11 out of 28, or 39 per cent, of the firms moved from the first tentative steps to public announcement in two months or less. For one half of Newbould's sample of firms the time lapse between serious merger intentions and public announcement was a month or less, leading the author to conclude that 'little serious analysis of the merger proposal may be typical'.[27] To take one extreme example from Newbould's period, within twelve days of the announcement of the merger between the National Provincial and Westminster banks in January 1968, Barclays, Lloyds and Martins banks announced merger plans. Although it may be argued that this response was necessarily rapid to meet a highly significant change in the external environment of the remaining independent banks, it does illustrate how very quickly merger proposals can be put together, and makes one wonder how much analysis has gone into the plan.[28] As in the case of Newbould's analysis as a whole, it is difficult to avoid combining this general and particular evidence with our other findings above regarding the failure to compare potential acquisitions with internal expansion, or the apparently casual or 'opportunistic' approach to merger pricing. These findings, taken together, again suggest a lack of rigour in this area at the pre-merger stage, which may indeed make some outside observers marvel at the success of any mergers or acquisitions.

As we shall emphasise below in considering guidelines for mergers and acquisitions, the post-acquisition phase is arguably as important for the success of the venture as the circumstances leading up to the event. This is certainly recognised in the textbook literature on the topic;[29] and as an example in his study on merger failure Kitching commented that 'The nature of the reporting relationships set up between parent and acquired companies, along with the organizational responsibilities and control systems established, is a dominant influence on the success or failure of the merger'.[30] The empirical literature is again disappointing in this area so far as omens for merger success are concerned. Newbould found that his sample of firms was exactly split in half between those which had and had not taken positive steps after the merger to benefit from the combined operations.[31] There are too many examples of unconsummated corporate marriages for this to be dismissed as an unimportant area of merger or acquisition strategy. Many a UK company could be characterised, as Chloride was in its pre-Michael Edwardes days, as having shown 'more eagerness for acquisition than for rationalisation. Indeed for many years, group companies continued to operate independently and in competition with each other'.[32] Such an apparent lack of management action in the post-merger period, following upon the rapid and unsystematic pre-merger phase, again must weigh the scales heavily against merger success.

10.5 Merger Guidelines

Having outlined some of the reasons for merger failure, we now consider guidelines for merger success. The areas for consideration fall under five headings:

1. Planning of mergers in the context of corporate strategy.
2. Consideration of alternatives to merger or acquisition.
3. Development of merger criteria.
4. The process of selection.
5. Post-merger implementation.

Mergers or acquisitions, like all corporate activities, require planning; and there is evidence to suggest that firms that have planned their acquisitions in terms of predetermined policies, searching for opportunities, evaluating and integrating acquisitions, have performed significantly better across a range of financial variables in comparison with a group of firms characterised as 'non planners'.[33]

Planning for acquisition must start with a review and restatement of the objectives of the firm, and an analysis of the strengths and weaknesses, opportunities and threats (SWOT) which form the internal and external environments of the organisation. Comparison of the objectives of the business with the present performance reveals the gap, if any, that is to be filled. SWOT analysis indicates the possible directions and approaches that may be adopted. This analysis will determine not only the major characteristics being sought by the business (for example, increased profitability, growth, stability of earnings, etc.) but also the broad product-market sectors that should be considered. Kitching gives a very good example of the conversion of product-market characteristics into appropriate corporate strategies and thus to possible acquisition objectives by reference to the Boston Consulting Group Matrix. This is reproduced in Table 10.1.

Table 10.1 illustrates clearly the link between product-market characteristics and acquisition criteria. In a 'Question mark' situation (low share of a growth market), given a 'go for broke' strategy a business is looking for a cash-rich acquisition, whereas in a 'Cash Cow' position (high market share in a low growth market) the firm has surplus cash resources with which to acquire a business with a low market share in a potentially high growth market and which requires considerable cash resources. This example illustrates the way in which specific acquisition criteria, to which we turn below, should derive from the broad strategic goals of the business.

At this stage a vital decision has to be made: is the strategy arrived at by the analysis above to be achieved by external or

Table 10.1
Product Market Strategy and Acquisition Objectives

1. FINANCIAL CHARACTERISTICS

	High Market Share	*Low Market Share*
High Growth	Self-financing to cash hungry	Really cash hungry
	Good to low reported earnings	Really low reported earnings
	High price/earnings ratio	Good price/earnings ratio
	Debt level low to moderate	Debt level high
Low Growth	Cash rich	Fair cash
	High earnings	Low earnings
	Fair price/earnings ratio	Low price/earnings ratio
	No debt, high debt capacity	Low debt capacity

2. BASIC STRATEGIES

	High Market Share	*Low Market Share*
High Growth	Continue to invest heavily in market share even at expense of reported earnings	Go for broke to increase market share (probably in specific segment) or Cut your losses
Low Growth	Stable situation as long as returns greater than stockholder alternatives or Seek growth areas and fund entry	Optimise cash and withdraw

3.   ACQUISITION OBJECTIVES

	High Market Share	*Low Market Share*
High Growth	Product/market reinforcements Acquire funding sources, as needed Foothold to new growth areas	Reported earnings Cash flows Stand-by debt capacity
Low Growth	Acquire number two company in a growth industry and Fund aggressive market penetration	Sale or merger on best terms possible

Source: J. Kitching, 'The Strategy of Merging', *Management Today*, October 1969, p. 77.

internal means – by buying or building? It was suggested earlier that one of the main reasons for which mergers or acquisitions may fail, and hence a prime area for improvement, is that management, if they do not see mergers as an end in themselves, continue to see them as the only means of achieving growth, increased market share, etc. It was emphasised in Section 10.2 above that in respect of corporate strategies such as growth, market entry and diversification, the acquisition route had both advantages and disadvantages compared with internal expansion. The balance in favour of building or buying will vary from case to case and time to time. On each occasion, therefore, an expanding business must carefully assess the relative merits of these alternative approaches and choose the more appropriate one in the light of its individual circumstances. The conclusion once again here is that mergers or acquisitions must be seen as possible means to a strategic end, that there is always more than one means to such an end, and that mergers must not be undertaken for their own sake.

Having decided upon the direction in which the business is to move, and the advantage of the external route to corporate goals, the next step in the acquisition process may be described as search and screen: a search for possible candidates for acquisition, and the application to these of criteria based upon those established above as the outcome of the SWOT analysis but which will result in a much finer screening of chosen candidates.[34] Acquisition prospects may be identified on the basis of current informal knowledge of the industries or product markets selected, from published sources, as a result of an original survey of the markets, or through professional advisers such as merchant bankers or specialist corporate marriage brokers. The screening process, which may be carried out at a number of levels, involves the establishment of criteria and the application of these to businesses selected above. Obviously these criteria, or certainly their weight relative to one another, will vary according to the objectives that a merger is designed to achieve. The criteria shown in Table 10.2 should certainly be borne in mind.

Table 10.2
Acquisition Criteria

Performance criteria:	return on capital employed
	sales margin
	sales growth
	market share
Company characteristics:	size
	geographical location
	product range
	marketing or R & D strengths
Management:	quality of management
	compatibility between organisations.

The first set of criteria in Table 10.2 is the most obvious. If the purpose of an acquisition is to increase return on capital employed or to expand, or if a particular market share goal has been established, then clearly the acquisition must satisfy such criteria.

Turning to the second set of criteria, a merger or acquisition involves the coming together of two companies. It is therefore important not only to consider an acquisition in the light of certain absolute standards, but also relative to the acquiring business.

Size of acquisition relative to the bidding company is regarded as important.[35] Too large an acquisition can create problems of corporate digestion. Too small an addition to one's stable can result in management costs of acquisition that are out of all proportion to the impact upon profitability or growth that such an acquisition can have. As the architect of one corporate acquisition programme put it with inelegant forcefulness, 'To piddle around with very small companies is disproportionate in management terms. When they get into trouble it takes too much time to sort them out'.[36] Ansoff uses the expression 'size mismatch' to indicate in particular a situation where the acquired business is too small to justify the effort to manage it. Kitching noted that 84 per cent of his merger failures were characterised by a size mismatch, i.e. the acquired firm's sales were less than 2 per cent of the acquiring company pre-merger sales.[37]

Geographical location relative to the parent company may determine the ease or otherwise with which control can be exerted over an acquisition. Equally, an acquiring company may have a clear idea of geographical gaps in its market which it wishes to plug, or countries in which for a variety of reasons it may not wish to operate.

Both at a broad and more specific level an acquiring firm will want to ensure that the victim firm's products fit with its own. At a broad level the acquiring firm will either be seeking the synergy benefits of a related product range, or the diversification benefits of a contrasting one. Even within the same market the acquiring firm will want to ensure that the acquired product range either falls within its own segment of the market if it is seeking simply to expand its share of that market, or that the acquired business's product range is in precisely that part of the market which it is appropriate to be expanding into.

Finally in terms of company characteristics, the acquiring business should consider the underlying marketing or research and development strengths of the potential acquisition. Are these sufficient for that business itself? Are there potential synergy gains between the marketing or research teams of the two firms? This second set of acquisition criteria is thus concerned with the more obvious elements of fit between the two potential partners.

There is, however, a third dimension to acquisition criteria, some aspects of which are less obvious than those of the other two. A vital component of an acquisition is its management. If the process of acquisition itself places a strain upon the acquiring company management, then it is essential that the acquired firm is well managed, that that management will remain with the business after the acquisition, and that it will be compatible with the management of the dominant firm. Although the quality of the victim firm's management and its future loyalty to the acquiring firm are subjective and conjectural matters, these concerns and the issue of compatibility between the two management teams are very important. Compatibility may depend upon insubstantial characteristics such as management style or ethos, but significant differences in this area (for example, between bureaucratic and entrepreneurial styles of management) may add significantly to the difficulties of integrating two firms and reduce the likelihood of achieving merger gains.[38]

Acquisition criteria should thus reflect the needs of the acquiring firm based upon gap analysis and the external and internal audit of the organisation. As an example, at the end of the 1960s Brooke Bond found itself in the situation of a dominant share (more than 25 per cent worldwide and 38 per cent in the UK) of the stagnant tea market on which it depended for 90 per cent of its revenue. The company faced high costs of overseas expansion, and in home markets was meeting stiff competition from more specialist tea producers as well as facing problems over its distribution policy involving a dependence upon small shopkeepers at a time when supermarket chains were becoming increasingly important distributors of food products. The company was thus concerned to broaden its product base and at the same time to achieve a blend of the benefits of diversification and synergy. It recognised the advantages of trying to achieve this strategy by acquisition both as a means of achieving its goals rapidly and also as an acceptance of its limited management resources and range of expertise. The company's acquisition criteria were set out as follows:

1. Any company we buy must have good management. We do not have unlimited management resources, and our capabilities largely lie in handling problems in the unique tea business.
2. The products or services acquired must have significant growth potential.
3. The firm's profit-to-sales ratio must be better than the industry average.
4. The products must be branded and hold a reputation for high quality.
5. The firm must have sufficient size and strength to provide a springboard for becoming a significant market force in its industry.
6. The purchase price should probably not be less than £5 million or more than £10 million. We do not want to spread our management talents over a variety of ventures that are too small to be significant; yet we do not want to overly consume our financial strength on one acquisition.
7. The financial arrangements necessary for acquisition should not cause our shareholders serious earnings dilution or weaken their dividend safety.[39]

In choosing its acquisition the company thus had regard to its corporate goal of broadening its base in the food market, its own managerial and financial strengths and weaknesses, and the issue of compatibility between the two organisations. The result of the application of these criteria was the 1968 acquisition by Brooke Bond of Liebig, the Oxo and Fray Bentos manufacturer. *Management Today* paid the resultant merger the compliment of describing it as 'certainly the result of a perfectly rational assessment. Indeed, seldom in recent years has a merger looked more completely logical'.[40]

The next step in the merger or acquisition process is financial evaluation. This involves the calculation of the maximum price to be paid for the acquisition, recognising the cash flow and balance sheet implications, and consideration of the best way of financing the purchase. A number of approaches can be taken to determining the maximum value of an acquisition. Unfortunately the correct approach – discounted cash flow analysis – is more complicated than alternatives such as asset valuation of the victim firm or capitalisation of earnings, or the arithmetic relating to short-term dilution of earnings per share.[41] The most correct approach to acquisition is, as one author has put it, to regard the acquisition as a money-making machine.[42] An acquisition or merger results in an increased cash flow in return for an initial investment. The increased cash flow comes from the earnings of the acquired business, and also possibly increased earnings or reduced costs associated with the firm's existing activities arising from synergy. This incremental cash flow should be discounted at the acquiring firm's marginal opportunity cost of capital, and the resulting gross present value represents the maximum value of the victim business. Despite problems associated with the application of this approach, such as the estimation of all of the cash flows, the treatment of inflation, and the choice of a discount rate, this method should be used in all cases of acquisition. Once this value has been computed – a value which quite explicitly reflects the incidence of all cash flows – the company's financial advisers will recommend the appropriate form (cash, fixed interest securities, equity) in which the acquisition shall be paid for.

The final, but often neglected, step in the merger or acquisition process is implementation, involving in particular the integration of the two businesses. Implementation of a merger or acquisition is something to which senior management has to be prepared to devote considerable attention and resources. Once a victim firm has been legally acquired, one cannot just stand back and assume that all of the pieces of the corporate puzzle will fall into place. Merger success is crucially dependent upon management action at this stage. Indeed, despite the stress that is is quite rightly placed upon the strategic dimension of acquisition activities, Kitching emphasises in his classic study that 'The key variable for success . . . is not superior strategy; it is the managers of change . . . In the time period immediately following the merger, the quality of management talent determines the success or failure of the venture'.[43]

Perhaps the greatest post-merger problem to be overcome is realising how great a task lies ahead of the acquiring management, particularly, as one author puts it, 'because of the natural tendency to relax once the merger is legally consummated and the usual premerger hassles have faded into memories'.[44] Integration, motivation and control are the three key areas at this stage. Integration, where appropriate, of manufacturing, purchasing, marketing, sales and other functions such as administration and research and development is an important determinant of synergy. It requires decisions at the highest and at the most modest levels: from new products to notepaper. But without action in this area the two businesses run the risk of continuing as before. The actual form and extent of integration that is desirable will, of course, vary from one situation to another depending upon the basis of the acquisition or merger. Where the rationale of the combined business is entirely financial, as in the case of a conglomerate acquisition, then the control and reporting relationship may confer upon the acquired company a considerable degree of autonomy. On the other hand, if the acquisition is a horizontal one the gains from the merger will only accrue if there is full integration of purchasing, production, distribution, etc., and management of the acquired business will require to be subsumed within the parent organisation.[45]

At the same time as this drive for improved efficiency most writers emphasis the human relations side of merger or acquisition activity; and this is one aspect where it is important to be aware of whether the union of two businesses has been the result of a genuine merger of equals or an acquisition by the dominant firm of a much less significant victim organisation. The feelings and attitudes of both senior management and the workforce of the acquired business are likely to have a considerable impact upon acquisition success or failure. A general allaying of anxieties, combined with positive efforts to motivate those concerned, and a sensitive approach to surplus management or shopfloor employees are likely to pay considerable dividends.[46] Such issues raise the question of the timing of change following an acquisition. As in all such matters there is no set of rules that can be laid down. In general, although there may be a temptation to delay post-acquisition change until more information is available, or to avoid making any decisions which may later have to be reversed, the climate for instituting change is likely to be best in the immediate post-merger period. Indeed, failure to make necessary changes then may considerably reduce the momentum of the acquisition or merger process as a whole.[47] Whatever the timing to be adopted, the process of implementing an acquisition should itself be carried out within a framework of objectives, a timetable by which certain goals are to be achieved, and a system of controls that enables performance to be set against objectives and necessary corrective action to be taken.

10.6 Conclusions

Acquisitions and mergers are an important part of corporate strategy and business activity. From the point of view both of individual firms and the economy as a whole it is therefore important that acquisition and merger decisions are made on a rational basis and effectively implemented. Despite the growth of the normative management literature in this area, evidence suggests that all too often a less than rigorous approach is adopted to planning and implementing mergers, with the not surprising result that the financial outcome of such strategies is unimpressive.

This chapter has emphasised that an acquisition can be appropriate for achieving certain corporate goals, but that care has to be taken over such a strategy. In particular one would emphasise the need to plan mergers in the context of the overall corporate strategy, to consider carefully the relative merits of the internal and external routes to business goals, to develop clear criteria and adopt these in choosing corporate partners, and to be prepared to invest significant managerial resources in the appropriate integration of acquisitions. Kitching once described British managers in their acquisition strategy as 'snappers-up of unconsidered trifles'.[48] Today the average acquisition is for most businesses too significant a deployment of its resources to be carried out in such an allegedly cavalier manner. This chapter has indicated the broad guidelines for a more successful acquisition policy in an attempt to encourage an improvement in this important dimension of business strategy.

Appendix Table 10A.1
Acquisitions and Mergers of UK Industrial and Commercial Companies (based upon reports in the financial press, supplemented by special enquires)

| | Within UK | | | Acquisition of foreign companies | | |
| | No. of firms | | | No. of firms | | |
	Acquiring	Acquired	Expenditure (£m.)	Acquiring	Acquired	Expenditure (£m.)
1969	686	846	1,068.9	34	43	29.2
1970	629	793	1,122.5	46	52	105.7
1971	687	884	911.1	53	62	73.0
1972	928	1,210	2,531.6	69	85	90.4
1973	929	1,205	1,304.3	80	88	178.5
1974	427	504	508.4	49	53	120.6
1975	276	315	290.8	17	18	41.3
1976	315	353	448.1	17	17	64.6
1977	427	481	823.8	18	18	142.8
1978	484	567	1,139.5	29	30	349.5
1979	447	534	1,656.4	55	63	344.8
1980	404	469	1,475.4	51	51	941.0
1981	389	452	1,143.7	139	150	726.2
1982	399	463	2,205.5	92	95	770.3
1983	391	447	2,342.9	69	71	367.4
1984	444	507	5,243.4	86	92	938.1

Source: Business Statistics Office, *Business Monitor MQ7: Acquisitions and Mergers of Industrial and Commercial Companies* (London: HMSO).

194

Appendix Table 10A.2
Acquisitions and Uses of Funds by UK Industrial and Commercial Companies

	Total uses of funds (£m.)	Expenditure on acquisitions and mergers within the UK (£m.)	%
1970	6,770	1,122	16.6
1971	7,153	911	12.7
1972	10,484	2,532	24.2
1973	15,088	1,304	8.6
1974	15,039	508	3.4
1975	12,506	291	2.3
1976	18,139	427	2.4
1977	18,417	814	4.4
1978	19,552	1,140	5.8
1979	32,338	1,656	5.1
1980	28,640	1,475	5.2
1981	31,539	1,144	3.6
1982	28,018	2,206	7.9
1983	34,905	2,343	6.7
1984	43,315	5,243	12.1

Sources: Business Statistics Office, *Business Monitor MQ7: Acquisitions and Mergers of Industrial and Commercial Companies* (London: HMSO); Central Statistical Office, *Financial Statistics* (London: HMSO).

Appendix Table 10A.3
Proposed Mergers Classified by Type of Integration

	Horizontal		Vertical		Conglomerate	
	No.	Value	No.	Value	No.	Value
1965	78	75	12	13	10	12
1966	76	84	12	9	12	7
1967	86	91	5	4	9	5
1968	81	79	4	4	15	17
1969	80	83	2	1	18	16
1970	84	70	1	–	15	30
1971	75	62	6	4	19	34
1972	65	40	7	9	28	51
1973	70	76	4	2	26	22
1974	68	65	5	2	27	33
1975	71	77	5	4	24	19
1976	70	66	8	7	22	27
1977	64	57	11	11	25	32
1978	53	67	13	10	34	23
1979	51	54	7	4	42	42
1980	65	68	4	1	31	31
1981	62	71	6	2	32	27
1982	65	64	5	4	30	32
1983	71	73	4	1	25	26
1984	63	79	4	1	33	20

Sources: W. S. Howe, *Industrial Economics* (London: Macmillan, 1978) p. 152; and *Annual Reports of the Director General of Fair Trading* (London: HMSO).

References

1. See M. A. Utton, *The Political Economy of Big Business* (Oxford: Martin Robertson, 1982) p. 24.
2. See E. T. Penrose, *The Theory of the Growth of the Firm* (Oxford: Basil Blackwell, 2nd edn, 1980) Ch. 4, and especially pp. 44–56 for Penrose's views on the limitations placed upon the rate of growth of a business by its existing management team.
3. See T. E. Chester, 'Mergers and Opportunities for Managers', *National Westminster Bank Quarterly Review*, May 1969, p. 13; and G. D. Newbould, *Management and Merger Activity* (Liverpool: Guthstead, 1970) p. 160.
4. See C. J. Sutton, *Economics and Corporate Strategy* (Cambridge: Cambridge University Press, 1980) pp. 113–115.
5. See Sutton, *Economics and Corporate Strategy*, p. 113.
6. See A. Silberston, 'Economies of Scale in Theory and Practice', *Economic Journal*, March 1972, Vol. LXII, pp. 369–91.
7. See P. E. Hart *et al.*, *Mergers and Concentration in British Industry* (Cambridge: Cambridge University Press, 1973) pp. 43–8; and R. W. Shaw and C. J. Sutton, *Industry and Competition* (London: Macmillan, 1976) pp. 96–7.
8. See Monopolies Commission, *British Match Corporation Ltd and Wilkinson Sword Ltd: A Report on the Proposed Merger* (London: HMSO, 1973, Cmnd 5442) para. 46.
9. J. Kitching, 'Why Do Mergers Miscarry?', *Harvard Business Review*, November–December 1967, p. 93.
10. Newbould, *Management and Merger Activity*, pp. 162–8.
11. G. A. H. Cadbury, 'Mergers', *The Business Economist*, August 1973, Vol. V, p. 160.
12. C. Raw, *Slater Walker* (London: Hodder & Stoughton, 1977) p. 253.
13. Hart *et al.*, *Mergers and Concentration*, p. 102.
14. See D. Swann *et al.*, *Competition in British Industry* (London: Allen & Unwin, 1974) pp. 172–8.
15. M. Hope, 'On Being Taken Over by Slater Walker', *Journal of Industrial Economics*, March 1976, Vol. XXIV, p. 165.
16. M. A. Utton, 'On Measuring the Effects of Industrial Mergers', *Scottish Journal of Political Economy*, February 1974, Vol. XXI, pp. 13–28.
17. G. Meeks, *Disappointing Marriage: A Study of the Gains From Merger* (Cambridge: Cambridge University Press, 1977).
18. M. Firth, 'The Profitability of Takeovers and Mergers', *Economic Journal*, June 1979, Vol. LXXXIX, pp. 316–28.
19. W. S. Howe, *Industrial Economics* (London: Macmillan, 1978) pp. 26–36.
20. S. R. Reid, *Mergers, Managers and the Economy* (New York: McGraw-Hill, 1968) Ch. 8.

21. J. Kitching, 'The Strategy of Merging', *Management Today*, October 1969, p. 75.
22. C. M. Leighton and G. R. Tod, 'After the Acquisition: Continuing Challenge', *Harvard Business Review*, March–April 1969, p. 93.
23. Newbould, *Management and Merger Activity*, p. 117.
24. T. Lester, 'The Business Marriage Brokers', *Management Today*, October 1969, p. 58.
25. G. D. Newbould, 'Implications of Financial Analyses of Takeovers', in J. M. Samuels (ed.), *Readings on Mergers and Takeovers* (London: Paul Elek, 1972) pp. 12–24.
26. See C. S. Jones, *Successful Management of Acquisitions* (London: Derek Beattie, 1982) Chs 4–6.
27. Newbould, *Management and Merger Activity*, pp. 115–16.
28. See Introduction to B. W. Denning (ed.), *Corporate Planning: Selected Concepts* (London: McGraw-Hill, 1971), p. 5.
29. See Jones, *Successful Management of Acquisitions*, Chs. 9–11.
30. Kitching, 'Why do Mergers Miscarry?', p. 91.
31. Newbould, *Management and Merger Activity*, p. 169.
32. G. Foster, 'How Chloride Got a Charge, *Management Today*, January 1975, p. 45.
33. See H. I. Ansoff, 'Does Planning Pay?', *Long Range Planning*, December 1970, pp. 2–7.
34. See A. Rappaport, 'Strategic Analysis for More Profitable Acquisitions', *Harvard Business Review*, July–August 1979, pp. 99–110.
35. Ansoff is credited with the formulation of the concept of size mismatch to describe a situation in which there is too great a disparity between the size of a bidding company and its victim. See H. I. Ansoff, *Corporate Strategy* (Harmondsworth: Penguin, 1968) Ch. 9.
36. See S. Salmans, 'Lift-Off at Low & Bonar', *Management Today*, August 1980, p. 29.
37. See Kitching, 'Why Do Mergers Miscarry?', p. 92.
38. See, for example, R. E. Davis, 'Compatibility in Corporate Marriages', *Harvard Business Review*, July–August 1968, pp. 86–93; and M. S. Salter and W. A. Weinhold, 'Choosing Compatible Acquisitions', *Harvard Business Review*, January–February 1981, pp. 117–27.
39. See *Brooke Bond & Co. Ltd* (Bedford: Case Clearing House of Great Britain and Ireland, Cranfield Institute of Technology, 1970) p. 6.
40. G. Foster, 'Blending Brooke Bond Liebig', *Management Today*, October 1969, p. 84.
41. These various approaches to the valuation of an acquisition are outlined in C. S. Jones, *Successful Management of Acquisitions*, Ch. 6.
42. See M. L. Kastens, 'How Much is an Acquisition Worth?', *Long Range Planning*, June 1973, p. 54.
43. Kitching, 'Why Do Mergers Miscarry?', pp. 94 and 98.
44. F. W. Searby, 'Control Postmerger Change', *Harvard Buiness Review*, September–October 1969, p. 5.

45. See R. A. Howell, 'Plan to Integrate Your Acquisitions', *Harvard Business Review*, November–December 1970, pp. 66–76.
46. See the article by C. M. Leighton and G. R. Tod, 'After the Acquisition' (note 22.)
47. See Searby, 'Control Postmerger Change', p. 12.
48. J. Kitching, 'Why Acquisitions Are Abortive', *Management Today*, November 1974, p. 85.

Divestment

11

All the evidence points to divestment continuing to be an important tactical option for firms in a competitive world. — R. Cohen and S. Slatter, 'How to Divest', *Management Today*, May 1983, p. 136.

11.1 Introduction

In November 1983 European Ferries, with 1982 sales of £293 million spread across shipping, harbour operations, banking and property, announced that it intended to sell its merchant banking subsidiary Singer Friedlander which it had acquired three years previously. European Ferries' expressed opinion was that Singer & Friedlander had 'strong profit growth and excellent prospects', but that following the appointment of a new managing director the company 'had been reviewing its strategy and concluded that it should concentrate on the shipping, harbour and property sectors'.[1]

Divestment – the selling off of part of a business by its management – is a not uncommon strategy, and appears to have become increasingly popular in the 1980s. Liquidation, i.e. the piecemeal sale of individual business assets – is obviously a form of divestment, but is normally regarded as a last resort by management, and our assumption here is that wherever possible a firm

199

will wish to divest itself of an unwanted subsidiary as a going concern. Our definition emphasises that divestment is a conscious decision by a company to sell a part of the firm to another organisation. The latter may include the management of that subsidiary as exemplified by the recent increase in the number of management buyouts.[2] It may also include demergers, under which large organisations float off prevoiusly wholly owned subsidiaries as independently quoted companies. Trafalgar House's 'demerger' of Fleet Holdings, the Express Newspapers business, in 1983 and Reed International's plans (at the time of writing) to follow the same strategy with respect to its Mirror Group Newspapers subsidiary, thus anticipating raising some £100 million, suggest that this too may become an important form of divestment.[3]

Thus it is not correct to suppose, as some authors have, that divestment and acquisition are opposite numerical sides of the same coin. This is demonstrated in Table 11.1 in comparing the first two data columns.[4] These data indicate that although the greatest proportion of acquisitions is accounted for by the purchase of independent companies rather than the acquisition of other firm's divestments, divestment activity has nonetheless over the years taken place on a not insignificant scale compared with acquisitions, which have normally been considered to be much more important both by industrial economists and those concerned with business strategy. These data further indicate that although the average divestment is normally of very much lower value than independent companies acquired, the divestment form represents by number about one-quarter of all acquisitions and that in peak years the value proportion has also reached this level.

Although divestment is a not uncommon strategy, its relative infrequency means that much less experience has been accumulated of divestment than, say, of acquisitions. The circumstances surrounding divestment also make the strategy more difficult to pursue. This is likely to be so for two reasons. First, a specific divestment is an irreversible decision so far as the seller is concerned. It is extremely unlikely that a subsidiary once divested can be re-acquired at a later date. By contrast, a corporate acquisition can normally be reversed by means of divestment, albeit in some cases at a loss in terms of a reduction in the value of

Table 11.1
Divestments in UK Industry

Year	Subsidiaries sold	All companies acquired	Sales of subsidiaries as proportion of acquisitions	
	No.	No.	No. (%)	Value (%)
1969	102	844	12.1	9.4
1970	179	787	22.7	11.7
1971	264	884	29.9	18.2
1972	272	1,203	22.6	7.4
1973	254	1,203	21.1	19.0
1974	137	503	27.2	9.8
1975	115	312	36.9	24.5
1976	111	352	31.5	22.3
1977	110	481	22.9	12.2
1978	125	567	22.0	12.7
1979	117	534	21.9	11.2
1980	101	469	21.5	14.3
1981	125	452	27.7	22.9
1982	164	463	35.4	36.4
1983	142	447	31.8	18.6
1984	155	507	30.6	21.4

Source: Business Monitor MQ7, *Mergers and Acquisitions* (London: HMSO).

the business since acquisition. Second, and again in contrast to acquisitions, divestment often appears to be a negative strategy – a confession of failure. While acquisitions may be undertaken confidently or even aggressively, a divestment is in a large proportion of cases taken to be an expression of failure. A further institutional characteristic of divestment decisions is the secrecy that inevitably has to surround such a policy. While this may also be a feature of acquisitions in so far as the acquiring firm may not wish its intended victim to be aware of its intentions until the last moment, in the case of divestments it is members of one's own organisation from whom one may be withholding knowledge of one's intentions as well as the world at large.

The plan of this chapter is now to consider the reasons for which firms may decide to divest some of their areas of activity, and to follow this with a consideration of the particular difficulties in implementing this strategy.

11.2   Reasons for Divestment

Although the predominant view in much of the management literature is that the need to make a divestment is a sign of failure, there are circumstances in which a positive decision to divest a subsidiary operation is a perfectly sensible one. First, following an acquisition a firm may find that there are some parts of the newly acquired business, which possibly had to be bought as a whole, that the acquiring firm does not require. In such a situation the acquiring firm will dispose of these unwanted components and thereby recoup some of the expense involved in the acquisition. Thus following any upsurge in the level of acquisition activity in the economy, one might expect to find an increased number of divestments.

Second, a firm may have entered a product-market area in which its market position and current profitability are satisfactory, but which is likely to demand considerable resources for development. If the firm does not possess sufficient resources – technical, financial or managerial – to develop and exploit its present market position, or if these resources could be better used elsewhere in the firm, then the correct strategy is to divest this particular market interest. The finance so released may then be put to more effective use elsewhere in the firm's product porfolio. This aspect of divestment emphasises the need for firms to carry out a thorough analysis of the anticipated opportunities and threats associated with a market in relation to the strengths and weaknesses of the organisation. Many of the divestments currently characterising the American business scene have involved diversified corporations selling off previous energy-sector acquisitions. What these corporate parents appear to have failed to realise is the size of the sums of money that have to be invested in gas and oil exploration and development over a long period of time before there is any prospect of reasonable returns.[5] This may not therefore be an appropriate field of investment for firms without considerable financial resources and a willingness to take a long-term view of investments.

A third and very obvious reason for divestment is dissatisfaction with the current profit or growth performance of a subsidiary. If no improvement is foreseen in this situation then again the most appropriate policy is to divest from the market sector and achieve a better return on the company's resources in other areas. This situation is likely to arise where a firm has been over-optimistic regarding prospects in a particular product-market sector, and as one manifestation of this may have paid an unduly high price for an acquisition in this field. Markets that appeared to promise profits and growth may turn out to provide neither if demand falls off, costs rise or unexpectedly strong competitors emerge. The US computer market, for example, has witnessed a number of very large corporations such as (American) General Electric and RCA withdrawing from this sector in the face of their failure to cope with rapidly changing technology and markets, and in particular competition from IBM.[6]

One factor that a firm may take account of in this context is the scale of some of its subsidiary activities both in relation to the parent company and relative to the markets in which they operate. When a subsidiary is generating indifferent returns and is at the same time a small part of the total enterprise relative to the efforts involved in its management, or when the prospects of increased profit from a subsidiary are limited by its market share, then senior management may regard such activities as primary candidates for divestment, with the resources released being channelled into the company's core businesses. Thus, commenting on the divestments from textile polypropylene, telephone call logging equipment, computer software and hardware distribution, self-adhesive labels and flexible packaging which were part of Bunzl Pulp & Paper's profit recovery in the early 1980s, the new chief executive explained: 'We were in a number of peripheral businesses not sizeable enough to grow into divisions, not making the sort of returns we were looking for, and not worth the effort to control and develop'.[7] By contrast, the rather more dramatic strategy followed by Fisons in 1982 was to divest itself of its core activity – fertilisers – and concentrate largely upon pharmaceuticals. Fertilisers, a cyclical market demanding high volume and large-scale investment, had become in *Management Today*'s word Fisons' albatross.[8] The problem for the company was that although fertilisers constituted a preponderant part of Fisons' sales, the firm enjoyed neither size nor market share in this sector compared with its main rival ICI. In the mid-1970s fertilisers accounted for more than half of Fisons' sales. However, an analysis in the early 1980s of the fertiliser market and of the company's own resources – that is, of the market opportunities and threats, and the firm's strengths and weaknesses – led Fisons, in the words of its new chief executive, to the following conclusion:

> **[It] was patently obvious that we didn't have the capacity to compete. The people growing in fertilisers are very, very deep-pocketed. Either they're the chemical giants, who themselves find it a bit of a strain, or they're governments: so they're very, very big investors. So strategically, it was a prime candidate for divesting. And if we could divest, it would go a long way to freeing our resources.[9]**

The outcome of this analysis was that Fisons sold its fertiliser business to the Norwegian state-owned Norsk Hydro, merged its agrochemicals interests with Boots, and is now based upon pharmaceuticals, horticulture and scientific equipment. The sale of its fertiliser division reduced Fisons' capital employed by some £30 million, and between 1981 and 1982 sales fell by 29 per cent. The result of these changes, however, was that although in 1982 Fisons' total of net assets was below that of 1978, and its 1982 total sales in money terms were virtually the same as those of 1978, earnings per share and return on capital employed both recovered sharply from the levels of the turn of the decade. Return on investment in 1982 was a record since 1976. The result of this divestment was that Fisons was able confidently to preface its 1982 Annual Report with the following strategic picture of itself:

> **Fisons is now engaged in business areas well suited to its skills and scale. These businesses are in attractive and inherently profitable markets, and the Company is competitively equipped**

for growth. Each division is a market leader in its field of activity, and is well placed to grow internationally.

The example of Fisons illustrates clearly how divestment can be used as a positive business strategy to allow a firm to achieve its objectives. In particular the full story of Fisons over this period shows how strategic analysis by a firm of the relevant characteristics of its present markets and of those available to it, combined with an assessment of the organisation's strengths and weaknesses, can lead to a significant change of strategic direction for the firm in pursuit of its objectives.

Finally, a business organisation may divest some of its traditional activities in order to reposition itself *vis-à-vis* the several markets in which its operates. Divestment may thus be part of the process of strategic shrinking discussed in Chapter 4 above. The logic behind this type of divestment is a natural application of the product portfolio strategy involving the channelling of resources released by Cash Cows and divestments into the high growth and profitability sectors of the future. The firm in this situation is not necessarily experiencing a low present return on its investment in this area, nor is it likely to face difficulty in remaining in the product-market sector in the short term. Indeed, the potential strategic error is that of remaining in the market for too long until decline has well and truly set in, by which time divestment may be far more difficult to achieve. Divestment at an early stage in a market's decline, and a subsequent reallocation of the firm's resources into potential growth markets represents a positive approach to product portfolio planning by multi-product firms.

While the cases discussed above illustrate a number of positive reasons for divestment, it is unfortunate that divestments appear to be undertaken in all too many cases for shorter-term negative reasons. Among the more understandable of these is the simple failure of an acquisition to 'work out' for the parent organisation. This failure may be aggravated by an excessively high price having been paid for the acquisition, and the fact that the acquisition may have been part of an unwise strategy on the part of the parent, as in the case of an uncritical diversification policy by many firms on both sides of the Atlantic in the late 1960s and early 1970s. In the author's own research concerning the reaction by traditional industrial textile manufacturers to the rapid decline in demand for spun and woven jute in the 1970s, a number of instances were found of firms acquiring subsidiaries in other markets – for example, hardware wholesaling, and mechanical and electrical engineering – only to discover that these investments did not provide the growth, profits or stability anticipated at the time of their acquisition. In most instances these acquisitions were held for less than five years.[10]

Associated with this selling off of recent acquisitions are the apparently high prices paid for these. Newbould's research, for example, already drawn upon in Chapter 10 above, revealed that the prices paid for acquisitions have often been totally unrealistic when these are compared with the implied earnings growth of acquired subsidiaries.[11] As the reality of such circumstances dawns upon management, then perhaps the most positive reaction is to sell the acquisitions to someone else rather than saddle the firm with inevitable loss-makers for years to come.

A particular stimulus to divestments has been what one observer of the American business scene has referred to as 'a radical strategic reassessment of the quality and extent of business diversity'.[12] Divestment is thus seen as part of a process comprising 'a swing back towards simplifying the corporation into an enterprise of related business activities. It could mean better management and improved efficiency for a sizable segment of US business'.[13] British data relating to the late 1970s also imply that the current pattern of divestment in this country tends to create a less diversified industrial structure. Chiplin and Wright studied divestments which took place from the second quarter of 1977 to the first quarter of 1979 inclusive, and their results are reproduced in Table 11.2.

The data in Table 11.2 indicate the very high proportions of all types of divestment that are horizontal acquisitions. In particular, while 22.9 per cent and 23.8 per cent of the horizontal and vertical divestments respectively covered by this study were regarded as conglomerate acquisitions, not only were 60.0 per cent of horizontal divestments made to firms at the same stage of production in the same industry, but more than one-third of vertical divestments and almost half of conglomerate divestments in turn constituted horizontal acquisitions for the acquiring firms. These data strongly suggest that divestment activity has contributed to a trend away

Table 11.2
Destination of Divestments by Type

Type of acquisition	Type of divestment		
	Horizontal	Vertical	Conglomerate
Horizontal	60.0	35.7	47.2
Vertical	10.0	31.0	10.3
Conglomerate	22.9	23.8	35.6
Other*	7.1	9.5	6.9
	100.0	100.0	100.0

*includes financial, brewery, hotel, leisure and foreign

Source: B. Chiplin and M. Wright, 'Divestment and Structural Change in UK Industry', *National Westminster Bank Quarterly Review*, February 1980, p. 48.

from diversification in the UK economy, reflecting a positive strategy in this direction by the firms involved.

Of more immediate concern to many divestors, however, may be the financial health or even the survival of the business as a whole. An almost random sample of divestments at the time of writing this chapter reveals the 'cash-starved' Tootal, one of the leading UK textile groups, selling its Australian associated Bradmill with one of the main aims being to reduce its £60 million of borrowings,[14] while the 'debt-ridden giant' Dunlop continues to try to dispose of most of its European tyre businesses to the Japanese Sumitomo and a major stake in Dunlop Malaysian Industries to the Malaysian group Pegi. These Dunlop divestments were anticipated to raise some £168 million.[15]

One particular characteristic of this type of situation is highlighted by the reference in the case of European Ferries' sale of Singer

& Friedlander to the intention of its management 'to concentrate resources on its core businesses and, as these have been draining cash, the disposal proceeds will come in very handy'.[16] The danger in this situation is that the divestments carried out will comprise not necessarily the most logical product-market sectors from which a firm should withdraw, but simply the most realisable components in its balance sheet. This represents a case of immediate financial liquidity having to be given priority over longer-term corporate strategy. These circumstances may be the particular outcome of the present economic recession in which relatively high growth in many markets, buoyant share prices and low real rates of interest have given way to slow economic growth generally, low stock market prices and higher real rates of interest. Whatever the reason, it seems to be agreed that divestments under these circumstances have often resulted in companies being forced by financial pressures into selling off businesses which from a longer-term strategic point of view they would much rather have retained.[17]

Divestments may therefore take place for a number of reasons. Constructively used, a divestment strategy can play a vital part in the achievement of business goals. In the case of Fisons we saw that divestment was a crucial part of a major change of strategic direction. Equally, however, divestment may be a reaction to which a business is forced to resort because of strategic failure. This may occur either because a previous strategy – involving perhaps an acquisition – has turned out to be incorrect, or when a firm has so lost its strategic direction that the motive for divestment is a crisis financial one to ensure the survival of the firm rather than part of a considered strategy. Because the differences behind all of these circumstances may be related to management attitudes to divestment as such, we turn now to consider the management implications of this strategy.

11.3 Management Considerations

One of the range of management variables associated with divestment is that of making the divestment decision sufficiently early to enable management to carry out a careful analysis of how the divestment should be undertaken and to avoid a piecemeal liquidation of the assets involved. In part the problem is a motivational one. A decision to divest is normally taken to be a regrettable one. Such a decision 'hurts emotionally, because a divestiture almost invariably reflects a mistake in judgment, a broken commitment, or incompetence on somebody's part. A divestiture is an expression of failure'.[18] As another American author has put it in discussing strategic exit barriers from a market, 'A consideration that turns up in case study after case study is management's emotional attachments and commitment to a business, coupled with pride in their abilities and accomplishments and fears about their own future'.[19] To this may be added a tendency expressed by Jim Slater of Slater Walker Securities for British boards of directors to be over-optimistic regarding their ability to turn round loss-making enterprises. Slater's view of many British managers was that 'if they have a loss-making business on their hands, they work like fury to pull it round, while I would sell it'.[20] While a great deal of the gilt has been knocked off the Slater Walker Securities gingerbread since its heyday in the late 1970s, Slater's comment adds further weight to the earlier conclusions regarding a psychological problem affecting the pursuit of a divestment strategy. So long as divestment is viewed as a negative strategy, then the decision to divest is likely to be left until it is too late to be effective. Such decisions may also be left to be implemented by less senior management than the situation demands or deserves. The outcome of this whole approach is almost certain to be that fewer resources are released by the divestment than may have been possible – both because the asset to be disposed of has lost some of its attractions to potential buyers during the interim of delay, and because the matter is being dealt with by less competent managers. There will also have been a delay in releasing the resources arising from the divestment, and possibly even further months of unproductive negative cash flow, with a corresponding delay in the redeployment of the released resources by the firm.

If divestment is going to be carried out effectively, then the redundant assets require to be disposed of in a manner and at a time that is optimal from the point of view of maximising the value of those assets and the replacement investment. This will involve management in a combined study of the implications of divesting from a particular product-market area at different times, and the likely returns from various possible sectors in which the funds may be reinvested. As in the case of the findings on merger analysis reported in Chapter 10 above so in respect of divestments, there often appears to be little financial analysis undertaken. As Hayes reported in the early 1970s, despite the growing awareness by management of capital investment appraisal techniques, 'They seldom attempt to anticipate the possible uses of the funds that will be made available, or even to evaluate the changes in net cash flow that are likely to occur. They appear to make their divestiture decisions largely on an *ad hoc* basis. Indeed, in a surprising number of decisions, financial factors are given little weight'.[21] For reasons of short- and long-term survival it is necessary for a divesting firm to link closely its realisation of cash resources from disposals and their subsequent investment in new market areas. Unless this is achieved, then in the short run the company may itself become a takeover victim during a period when it has an attractive cash-laden balance sheet combined with a low stock-market value resulting from its reduced earnings and the uncertainty regarding the returns from future new investments. For the longer term, apart from eliminating any losses, a divestment is hardly going to assist the business in achieving its goals if no prospective uses of the released funds have been assessed, although as we have seen in a number of cases divestments have had to be made very largely to allow firms to reduce excessive levels of fixed-interest borrowing.

One alternative danger faced by management in divesting is that of failing to recognise interdependencies between a loss-making activity which management feels the firm ought to divest and the remainder of its product market areas. The potential error here is that of looking at such a loss-making activity in too marginalist or incremental a manner. Divestment from one product-market area may leave fixed overhead costs to be spread over a smaller level of output. Purchasing and other economies of scale may also be sacrificed by such a move. On the demand side customers may be lost if buyers prefer to purchase a complete package of goods from sellers and value the availability of a full line of products in choosing among competing suppliers. Manufacturers who are vertically integrated may have to be prepared to carry some of their market linkages at a low profit in order to enjoy the strategic advantages of their integrated position. As one author warns,

'This is not to suggest that there is never a case for dropping unprofitable products from the range . . . The long term purpose of the company and its strategy are important if it is to be successful. If products are to be dropped, it must be to strengthen the company's position in order to launch new ventures or to concentrate efforts in areas where there are real marketing advantages.'[22] The Boston Consulting Group report on the UK motor cycle industry suggested that a gradual retreat by British manufacturers from 'unprofitable' sectors of that market had in fact led to a situation where the viability of home producers in this field became increasingly questionable.[23]

11.4 Conclusions

The data in Table 11.1 above indicate that divestment activity is a not insignificant part of business strategy. Furthermore, the limited statistical analysis in this area suggests that divestment activity combined with acquisitions provides scope for significant rearrangement of corporate assets on the part of divesting firms and may be responsible for important structural changes in British industry.[24] In particular, and to the extent that the divestment data portray a reversal of previous diversification moves in the UK economy, they support a 'correction of previous strategic mistakes' hypothesis behind divestment. It is, of course, appropriate that such a corrective avenue should be open to firms. It is, however, equally important that divestments should be regarded as a normal part of corporate strategy.

References

1. See *Financial Times*, 12 November 1983.
2. See J. Coyne and M. Wright, 'Buy Outs and British Industry', *Lloyds Bank Review*, October 1982, pp. 15–31.
3. See *Sunday Times*, 16 October 1983.
4. See R. H. Hayes, 'New Emphasis on Divestment Opportunities', *Harvard Business Review*, July–August 1972, p. 55.
5. See J. Thackray, 'The Disinvestment Boom', *Management Today*, January 1982, p. 47.

6. See J. E. Ross and M. J. Kami, *Corporate Management in Crisis* (New Jersey: Prentice-Hall, 1973). Ch. 5.
7. See D. Arnott, 'Bunzl's Unfiltered Future', *Management Today*, November 1982, p. 68.
8. N. Newman, 'Fisons' Unfertilised Future', *Management Today*, May 1982, p. 44.
9. *Ibid*., p. 48.
10. See W. S. Howe, *The Dundee Textiles Industry 1960–1977* (Aberdeen: Aberdeen University Press, 1982) Ch. 3.
11. See G. D. Newbould, 'Implications of Financial Analyses of Takeovers' in J. M. Samuels (ed.), *Readings on Mergers and Takeovers* (London: Elek Books, 1972) pp. 12–24.
12. Thackray, 'The Disinvestment Boom', p. 46.
13. *Ibid*.
14. See *Financial Times*, 17 December 1983.
15. See *Sunday Times*, 11 December 1983.
16. See note 1 above.
17. See R. Cohen and S. Slatter, 'How to Divest', *Management Today*, May 1983, p. 92.
18. Hayes, 'New Emphasis on Divestment Opportunities', p. 56.
19. M. E. Porter, *Competitive Strategy* (New York: Free Press, 1980) p. 263.
20. Quoted in C. Raw, *Slater Walker* (London: Deutsch, 1977) p. 243.
21. Hayes, 'New Emphasis on Divestment Opportunities', p. 58.
22. D. J. Spurrell, 'Business Strategy in the United Kingdom – The Challenge from Abroad', *National Westminster Bank Quarterly Review*, August 1980, p. 37.
23. See Boston Consulting Group, *Strategy Alternatives for the British Motor Cycle Industry*, A Report to the House of Commons (1975).
24. B. Chiplin and M. Wright, 'Divestment and Structural Change in UK Industry', *National Westminster Bank Quarterly Review*, February 1980, pp. 42–51; and S. Lye and A. Silbertson, 'Merger Activity and Sales of Subsidiaries Between Company Groups', *Oxford Bulletin of Economics and Statistics*, August 1981, Vol. XLIII, pp. 257–72.

Business Failure and Turnaround 12

At Vauxhall, he was responsible for pulling the company back from an £18 million loss in 1974 to its only year of profits since, £2 million in 1978. In turning round Vauxhall he shed labour by a ruthless 20%, changed management, put in new cost-control measures and introduced new product lines. — D. Arnott, 'How Vauxhall Shifted Gear', *Management Today*, July 1983, p. 47.

12.1 Introduction

The quotation above encapsulates the role of the incoming manager in a corporate turnaround situation. A previously desperate state of affairs is taken hold of by a single individual who assumes the authority to make sometimes dramatically unpleasant decisions as a result of which the dying corporate patient is revived. Sometimes there is a return to permanent good health. In other instances such as Chrysler in the USA the individual turnaround situation may be one of a series of apparent recoveries which in retrospect may be atypical peaks in an otherwise undistinguished performance.[1]

The business failure and turnaround situation is an appropriate one with which to drawn to an end a text on corporate strategy, for it is in these circumstances, as we shall see, that strategic management has most obviously failed, and in which a new strategy is needed – one that is often clearly the work of a single individual or group of individuals. That is, at a simple level corporate turnarounds are required by strategic failures and result from strategic successes. They also epitomise Drucker's aphorism that 'Every achievement of management is the achievement of a manager. Every failure is a failure of a manager'.[2]

Bibeault, the author of the most significant American study in this field, describes a corporate turnaround as 'a substantial and sustained positive change in the performance of a business'. This author estimated that over the period 1967–76 370 or 9 per cent of the 4,000 US Standard & Poor's companies (representing 70 per cent of US corporate assets) had experienced a turnaround in terms of net earnings losses or severe (80 per cent or more) earnings declines followed by recovery.[3] Equally interestingly the figure of 370 turnaround situations may be compared with that of the 1,100 cases out of 4,000 over the period where losses or severe earnings declines occurred. In other words, while turnaround situations are quite important relative to the total number of businesses, a disappointingly small proportion – about one-third – of firms requiring such treatment is actually saved.[4] So far as British data are concerned Argenti has suggested that in the early 1970s, at any one time 50,000 companies or 10 per cent of registered firms were in a state of failure, thus adding weight to his argument that relative to the importance of the phenomenon, corporate collapse and recovery is vastly underrepresented in the management literature.[5]

Bibeault's own thumbnail sketch of the turnaround situation is as follows:

The extended absence of properly timed, fresh management input causes the firm a slow but sure inevitable decline – first in gross margins, then in new orders, backlog, sales, and, finally, return on investment. The firm will then fail to invest (as a stop-gap measure to avoid pressing cash problems) and continue toward bottom line losses and ultimate oblivion. However, when sleepy or complacent management is replaced by new and eager management, this trend is reversed dramatically. Losses are stopped, employee morale is rebuilt, customer confidence is regained, and the company returns to robust and healthy growth. It sounds so easy, but in reality it is not easy at all.[6]

Our approach to analysing the business turnaround situation is to ask why the need for such action should occur in the first instance, and to consider in more detail the way in which corporate turnaround is achieved. This is followed by a consideration of a small number of actual cases of turnaround in the UK, both in order to make some general comparisons among these and also to compare them as a group with the analysis contained in the American literature. We shall also have some observations to make on the importance of strategy-making and strategic decision-makers to business success.

12.2 Business Failure or Decline

There are two broad approaches to analysing company failure. The first is based upon an examination of certain accounting ratios in an attempt to predict business failure. A group of such ratios may be combined in order to produce a single numerical indicator, the best example of this being the z-score technique developed by Altman.[7] Taffler, one of the foremost exponents of this technique in the UK, summarises the approach as follows:

> **By calculating a number of appropriately chosen financial ratios derived from the last set of published accounts, or in the course of an audit from pro-forma statements, weighting each and adding, the degree of solvency or otherwise of a business is exposed for all to see. If the z-score is above a cut-off, i.e., if it lies above the solvency threshold ($z = 0$) on the 'solvency thermometer', the comany is solvent and will not fail in the next year. However, if its z-score lies in the 'at risk' region, the company has the financial characteristics of previous failures, and recent experience indicates that this heralds a more than 50/50 chance of financial distress in due course.[8]**

The z-score in a four-independent-variable form appears to be a very good predictor of business failure. For example, one analysis of z-scores in 1983 showed that of those listed UK firms in manufacturing and construction which in 1976 had z-scores below zero, 43 per cent had failed financially and a further 29 per cent were still at risk. Using 1980 data, a company with a negative z-score at the beginning of the year had a one-third chance of failing by the end. By contrast, firms with positive z-scores exhibited a negligible risk of failure. Furthermore by computing z-scores for all companies in a particular product-market sector and comparing those of a single firm over a number of years, considerable advance warning of business failure can be obtained.

The z-score approach is not, however, designed to explain business failure. The independent variables in the z-score equation are financial ratios, including for example profitability and short-term liquidity. A poor performance in these respects is the outcome of poor strategy and thus not the fundamental cause of business failure. Analysis of the z-score factors alone is thus not likely to lead to improved business performance. In an attempt to examine some of the likely fundamental causes of business failure we must look at the topic from the point of view of corporate strategy. In terms of strategic decision-making, businesses decline because the policies they are following are not appropriate to their environment and resources. Either the environment has changed in such a way as to invalidate a strategy that was originally correct, or it may transpire that the original strategy itself was incorrect for the firm's circumstances. Bibeault recognises the former possibility – obsolete strategy as a result of changes in the environment – as being particularly likely in an era of increasingly rapid economic, technological and social change. Such changes may arise in the general environment in terms of macroeconomic decline or changes in social variables. Alternatively, there may be adverse developments in task environment features leading to increased competition. These 'external' factors, however, would appear to account for only a relatively small proportion of business failures. The results of Bibeault's survey of company chief executives indicate that in their view only 33 per cent at most of business declines could be attributed directly to such external factors, while on the other hand 52 per cent were ascribed by the same chief executives to 'internally generated problems within management's control'.[9] The study by Schendel *et al.* also found that neither business failure nor recovery could be explained by reference to the industry of the individual firms, thus implying the importance of management or internal factors in such situations.[10] These findings simply emphasise that businesses are not necessarily the prisoners of their general or specific (task) environments, but that the key to business success or failure is the quality of the strategic reaction by firms to their environments.[11] As Argenti puts it, 'The prime cause of [business] failure is bad management. Good managers will seldom make the same fatal mistakes as poor managers'.[12] These management failings may range from downright incompetence, lack of management depth, or inadequate financial control, to failure to carry out any strategic decision-making. The errors that Bibeault highlights are failure to keep pace with changes in the product market, lack of business controls, over-expansion, excessive diversification, and poor financial policies.[13]

As a result of research in this area a number of factors have been identified which typically are associated with business failure. Study of such phenomena is designed to provide practising business people with a list of 'don'ts' or warning signals regarding corporate decline. These common themes from individual studies of corporate failure are well represented in Argenti's writing. Drawing upon his own studies and also upon American material, Argenti puts forward a comprehensive list of what he refers to as causes and symptoms of corporate collapse, and these are set out in Table 12.1 below.[14]

Argenti's conclusion is that businesses that exhibit the fundamental weaknesses set out in Table 12.1 by breaking some of his apparent management rules, by being ignorant of constraints or unresponsive to change, by not collecting or using appropriate accounting information, or by failing to cope with normal business hazards, or through committing what he refers to as gross errors, are likely to fail. Such businesses may also be identified through an examination of certain accounting ratios, by their indulging in unconventional accounting practices, or by the low morale or unhealthy management attitudes that they exhibit. The problem, however, with Argenti's list of causes and symptoms – twenty-one individual aspects – is that it merely amounts to a series of errors encountered in unsuccessful businesses.[15] Not only is there no indication of the relative importance of these features and what degree of error is likely to lead to corporate failure, but businesses can also exhibit some of these failings – for example, one-man rule – and achieve considerable success. Indeed, so extensive is the list of failings that there must be few if any companies which have not committed some of them! Such a comprehensive shopping list of

Table 12.1
Causes and Symptoms of Corporate Collapse

Causes

Management:

One-man rule
Non-participating board
Unbalanced top team
Weak finance function
Lack of management depth
Combining of role of chairman
  and chief executive

Constraints:

Social pressures
Government intervention

Gross errors:

Overtrading
'The Big Project'
Excessive gearing

Accountancy information:

Budgetary control
Cash flow forecasts
Costing systems
Valuation of assets

Response to change:

Competitive trends
Political change
Economic change
Societal change
Technological change

Normal business hazards:

Symptoms

Creative accounting:

Delays in publication
Capitalisation of recurrent costs

Financial ratios:

Non-financial symptoms:

Low morale
Management attitudes

strategic and management errors, although it offers scope for a more fundamental approach to understanding business failure than z-score analysis, is likely to do little more than provide managers with a checklist of possible danger areas in making strategic decisions. Nonetheless, in the light of some of the strategic errors which we shall come across below in our case studies of business failure and turnaround, it is clear that many firms could benefit from this approach.

The point is that the root of business decline is overwhelmingly management or strategic inadequacy. Correspondingly turnaround is a management issue, and can only be achieved by a strategic rethink for the business. Having emphasised the place of management or strategic variables in corporate decline, we shall now examine the sequence of decision-making in the turnaround situation.

12.3 The Corporate Turnaround Process

This section is concerned with the way in which management can turn poor business performance into good. It is concerned with the process involved in the turnaround situation where the major reason for a reversal of a company's poor performance is positive rather than a fortuitous favourable change in the firm's environment. Happily some firms do experience turnaround as a result of the demise of a major competitor or a sudden upsurge in the level of demand, and well-managed businesses should, of course, take advantage of such good fortune. Our concern here, however, is to examine how, unaided by such favourable changes in their environment, managements can effect a business turnaround.

Bibeault identifies five discrete stages in the turnaround process: recognition, evaluation, emergency, stabilisation, and return to normal growth.[16] The first stage, *recognition*, quite simply involves the business in recognising the full extent of its present problems. These have to be accepted as serious rather than minor, permanent rather than temporary, strategic rather than operational or administrative, and the result of previous management error rather than bad luck. Not until these facts have been faced and the truths recognised – which is by no means easy or palatable for the incumbent management – is the firm even in a potential turnaround situation. Indeed, the absence of such recognition or acceptance of the situation probably explains the delay in taking necessary action, and may also be one of the reasons for which most business turnarounds involve a change of management.

Evaluation, the second stage in the turnaround process, is an essential step to take prior to implementation of a new strategy despite the obvious time pressure in a turnaround situation. Evaluation involves an assessment of the seriousness of the firm's difficulties, the dimensions of the firm's environment and resources which are most responsible for the current difficulties, and the key direction in which the potential future success of the business lies. This is followed by the formulation of a broad recovery plan for the firm and the communication of this throughout the organisation.

One of the reasons for the relatively rapid rate at which evaluation must be carried out is the necessity for turnaround management to take *emergency action*, the third stage in the process. Indeed there must be a strong temptation for management to undertake emergency action before a complete evaluation. The question of precedence is a matter of degree, however, and although it is necessary to carry out an evaluation before major emergency decisions are made, minor but nonetheless significant resource savings can often be made at a very early stage in the turnaround process prior to a full evaluation being completed. Indeed, as in the case of post-merger rationalisation, there may be a psychological advantage to be gained in carrying out some savings at an early stage. This sort of action is almost expected of the turnaround manager, and such behaviour may be welcomed by employees in the organisation as indicating that the manager 'means business'. Thus, according to one writer, 'Experience indicates that the existing management will usually expect and want immediate action from the new man. Furthermore, people expect the action to be tough'.[17] Emergency action involves staunching the flow, to use the surgical metaphor so commonly adopted in this context. Such action most dramatically involves minimising cash outflow and maximising cash inflow: reducing current expenses (most frequently shopfloor wages) and realising cash from surplus assets. It is in respect of the latter programme that it is essential for evaluation to have preceded emergency action lest the goose which is potentially capable of laying the golden eggs is jettisoned along with less valuable corporate assets. That is, although in general there must be an emphasis on cutting back in all areas of the business, cutbacks in product development, marketing, etc. in sectors that are going to be crucial for the recovery of the firm are even in the medium term counterproductive. Emergency action, however, is a situation in which inevitably the short term has to take priority over the long. At this stage cash flow is more important than profitability, and actual survival the essence of the operation.

Once the emergency action has ensured its current survival, the business can turn to *stabilisation* – stage four in the turnaround process. This is the activity of returning the remaining business to profitability, maintaining pressure on all expenditures, and considering the future of the organisation. Management can and must at this stage make the necessary strategic decisions to carry the business forward to the final return-to-growth stage. The firm as part of the stabilisation stage realigns itself to its environment in the light of the assessment of its resources, making strategic decisions that are an improvement upon those which were originally responsible for the decline in the fortunes of the business. The final *return-to-growth* phase in the recovery process involves strengthening the balance sheet of the organisation, and generally preparing for selective additions to the firm's activities designed to enhance profits and sales at an acceptable degree of risk.

Although it is not possible to indicate precisely how long each of these five stages in the turnaround process should last, they represent an ordered sequence in which the whole process should be carried out. In order to take our understanding of the process further we shall now consider three short case histories of business turnaround, and base some of our conclusions in this chapter upon these and other examples of UK corporate turnaround situations.

12.4 Turnaround Case Histories

Ferranti

The case of Ferranti provides an example of a number of the phenomena of corporate collapse and turnaround.[18] Throughout this century Ferranti enjoyed a world-wide reputation in the electrical and electronic engineering industry. For Ferranti, however, technical excellence was accompanied by 'slipshod financial management', an overdependence upon government contracts, and a reluctance to move into new growth markets such as computing, while remaining more heavily committed to transformers on which the firm had been losing money for years. It was in fact the virtual collapse of orders for heavy electrical equipment from the CEGB in the late 1960s and the general impact of the recession of the early 1970s, combined with the company's heavy dependence upon short-term loans, that necessitated the £15 million rescue of the firm by the National Enterprise Board (NEB) in 1974. Under this financial umbrella, and with a new managing director installed by the NEB, Ferranti moved steadily from a pre-tax loss of £½ million in 1975 to profits of £9.8 million in 1978, while not quite doubling its sales figure. Although it may be argued that some of the urgency of the Ferranti turnaround was obviated by the financial involvement of the government via the NEB – some of which was in fact conditional on the maintenance of certain operations and of employment – the history of the firm during the late 1970s bears many of the hallmarks of the classic turnaround situation. Most obvious was the change in management – the bringing in of a new managing director and the installation of two additional board members by the NEB. Even more significant was the changed atmosphere regarding financial management. The new chief executive was reported as having brought to the firm 'a healthy respect for cash control' and a 'heavy emphasis on strict financial reporting'. One interesting aspect of this apparent change in the management philosophy of the company is that not only was there no resistance to it on the part of incumbent senior management, but that it was positively welcomed by those who for years had been critical of the previous financial systems (or lack of them) and who appreciated the benefits of operating within a set of clearly defined limits and objectives. Thus in the words of the new managing director and a *Management Today* writer,

> **I felt I had to change the atmosphere . . . I regard my job here as balancing the engineering judgment of my managers with a totally commerical approach. I assigned profit responsibility, set a lot of targets, and formalised planning and budget procedures.' Introducing genuine financial discipline to a company unaccustomed to such rigours is a notoriously difficult task. But, if the testimony of his senior managers is to be believed, Alun-Jones has succeeded without wholesale sackings or a completely new team.[19]**

Nonetheless the Ferranti turnaround was characterised by some
divestment and redundancy. The Canadian subsidiary was disposed of, as were peripheral activities such as cathode ray tube
manufacture and a helicopter operating business. It is more
difficult to discern any new direction in which Ferranti has gone as
a result of its turnaround. The company is perhaps now best
considered as a relatively small-scale avionics group continuing to
depend for its success upon technological flair, but combining with
this a much higher level of financial expertise, with the company
now shorn of its previous less related, low growth and unprofitable
interests. Turnaround has in this case introduced (or liberated) a
higher standard of financial management, forced the group to
divest itself of products that were less relevant to its core expertise,
and which in some cases were maintained because of historical
attachment, and refocused the business in high-technology growth
areas which fit best with its unique resources.

Montague Burton

Burton provides an example of corporate turnaround without
government intervention.[20] This vertically integrated menswear
group was established in 1900 by Sir Montague Burton and
controlled by its founder until his death in 1952, at which time the
firm had a 25 per cent share of the UK made-to-measure suit
market. A degree of succession to the founder was achieved by
Burton's takeover of Jackson the Tailor, whose family managers,
the Jacobsons, provided management until the late 1960s, when a
new outside team of professional managers was brought in by the
Jacobsons pending their own retirement. In the early 1970s Burton
found itself dependent for 86 per cent of its sales upon a static
market (made-to-measure suits) – one which was increasingly in
the hands of the under-30 age group. In response to this situation
the new management team embarked upon a seemingly obvious
course of operational and strategic improvements. The standard of
financial and property management expertise in the business was
improved, the former management information system having
been described as 'rudimentary, slow and short on detail'. The
company expanded the existing womenswear side of the firm

through the acquisition of Evans (Outsizes) at the same time as divesting itself of loss-making operations such as mail order (which at this time was losing £½ million each year) together with certain stores. Burton also began diversifying out of clothing altogether, for example through the purchase in the early 1970s of Ryman Conran, the office furniture manufacturers, and Greens Leisure Centres, the camera and hi-fi chain. The company also began to expand overseas through clothing manufacture and retailing in France and retailing in Belgium. Surprisingly, however, this policy turned out to be the prelude to a dramatic collapse of profits in the mid 1970s: from a pre-tax £8.7 million in 1973 to £1.3 million in 1975.

The basic problems for the group had been a failure to establish the respective roles of the Burton manufacturing and retailing operations (shops were in fact regarded as ordering points for the output of the factories), continued loss of custom in menswear as Burton failed to react sufficiently rapidly to changing patterns of custom, and the poor performance of the diversified and overseas interests. Referring to the absence of management concentration on the essence of the business, one writer summarised this period for Burton in concluding: 'The net effect of the diversification programme was to distract top management attention from the pressing problem of what to do with the Menswear part of the Group'.[21]

The turnaround at Burton which commenced in 1975 was precipitated by an unusual external agency: a firm of stockbrokers specialising in the retail trade issued to its institutional clients a highly critical report on the company. In reaction to this Burton sold off loss-making and peripheral operations, ninety unprofitable stores were closed, stockholding was considerably reduced, surplus properties were disposed of (these and staff reductions reportedly saving 'several millions'), and some senior managers left. The Burton group emerged from the turnaround with an explicit retailing orientation and a concentration on the range of clothing demanded by its customers, particularly younger buyers. The result of this action was that from the £1.3 million pre-tax profits of 1975 and the losses of 1976 and 1977, the firm returned to profits of £6 million in 1978 and £17.5 million in 1979.

Certain similarities emerge from the two business turnarounds described above. While the need for turnaround in both cases occurred at a time of generally poor economic conditions, there is no doubt that the major difficulties faced by these firms arose from management strategy and performance. Again in both cases a prime incentive to remedy business weaknesses came from outside the organisation: from its bankers it the case of Ferranti, and from a stockbroker in the case of Burton. In a number of respects, however, Burton represents a different turnaround situation from that of Ferranti. In particular, while some of the problems at Ferranti arose from the continued operation of an outdated approach to the business originating with the controlling family, in the case of Burton the need for a turnaround was brought about by new, professional managers implementing what appeared to be an exemplary changed strategy. This highlights the fact that it is quite possible for a younger group of managers to put a business into a situation where turnaround is required, just as it is often these people who effect a necessary rescue.

Dawson International

The case of Dawson International, the high-quality textile manufacturers, represents another instance of management implementing one seemingly appropriate strategy only to find that it has thereby created a need for considerable changes in the opposite direction if the business is to survive and prosper. In the case of Dawson, a significant drop in profits in the early 1970s (from £2.7 million in 1969 to £380,000 in 1971) followed a period of rapid expansion, including vertical integration, under a single dominant chief executive. The reorganisation that followed involved the introduction of centralised management and financial control systems, and in the wake of this profits recovered, rising to £3.1 million in 1973. Dawson too, however, became a victim of the mid-1970s downturn in the economy. But as in the cases of Ferranti and Burton, the difficult macroeconomic conditions merely exaggerated what turned out to have been inappropriate management decisions. In the case of Dawson management centralisation did not appear to work. According to one senior executive, 'At head office, we had too many cooks spoiling the broth. There were a lot of people not taking responsibility for anything. There was a lot of information around, but it wasn't being used'.[22]

As well as expanding corporate headquarters staff from virtually nil to more than forty the company had embarked upon a programme of diversification away from its previous commitment to top-quality yarns and knitwear. In the mid-1970s Dawson experienced another massive drop in profits: from £6.2 million in 1974 to £500,000 before extraordinary losses in 1975. Despite centralised control the firm proved to be extremely exposed to changes in demand. Furthermore, the new management system had not only created additional head-office costs but had also produced a situation at the local level where, according to another senior executive, 'About 70% of management's time was spent trying to get round the restrictions'.[23] Nor were the firm's diversification moves, which had helped to increase bank borrowing to high levels, the success which had been hoped for. The predictable result of this fall in profits was the virtually total disbanding of the head office, the disposal of some of the less logical acquisitions, and in particular stringent profit decentralisation combined with significant rewards for the achievement of profit targets. In the words of the chairman, 'I said to my managing directors, "You're running the group now", and built a substantial incentive scheme, and demanded that they either perform or get out'.[24] The results of these changes appear to be impressive, with turnover up almost three times from 1975 to the end of the decade and profits for 1980 of £18.2 million. Thus Dawson has twice in a decade had to undertake its own recovery from a significant decline in profitability caused not simply by a difficult macroeconomic environment but by inappropriate management decisions. This case illustrates again that on occasions the same management team has to accept not only the credit for achieving a business turnaround but also the blame for originating the crisis situation!

From these three examples above and others, a number of common features of business failure and turnaround emerge. Companies fail, in the sense either of going into liquidation or experiencing a significant drop in earnings, not simply as a result of a difficult general environment but because of circumstances internal to the firm. These circumstances fall into three groups: poor strategy, inadequate or inappropriate business control, and a miscellaneous category including in our examples unwise diversification. Thus Ferranti and Burton had both failed to react adequately to a changing demand for their output. They followed an unaltered strategy when their task environment had changed. ICL too, which experienced a dramatic turnaround between 1979 and 1983, had made two fundamental strategic errors. It tried to compete on the same basis as the giant IBM despite having a sales turnover of only 3 per cent of the latter, whose research and development budget matches ICL's sales; and it failed to react to the movement in its market from mainframe computers to distributed data processing.[25] We would argue that this is the major cause of business failure: an improper response by the firm to its environment – typically, a failure to change the business strategy as the environment itself changes. In addition to this, however, failing businesses are also characterised by a lack of financial or cost control. This was admitted to be the case at Ferranti and Burton; and in the case of ICL the firm appears to have been unduly optimistic in the way in which it depreciated the value of the computers it leased and was liable to have to buy back from customers.[26] Paradoxically Dawson's problems in the mid-1970s were made worse by excessive centralisation of management in a market in which rapid response to changes was essential. Thus poor strategic reaction to the environment is aggravated, and perhaps in some cases contributed to, by poor control of the organisation either in terms of financial discipline or organisation structure.

Finally, failing firms may also exhibit other strategic or organisational flaws, the one most obviously identified in our own limited survey being the irrelevant and distracting diversification policies pursued by Burton and Dawson. By contrast the actual turnaround process appears to vary from one situation to another. The stimuli for change may be internal or external, and the direction of change will of course vary as necessary according to the circumstances of the business. In some cases these changes will appear to come about fairly slowly, as in the case of Ferranti, and there may be little apparent drama in the situation. In other instances there may be a more sweeping and comprehensive change in the organisation. According to *Management Today* 'But for the familiar logo on the door (itself planned to go), the "new" ICL (as it is constantly referred to within the company) might well be mistaken for a completely different group. Hardly any of the top 20 executives of two years ago have survived; the corporate strategies which the all-new management is implementing are unrecognizable; the company style, its ethos, can't be compared'.[27]

The examples above are of instances in which a business turnaround was achieved; and the point has been made that management action was a crucial element in the turnaround process. Two American authors have examined turnaround policies more rigorously by matching thirty-six pairs of turnaround and non-turnaround businesses over the period 1952–71 and observing differences in the performance and policies of the successful and unsuccessful firm in each pair. The essence of the comparisons was, of course, that in all other respects such as opening size and industry classification each of the two firms in the pair was very similar.[28] The quantitative results of this study indicate that in their recovery phase turnaround businesses increased their investment significantly more rapidly than those firms that did not recover. For successful businesses, moreover, sales increased more rapidly than investment, increasing the capital turnover ratio and reducing the level of unit fixed costs. At the same time the ratio of cost of goods sold to sales decreased for turnaround firms and increased for their paired comparator. Although successful turnaround firms did experience much greater cash flow requirements than unsuccessful firms, their increased market share and superior performance in the remainder of the indicators above enabled them significantly to outperform the non-turnaround firms during the recovery phase. Particular differences brought out in multiple regression analysis of the respective performances of these two groups of firms are that whereas the superior profitability of the successful firms is accounted for by their increased sales and investment levels, the much less satisfactory profit levels of non-turnaround businesses are associated with efficiency measures such as profit margins, capital turnover and sales per employee. That is, business turnaround is associated by comparison with failure with increasing sales and investment while maintaining profit margins, as opposed to an over-concern with partial measures of business efficiency. Successful firms in some broad sense spend their way out of corporate recession. This, to the extent that it involves them in expanding sales, increasing market share and investing efficiently (expanding sales levels more rapidly than investment) implies superior management performance in a range of dimensions. By contrast, non-turnaround firms were not able to make such successful management decisions. This again appears to emphasise the vital role of management in the turnaround situation.

12.5 Conclusions

Reference to the litereature and to the individual examples in this chapter indicates that the causes of business decline and turnaround are varied. A number of common features nonetheless stand out. Despite the obvious impact that difficult macroeconomic or individual sector circumstances have upon businesses, corporate decline on any scale is not explained entirely by reference to such external events. The brief case histories above of Ferranti, Burton and Dawson International in particular reveal more fundamental management errors. Specifically these and other businesses in decline had lost touch with their markets, had become less efficient in operational terms, had in some cases strayed unsuccessfully into diversified product-market areas, and almost uniformly lacked adequate information regarding the monitoring and control of the business. Old, loss-making products were retained, new market areas neglected, and cost levels allowed to rise above those of competitors. In many cases management attempted to operate the business without possessing the necessary accounting information. It was thus a combination of these internal factors together with adverse external circumstances that precipitated business decline.[29] In order to bring about a potential turnaround situation these management shortcomings and adverse economic circumstances have to combine to reveal themselves in a dramatic downturn in the fortunes of the business; and in the cases of Ferranti and Burton it was necessary for the firm to be faced with the prospect of bankruptcy or to have its poor performance publicised by a third party before corrective action was initiated.

This illustrates one of the more severe management problems associated with turnaround situations. Management too often fails to react appropriately to a series of events that is potentially threatening, and sees these as short-term and caused by an unfortunate change in the external environment. This situation is met by a 'tighter' implementation of the firm's existing strategy, including some improvements in operating efficiency. Managers, particularly those whose experience is limited to one industry, may be reluctant to admit that poor business performance is due to inadequate strategic decision-making, and that recovery on the part of the firm may demand the formulation and implementation of radically different strategies. It is for this reason – the need to introduce new strategic thinking into the organisation – rather than because previous management has been totally incompetent, that business turnaround is often accompanied by the introduction of new senior management.

Both in the case of business failure and recovery, management and strategic decision-making emerge as fundamental variables. Thus although there are a large number of possible causes of business failure, including adverse changes in the external environment, the studies considered in Section 12.1 of this chapter emphasise the crucial role of management failure. Slatter, too, in a very recent study of forty UK business recoveries; found that lack of financial control and 'inadequate management' occurred as causal factors in three-quarters of his sample, by far exceeding in importance other factors such as changes in environmental variables.[30] In recovery also those businesses that are successfully turned round have to rely upon superior management rather than fortuitous changes in their environment. Thus Grinyer and Spender have emphasisd in their analysis of the turnaround of a number of ailing subsidiary operations in one engineering group that, 'Tight, financial control is simply not enough. While it minimises losses and clarifies the ailing firm's situation, it cannot be the basis for revival. This comes only from entrepreneurship, the development and implementation of more pertinent corporate recipes . . . The key to the turnaround ultimately lies in management'.[31] Slatter particularly emphasises that 'one big difference between recovery situations that are successful and those that fail is in the *quality* of implementation'.[32] In simple business policy language business failure is management failure to react appropriately or adequately to the firm's environment or to develop and exploit its resources, while business recovery is the result of a successful new analysis of these variables.

This, not surprisingly, brings us back to the importance for business success of analysing those factors upon which so much emphasis was placed in Chapter 3 of this text. By carrying out such an analysis of the business environment and the strengths and weaknesses of the organisation, management should be able to anticipate and react to changes, assess the quality of its resources, and make the necessary strategic decisions which avoid the need for the total, and not always successful, upheaval that has so often to take place if failing business is to be turned round.

References

1. See P. Bohr, 'Chrysler's Pie-in-the-Sky Plan for Survival', *Fortune*, 22 October 1979, pp. 46–52.
2. P. F. Drucker, *Management: Tasks, Responsibilities, Practices* (New York: Harper & Row, 1974) p. 49.
3. See D. B. Bibeault, *Corporate Turnaround* (New York: McGraw-Hill, 1982) pp. 10–11 and 82–3.
4. Data for an earlier, longer period but using a more restrictive definition of failure and turnaround suggest that over the 1952–71 period 37 per cent of the 1,800 Standard & Poor firms suffered a decline in net earnings relative to GNP, while only 68 of those firms (10 per cent of the failures, 4 per cent of the total sample) experienced a turnaround. See D. Schendel *et al.*, 'Corporate Turnaround Strategies: A Study of Profit Decline and Recovery', *Journal of General Management*, Spring 1976, Vol. III, p. 4.
5. See J. Argenti, *Corporate Collapse: The Causes and Symptoms* (London: McGraw-Hill, 1976) p. 6.
6. Bibeault, *Corporate Turnaround*, pp. 81–2.
7. See E. L. Altman, 'Financial Ratios, Discriminant Analysis and the Prediction of Corporate Bankruptcy', *Journal of Finance*, September 1968, Vol. XXIII, pp. 589–609.
8. R. J. Taffler, 'The Z-Score Approach to Measuring Company Solvency', *The Accountant's Magazine,* March 1983, p. 91.
9. Bibeault, *Corporate Turnaround*, p. 25.
10. See Schendel *et al.*, 'Corporate Turnaround Strategies', pp. 4–5.
11. See, for instance, the examples of how selected businesses have coped with difficult environments in D. K. Clifford Jr., 'Thriving in a Recession', *Harvard Business Review*, July–August 1977, pp. 57–65; and W. K. Hall, 'Survival Strategies in a Hostile Environment', *Harvard Business Review*, September–October 1980, pp. 75–85.
12. Argenti, *Corporate Collapse*, p. 122.
13. See Bibeault, *Corporate Turnaround*, Ch. 6.
14. See Argenti, *Corporate Collapse*, Ch. 7.
15. In fact they appear to be largely taken from the American study by J. E. Ross and M. J. Kami, *Corporate Management in Crisis: Why the Mighty Fall* (Englewood Cliffs: Prentice-Hall, 1973).
16. See Bibeault, *Corporate Turnaround*, Ch. 10.

17. B. Pearson, 'How to Manage Turnrounds', *Management Today*, April 1977, p. 75.
18. The material in the following pages is based largely upon D. Manasian, 'How Ferranti Fought Back', *Management Today*, January 1980, pp. 66ff.
19. *Ibid.*, p. 70.
20. This example is based upon T. Lester, 'The Retailoring of Burton', *Management Today*, February 1980, pp. 43ff; and the Burton Group Ltd case in J. M. Stopford *et al.*, *British Business Policy* (London: Macmillan, 1975) pp. 152–71.
21. H. Sharman, 'Tailor-Made Disaster at Burton', *Marketing*, September 1977, p. 25.
22. Quoted in N. Newman, 'Dawson's Well-Knit Whoosh', *Management Today*, March 1981, p. 78, upon which article this material on Dawson is based.
23. *Ibid.*, p. 78.
24. *Ibid.*, p. 79.
25. In the case of ICL pre-tax profits fell from a figure approaching £50 million in 1978 to losses of an equal magnitude in 1981. These recovered to a profit of £24 million in 1982 and £46 million in 1983. See N. Newman, 'Key Crunch at ICL', *Management Today*, February 1983, pp. 58ff; and 'ICL Fights for a Place in the Sun', *Financial Times*, 30 March 1984.
26. Newman, 'Key Crunch at ICL', p. 62.
27. *Ibid.*, p. 60.
28. For an account of the methodology of the study and the detailed results, see D. E. Schendel and G. R. Patton, 'Corporate Stagnation and Turnaround', *Journal of Economics and Business*, 1976, Vol. XXVIII, pp. 236–41.
29. See Schendel *et al.*, 'Corporate Turnaround Strategies', pp. 10–11.
30. See S. Slatter, *Corporate Recovery* (Harmondsworth: Penguin, 1984) p. 53. This chapter was in final draft form before the publication of Slatter's study, and it has not been possible to draw significantly upon this excellent study of UK business recoveries.
31. P. H. Grinyer and J–C. Spender, *Turnaround – Managerial Recipes for Strategic Success* (London: Associated Business Press, 1979) pp. 83 and 123.
32. Slatter, *Corporate Recovery* p. 121.

Conclusions

13

When the simplicity and intuitive appeal of strategic planning are combined with its promise to solve the problem of uncertainty facing professional managers, the rapid adoption of the concept is quite understandable. Nevertheless, after a decade or more of experience, it is reasonable to ask whether strategic planning has lived up to its promises and, if not, in what ways it has failed. — R. N. Paul *et al.*, 'The Reality Gap in Strategic Planning', *Harvard Business Review*, May–June 1978, p. 125.

13.1 Introduction

The purpose of this text has been to analyse and illustrate the way in which corporate strategy decisions should be taken. The explicit belief in writing such a text is that these decisions are important for individual businesses, and thereby for the economy as a whole. Moreover it is argued that the strategic decision-making process analysed here offers a more logical, systematic and effective way of arriving at corporate policy decisions than other less formal or intuitive systems.

13.2 Reservations

Studying the literature in the area of corporate strategy in the process of writing this text, one is conscious of a number of strands of criticism of the approach to the subject adopted here. First, there is still a view held by some business people that flair and intuition on the part of senior managers are more important than adherence to a formal system of corporate strategic decision-making. Sometimes this criticism is merely dismissive of the value of the formal process of strategic decision-making. Commenting on the causes of the undoubted success of Sainsbury in the grocery retailing market, the managing director was recently quoted as saying, 'We certainly did not sit down in the early 1970s and work out any corporate plan, or say that by a particular time we intended to be in a particular business or to be of a particular size'.[1] More vigorously, and around the time of his move from the chief general managership of the Abbey National Building Society to become managing director of Mirror Group Newspapers, Clive Thornton spoke of 'a corporate cancer of startling proportions which is assiduously eating away at the very foundations of business success'. The source of this disease?

> **The culprit in my view is all too clear: top management has allowed itself to be shackled by over-reliance on so-called management sciences, on analyses and gargantuan reports, on long-winded committees, detailed job descriptions and structure plans. It has forgotten the basic rules of success in business: simplicity, flexibility, action.[2]**

But these and similar criticisms appear to be based upon a dislike of the bureaucracy associated with corporate planning rather than a distrust of the concept itself. They are an argument for decentralisation of some decision-making in business and a possible relocation of some parts of strategy-making rather than the abolition of the practice altogether.

Indeed, for every business criticism of the concept and practices of corporate strategy there are examples in the press of companies going through the very process of identifying opportunities and threats and assessing their strengths and weaknesses in the manner described in this text. Among the most recently reported of these at the time of writing is that of British Home Stores, whose new executive chairman Sir Maurice Hodgson – 'the ex-ICI man, a brilliant corporate planner' – has presided over a rethinking of the store's role in a world of changing demand from its customers, and in the context of its rivals Marks & Spencer, Littlewoods, and Woolworth.[3] The group appears to have gone through a process of reassessing its product range, the customers to whom it is trying to appeal, and the presentation of its stores in an effort to maximise its performance in the market relative to its competitors. By contrast the emphasis upon corporate planning at GEC appears to be limited. The function is diffused in part throughout the organisation but essentially centred upon the managing director, Lord Weinstock, whose emphasis upon current business efficiency in terms of financial indicators was epitomised by a former GEC chairman's reference to Lord Weinstock's role being to 'mind the shop'.[4] According to the *Financial Times*, 'GEC has no elaborate mechanisms for formulating overall strategy. Its Stanhope Gate offices are leanly staffed, and central management style leans strongly towards pragmatism, responding to opportunities – often proposed from within the group – rather than spending long hours drawing up detailed blueprints for future development'.[5] While none can deny the impressive growth by GEC since the late 1960s, the build-up of a massive £1.6 billion cash reserve, apparently unclear policy on growth or divestment (including the on-off acquisition discussions with British Aerospace in the summer of 1984), and the firm's cautious approach in some markets such as information technology suggest that a reliance upon pragmatism for policy-making is insufficient.

A second criticism of corporate strategy as it has been developed in this text, and which again has come largely from practising business people, is concerned with an overselling of the possible benefits of the process. It is argued that the earlier commercial sellers of corporate strategy misled their clients into believing that it could do more for them than was reasonably possible. Corporate strategy was reduced to an over-simple list of concepts such as the product-portfolio matrix, the learning curve, and the association between market share and return on investment.[6] Writing of the reaction to this by the early 1980s in the United States, on journalist commented, 'if the apostles (of corporate strategy) have fallen on slightly hard times, the object of their devotion – the concept of strategy itself – is positively bedraggled'.[7] In particular corporate planning has been criticised for depending too much on quantitative analysis, which is now becoming less possible in an increasingly turbulent set of general and task environments for most firms.[8] The root of this second criticism of corporate strategy is thus not that the exercise is not worthwhile, but that business people may have been misled in taking on board a set of tools that are too simple for the task and some of which may be quite misleading or incapable of being realistically applied. Practising corporate strategists who were at one time highly receptive to the new techniques, now realise, as they perhaps should have done all along, that setting up Strategic Business Units (SBUs), filling in a product portfolio matrix, or being aware of the impact of learning curves does not of itself make good strategy. Indeed, we have pointed out in Chapter 5 above that certain strategic relationships such as the link between market share and return on investment are not invariable, and we have provided examples of firms achieving enviable records of profitability and growth in mature markets in which they hold low market shares.[9]

What surely cannot be disputed by any critics, however, is the appropriateness and the applicability of the intellectual building blocks of corporate strategy such as SWOT analysis and the sequence of strategic implementation covered in Chapter 6 above, or the value of the whole process of strategic planning. An understanding of strategy-making has allowed top management to take an overall view of the organisation; it has allowed these people to isolate from the vast amount of data available the key variables upon which the success of a business depends; and it has arguably permitted the successful development of large multi-product businesses beyond the point at which managerial diseconomies of scale were earlier assumed to inhibit expansion. Furthermore, it has potentially restored the most senior management to a position of power in the organisation in contrast to the Galbraithian picture of those at the top of the firm occupying largely honorific and ceremonial positions, 'rubber stamping' decisions made within Galbraith's technostructure.[10] We would thus argue that sensibly and realistically applied corporate strategy is an essential tool for senior management in any organisation.

A third criticism of corporate strategy, which has gained further momentum from the Peters and Waterman study, *In Search of Excellence*, is that it is only a partial approach to ensuring business success.[11] Corporate strategy as discussed in this text, it is argued, is over-concerned with the management science, quantifiable dimensions of the determinants of business performance. Critics of this approach argue that in addition to the 'hard S's' of strategy and structure, business success comes from attention to the 'soft' aspects of systems, skills, staff, style and shared values. Peters and Waterman themelves analysed sixty-two US companies which were selected on the basis of superior growth and profit performance over the period 1961–80. They found that associated with these companies, and presumably explaining their superior performance, were certain fundamental characteristics referred to by the authors as A Bias for Action, Close to the Customer, Autonomy and Entrepreneurship, Stick to the Knitting, etc. The case of the two authors is that it is by having regard to these values in an organisation, and in particular by ensuring that they are shared across the business, that firms succeed, thus reinforcing the authors' earlier research finding that 'companies whose only articulated goals were financial did not do nearly so well financially as companies that had broader sets of values'.[12]

It would be hard to disagree with much of what Peters and Waterman say in their example-upon-example analysis. Indeed we recognised in Chapter 6 of this text the importance in strategic implementation of some of the 'soft S's', such as the need to choose managers to suit a particular strategy, the requirement to motivate managers in accordance with the chosen strategy, and the importance of communicating strategy within the organisation. Nor would one deny the virtues of firms being customer-oriented, encouraging entrepreneurship or being healthily sceptical about the possible advantages of diversification strategies. The concept of corporate culture, however, seems as yet to have been insufficiently analysed for it to play a major role in influencing strategy, and is certainly not in a position to supplant the more traditional approach to the determination and implementation of strategy. Not only is it the case that much of the material in this area is descriptive rather than prescriptive, but what evidence there is suggests that the process of changing corporate culture is extremely costly in terms of management effort, and may take from six to fifteen years to achieve. Moreover, if a strongly held culture becomes inappropriate to a new strategy introduced because of a fundamental change in environmental variables, then the culture becomes dysfunctional in a strategic context.[13]

A final example of the reservations expressed regarding the usefulness of corporate strategy concerns the appropriateness of the approach in a rapidly changing environment, and the fact that

present day strategic planning may have distracted senior management from a more relevant concern with technology. It is pointed
out by such critics that not only has the environment of strategic
planning become much more complex, dynamic and unpredictable, but that technology and other factors have at the same time
made businesses more complex organisations requiring extended
lead times in making important strategic decisions. These two
changes – increased unpredictability of the environment and
simultaneously a need for a longer planning horizon – have, it is
argued, combined to reduce considerably the value of corporate
planning.

One result of an overselling of the advantages of corporate
planning has been that when an unforeseen event occurs, such as
the quadrupling of crude oil prices in 1973–4 and the onset of
world recession, then corporate planning or strategy as a whole is
jettisoned. There is certainly evidence to suggest that there was an
adverse reaction of this kind to corporate strategy in the United
States in the late 1970s.[14] However, this disillusionment fails to
recognise what it is that corporate strategy can do and is intended
to do. In so far as it looks at possible future events (and it certainly
should be looking to the future) corporate strategy is concerned
with the likely market conditions, the identity of customers and
competitors, and the way in which the company's resources can
best be used or developed to meet these conditions. In this context
a view must, of course, be taken of the likely future business
environment. But no strategist should claim that part of his or her
talent is for detailed forecasting. The task, without being irres-
ponsible in the advice he or she gives, is to provide insight and not
foresight. Or as the planning director of Shell UK Ltd put it
recently, responding to the argument that strategic planning loses
its value in an uncertain environment: 'What, after all, is the
purpose of planning? Basically, it is to provide a framework within
which decisions throughout an organization can be taken. While
this implies an understanding of the forces that will mould the
future, it does not necessarily imply a need for single-line
forecasts'.[15] Our case is that much of the benefit of corporate
strategy-making derives from the very carrying out of the exercise
itself. It is the process of strategy-making as much as the resulting
plan that should be of value to the business: 'the value of bringing
managers together and directing their attention away from current

problems to the problems and opportunities which may occur next year and thereafter; to think about the broad trends in market and technological developments'.[16]

It is the absence of an explicit technological dimension to corporate strategy, and a corresponding overemphasis upon excessively detached, shorter-term , 'financial' corporate management that has drawn the fire of some American writers with an operations management background.[17] In their observation, 'High quality, reliable performance, relatively low cost based on real manufacturing efficiencies – these have been, time and again, at the heart of the competitive strategy that has enabled foreign producers to outflank, outfox, and outperform their American counterparts'.[18] Their argument is that while some markets have matured in ways that have reduced the competitive significance of product and process innovation and correspondingly elevated the role of marketing and finance as key factors for success, there are others in which competition is becoming more commonly based upon technology, including of course those which we loosely refer to as 'high technology' industries. Abernathy *et al.* suggest that a variety of environmental and competitive forces are now creating a broad de-maturing of a number of manufacturing industries, and that corporate strategy must respond to this trend by an increased emphasis on product and process competitiveness.[19] In contrast to the demands of this environmental trend, senior management is often found moving in an opposite direction, and with dire consequences: 'By their preference for servicing existing markets rather than creating new ones and by their devotion to short-term returns and "management by the numbers", many of them have effectively forsworn long-term technological superiority as a competitive weapon. In consequence, they have abdicated their strategic responsibilities'.[20] Convincing though part of the rationale for this attack on the attitudes of some managers is, it should be regarded as just that: a criticism of shortsightedness, timidity and in some instances an over-reliance upon distant financial controls over business ventures rather than a desire to be more closely involved, to take risks, and in particular to compete by means of new products and processes (albeit at a cost of writing off one's existing investment) rather than market-led proliferation of current product offerings. It is a criticism of certain attitudes and not of the fundamental concepts of corporate strategy.

13.3   Conclusions

Although corporate strategy as practised by senior managers is as
old as businesses of any significance themselves, as a topic in the
management literature it is relatively new. Writing in the mid-
1980s, the subject is only twenty-five years old.[21] The topic has
progressed from the earlier, more descriptive texts whose material
derived very largely from the experiences of successful business
executives. The subject of corporate strategy and the concept of
the strategic decision-making process and sequence has now begun
to settle into a more established framework. It is this framework
that provided the basis for Part I of this text.[22] Furthermore,
although a number of other disciplines such as economics and the
behavioural sciences have contributed and continue to contribute
usefully to an understanding of corporate strategy, the subject is
now recognised on both sides of the Atlantic as having a separate
existence of its own. A further development is that it is becoming
more common for middle as well as senior management courses to
have a corporate strategy component. No apology is needed here
for teaching material that is beyond the immediate direct requirement of the students. For it is increasingly recognised that an
understanding of the pressures involved in corporate strategy-
making and the process of arriving at these decisions are topics
which managers across the organisation should know something
of. Corporate strategy in terms of the assessment of the environment, and again at the point of implementation, after all begins
and ends at divisional or SBU level. The more managers in these
units understand of corporate strategy, the better managers they
will be in their present positions, and the better prepared they will
become for senior management. Thus, responding again to criticism of corporate strategy as being simply a set of tools and
procedures, one McKinsey consultant emphasised that it should
rather be regarded as 'a frame of mind and a set of behavioral
patterns ... This frame of mind, this mind set toward turning
change into competitive advantage, must be deeply ingrained in
line managers, so that they can become the driving force behind
strategic management'.[23]

One recent survey of business practice concluded that the
existence of an integrated, clearly understood strategy for the firm
as a whole is yet 'disturbingly rare outside the top elite of British

companies'.[24] Obviously there must be many contributing factors
to Britain's relatively lacklustre industrial and economic performance over the past decades, and we would not argue that corporate
strategy is a panacea for these or other ills. But the concepts and
processes put forward in Part I of this text and the applications
continued in Part II are not themselves obscure, difficult or
impracticable. On the contrary, we would argue that they are
relatively straightforward, easy to comprehend, and capable of
being implemented in a wide range of organisations. The purpose
of this text has been to indicate the nature of the corporate
strategy process, to discuss the advantages and weaknesses of the
associated techniques and their implementation, and to analyse
the situations in which corporate strategy can be applied. It is
hoped that a contribution has thereby been made to the further
adoption of the practice of corporate strategy and an improvement
in business performance.

References

1. Quoted in *Sunday Times*, 13 November 1983.
2. C. Thornton, 'What's Wrong with Corporate Management?', *Management News*, October 1983, p. 4.
3. See *Sunday Times*, 13 May 1984.
4. Quoted in *The Director*, December 1983, p. 42.
5. *Financial Times*, 18 July 1984.
6. See W. Kiechel, 'Corporate Strategists Under Fire', *Fortune*, 27 December 1982, pp. 34–9.
7. *Ibid.*, p. 34.
8. See R. N. Paul *et al.*, 'The Reality Gap in Strategic Planning', *Harvard Business Review*, May–June 1978, pp. 124–30.
9. See J. Thackray, 'The Corporate Strategy Problem', *Management Today*, October 1979, pp. 87ff.
10. See J. K. Galbraith, *The New Industrial State* (London: Hamish Hamilton, 1967) Ch. 6.
11. T. J. Peters and R. H. Waterman, *In Search of Excellence* (New York: Harper & Row, 1982).
12. *Ibid.*, p. 103.
13. See 'The Perils of Trying to Change Corporation Culture', *Financial Times*, 14 December 1983.
14. See 'Corporate Strategy in the Wilderness', *Financial Times*, 29 June 1979.
15. P. W. Beck, 'Corporate Planning for an Uncertain Future', *Long Range Planning*, August 1982, p. 17.

16. *Financial Times*, 29 June 1979.
17. For a review of this see R. H. Hayes and W. J. Abernathy, 'Managing Our Way to Economic Decline', *Harvard Business Review*, July–August 1980, pp. 67–77.
18. W. J. Abernathy, K. B. Clark and A. M. Kantrow, *Industrial Renaissance: Producing a Competitive Future for America* (New York: Basic Books, 1983) p. 11.
19. *Ibid.*, Ch. 2.
20. Hayes and Abernathy, 'Managing Our Way to Economic Decline', p. 70.
21. R. N. Paul *et al.* (note 8) date the subject from the publication of David E. Ewing's *Long Range Planning for Management* in 1958.
22. See the book by Harvey referred to at various points in this text: D. F. Harvey, *Business Policy and Strategic Management* (Columbus, Ohio: Merrill Publishing, 1982); and also A. A. Thompson and A. J. Strickland, *Strategic Management* (Plano, Texas: Business Publications, 3rd edn, 1984) as examples of the American literature. The most recent UK text in this field adopts a not dissimilar approach: see G. Johnson and K. Scholes, *Exploring Corporate Strategy* (London: Prentice Hall, 1984).
23. F. W. Gluck, 'Strategic Management for the Eighties', *The McKinsey Quarterly*, Summer 1983, p. 14.
24. See *Arthur Young Business Review*, Spring 1984, p. 12.

Index